Screw Consent

Screw Consent

A Better Politics of Sexual Justice

Joseph J. Fischel

UNIVERSITY OF CALIFORNIA PRESS

University of California Press, one of the most
distinguished university presses in the United States,
enriches lives around the world by advancing scholarship
in the humanities, social sciences, and natural sciences. Its
activities are supported by the UC Press Foundation and
by philanthropic contributions from individuals and
institutions. For more information, visit www.ucpress.edu.

University of California Press
Oakland, California

Library of Congress Cataloging-in-Publication Data

Names: Fischel, Joseph J., author.
Title: Screw consent : a better politics of sexual justice /
    Joseph J. Fischel.
Description: Oakland, California : University of
    California Press, [2019] | Includes bibliographical
    references and index. |
Identifiers: LCCN 2018020265 (print) | LCCN 2018026660
    (ebook) | ISBN 9780520968172 (ebook) | ISBN
    9780520295407 (cloth : alk. paper) | ISBN
    9780520295414 (pbk. : alk. paper)
Subjects: LCSH: Sexual consent. | Sex—Political aspects. |
    Sexual ethics. | Sex and law.
Classification: LCC HQ32 (ebook) | LCC HQ32 .F573 2019
    (print) | DDC 176/.4—dc23
LC record available at https://lccn.loc.gov/2018020265

Manufactured in the United States of America

28 27 26 25 24 23 22 21 20 19
10 9 8 7 6 5 4 3 2 1

Contents

Acknowledgments

I meant to write this book about a decade ago but accidentally wrote another one instead. That book is pretty nerdy and includes a lot of polysyllabic words, and its critique of consent owes a bunch to Foucault. This book, which I hope is accessible, compelling, and occasionally titillating, has fewer five-dollar words (but I make up ones too, like *corporanormativity*), and its critiques of consent owe more to feminist theorists and student activists against sexual violence. My first debt of gratitude, then, is to those feminist theorists and student activists, at my university and beyond, collaborating to build more nonviolent, democratically hedonic sexual cultures. By "democratically hedonic culture," I mean a world where access to pleasure and intimacy is not so systematically and unfairly apportioned to the privileged few.

I am grateful for the intellectual camaraderie of the Women's, Gender, and Sexuality Studies (WGSS) program at Yale University. I treasure support and interlocution from WGSS faculty and fellow travelers: Melanie Boyd, Inderpal Grewal, Margaret Homans, Rodion Kosovsky, Greta "Doug" LaFleur, Katie Lofton, Ali Miller, Eda Pepi, Chamonix Adams Porter, Linn Tonstad, and Laura Wexler. Robin Dembroff offered excellent advice for the third chapter of the book, as did Laurie Santos for the fourth. Many thanks to Linda Hase and Moe Gardner for enabling my colleagues and me to pursue our research.

Discussions with the speakers of the 2017 Race, Sex, and Ethics Speaker Series at Yale were enormously helpful in advancing the project.

Thank you to Michael Burroughs, Adrienne Davis, Charles Lawrence, Mari Matsuda, and Kathryn Stockton.

The undergraduate students across the several iterations of my Theory and Politics of Sexual Consent seminar provided rich input for the arguments of this book and for my thinking more generally about sex, consent, and inequality. The splendid insights of Connie Cho, Alexa Derman, Hilary O'Connell, and Grace Paine especially reverberate in *Screw Consent*. Two graduate student advisees, Charlotte Jeffries and Matt Shafer, offered most thoughtful suggestions too.

This book—its collected and coded data, its arguments, its existence in your hands or on your screen—materialized only because of the fantastic, diligent work of several research assistants: Jenny Friedland, Jim Huang, Emma Thurber Stone, and Becca Young. Thanks too to Emmanuel Cantor for assistance with copy editing.

I sent out (or just talked out) chapters of the book to many colleagues and friends who kindly responded with necessary criticisms and terrific source suggestions. Thanks to Susan Appleton, Mary Anne Case, Andrea Long Chu, Zach Herz, Aeyal Gross, Ron Den Otter, and Gabriel Rosenberg; to Ummni Kahn, Ann Pellegrini, and the participants of the 2016 Dangertalk Forum at New York University; to Ann Cahill, Harriet Gray, Tanya Palmer, Maria Stern, and all the engaged and engaging scholars of the Unpacking Consent Workshop at the University of Gothenberg. My thinking, writing, teaching, advising, and imagining have been deeply enriched by Lauren Berlant. Over the past ten years Lauren has been a most generous adviser, beautifully brilliant colleague, and true friend.

I owe gratitude to Maura Roessner at the University of California Press for seeing promise in *Screw Consent* and shepherding it along with creativity and efficiency. Thanks too to Sabrina Robleh, the UC Press staff, and the anonymous readers who offered such valuable feedback for the book's direction.

My sister, Rabbi Eliana Fischel, reminds me of the many sacred things in this world; her goodness infuses the book throughout.

My husband, Igor Souza, scholar of commentary, gave me all the right comments. He also gives me patience, stability, fun times (high five!), impossibly delicious food, and love.

On nearly every morning of the summer months of 2017—usually before 7 AM—my mother suffered through breakfast as I expounded my zany ideas about weird sex or weird sex laws with (at) her. Shelley Fischel is an exacting, phenomenal editor. She spent many unpaid hours reviewing the manuscript. She made the book better. For this, as for everything else, I am eternally grateful.

During the time I wrote this book, two members of my family grew increasingly ill: my father, Robert Fischel, and Elva Neyra. Dad and Elva both are warm, kind, caring, and joyous. Disease is crushing in too many ways, and I wish more than anything they could be well again. This book is for them.

Introduction

When Consent Isn't Sexy

Enthusiastic consent is necessary for both parties to enjoy the experience.

—Gigi Engle

In the summer of 2017, *Teen Vogue* taught its young, impressionable readers how to have butt sex. Well, not exactly, but that is what you would have gathered from the fury that followed the publication of the essay. The self-proclaimed "Activist Mommy," Elizabeth Johnston, posted a video of herself burning the magazine in outrage (Activist Mommy 2017). The video has been viewed by millions reports Fox News, and the Activist Mommy used it to spearhead a campaign to boycott the magazine. Conservative parent activists are as impassioned as they are unoriginal, and so Johnston predictably tarred *Teen Vogue* as a pedophilic peddler while posturing her politics as above politics: "They should not be teaching sodomy to our children. [. . .] This is not a Republican issue or a Democratic issue. This is not a conservative issue or a liberal issue. This is a parent issue" (Starnes 2017; see also Edelman 2004, 1–32).

I will have more to say about *Teen Vogue*'s article "Anal Sex: What You Need to Know" in the fifth chapter of the book, but for now I note simply that the article is pretty rad and young people ought to have accurate sexual information more readily available to them. The essay, penned by author and sex educator Gigi Engle, is written candidly and cutely ("Here is the lowdown on everything you need to know about the butt stuff") and emphasizes the importance of sexual communication between partners. While Engle does not shy away from explaining the pleasures of anal sex (for example, nerve endings for all, prostate massages for some) and its possible problems (for example, tightness of the anus, poop), she stresses dialogue: "Whether you are planning to give or receive anal sex, a conversation must take place beforehand." She encourages her young readers to be "honest about your feelings," and returns to the importance of maintaining "regular communication" during the act itself so that partners can convey their pain or discomfort. Engle enjoins her readers to start small (begin with a finger or small toy in the anus before graduating to a penis or bigger toy) and to always use lubricant for the at-first-unreceptive orifice—gems of insight that I imagine especially inflamed conservative ire (Engle 2017).

The values and lessons of the anal sex guide resonate with the arguments and provocations of *Screw Consent*. The more accurate and accessible sexual information for young folks, the better, and the more we can destigmatize sex talk, the more likely we are to have pleasurable, not just bearable, sexual experiences.

But—and it is a big *but* (see what I did there?)—as the reader might gather from the title of this book, I cannot sign on to Engle's pitch for consent: "Enthusiastic consent is necessary for both parties to enjoy [anal sex]." Neither, I think, should you.

Permit me to start with the empirically obvious. However we define the "enthusiastic" element of "enthusiastic consent," it is simply untrue that enthusiastic consent—or for that matter, and here is a phenomenological whopper, *any* consent—is *necessary* for a sexual experience to be enjoyable. Teenage Billy or teenage Becky might hesitantly consent to butt sex, or vaginal sex, or oral sex, that turns out to be the best, most mind-blowing sex ever. Becky might even slip a finger in Billy's butt without Billy consenting in advance, and Billy might absolutely, unequivocally love the sensation. Conversely, Billy and Becky might emphatically consent to penetrate each other's anuses; they might even discover sexual pleasure in the very agreement. And yet the ensuing anal sex might be thoroughly terrible. It might be unenjoyable, painful, and . . . shitty (see what I did there?).

So we can haphazardly or ambivalently consent to sex that is fantastic, and consent fantastically to sex that is resolutely unfun. This latter observation is perhaps not entirely fair as a critique of Engle's point, for she argues that "enthusiastic consent" is necessary for sexual experiences to be enjoyable (it is not), but she never states outright that it is sufficient. Still, insofar as we can assume that "enthusiastic consent" signals desire for Engle, and insofar as "enjoy the experience" signals pleasure, then Engle is saying something like this: *Enthusiastic consent, from which we can read desire, is not simply a baseline for sexual pleasure but nearly its guarantor.* In that case, "enthusiastic consent" is pretty darn close to being held up as both necessary and sufficient for experiencing the joys of anal sex, with the provisos that Billy and Becky use lube, go slowly, and initiate penetration with small toys or fingers. More precisely, these provisos are meant to ensure ongoing desire: who would enthusiastically consent to rapid anal penetration with a nonlubricated enormous dildo?

Still, Becky might strongly dislike being anally penetrated, even gently, by Billy's small and lubricated penis, however enthusiastic Becky's consent.

Whether Becky's slipping her finger unannounced into the anus of the pleasantly surprised Billy ought to be lawful or morally permissible, and whether that slipped finger is enjoyable or unenjoyable, are separate questions that we should continue to keep separate, not only for legal but also for political and philosophical reasons. One worry running under this book is that in the current moment of sexual politics— let's call it the Consent Moment—we risk collapsing consent into desire into pleasure, not (yet) as a matter of law or policy (more on this below) but as a matter of political rhetoric and quite possibly phenomenological experience (more on this, too, below).

SCREW CONSENT, KIND OF

I will take the opportunity offered by Gigi Engle's anal sex guide, with its meditations on consent, pleasure and pain, to telegraph now—but to be elaborated later—what I do and do not intend by "screw consent." Perhaps to the relief of many but to the disappointment of a few, by "screw consent" I do not mean *fuck consent, go ahead and have whatever sex you wish, unimpeded.* Nor do I advocate screwing, as in jettisoning, consent as a core component of sexual assault law. In fact, I shall argue that an "affirmative consent" standard is the least-bad standard available for sexual assault law, compared to "force," "resistance," or nonconsent standards. So if we should screw consent neither when it comes to *sex* nor when it comes to sex *law,* where should we screw it? In our sex *politics*. In our activism and advocacy for an egalitarian, feminist, and more democratically hedonic sexual culture, consent talk at best diminishes and at worst perverts our sexual justice politics. And if we cannot jettison *consent* from our sexual justice politics altogether, we should, taking our cue from the *Oxford English Dictionary,* "exert pressure" on consent by "twisting, tightening, or pressing" upon it,[1] releasing consent's capture of our imaginations in order to invite more-promising values, norms, and concepts into our efforts for building a safer, more democratically hedonic culture.

One key problem with the primacy of consent in our sex politics is that its conceptual thinness has been remedied by increasingly more robust, sometimes ridiculous redefinitions of consent as enthusiastic, imaginative, creative *yes*-saying. But the unfortunate corollary is the cultural coding of nonenthusiastically desired sex as sexual assault, which generates conservative and sometime feminist backlash ("Bad sex is not *rape,* after all," sings this chorus) and perhaps exacerbates one's sense of injury when sex goes awry (Way 2018; B. Weiss 2018).[2]

A second key problem with the primacy of consent in our sex politics cuts the other way. Bad sex, even if consensual, can be really bad, and usually worse for women: not just uninspired, unenthusiastic, or boring, but unwanted, unpleasant, and painful (Loofbourow 2018; Traister 2015). *That* problem cannot be addressed by consent. Worse still, the problem of bad-as-in-really-bad sex is automatically deprioritized by the consent-as-enthusiasm paradigm, which divides sex into the categories *awesome* and *rape* and leaves unaccounted and unaddressed all the immiserating sex too many people, typically women, endure.

I revisit these two key problems of the consent paradigm for sexual justice politics in chapter 5 and the conclusion of this book, and later in this introduction. In the chapters in between, I address these key problems obliquely, shoring up the limitations of consent for thinking about and regulating sex across encounters and intimacies that are nonnormative, atypical, or weird.

In any case, it is these concerns with and for sexual politics that animate my wish to screw—tinker, tighten, and pressure, rather than altogether dispense with—consent. And so I want to rupture the chain of equivalences that are not quite made by Gigi Engle but are well on their way, in which consent = desire = pleasure. These are dangerously mistaken equations, though not, I believe, for the reasons other feminist and legal scholars have suggested. The following section ("Is Consent the End of Liberal Democracy?") challenges objections that consent reforms have gone too far, wrongly emboldening federal and bureaucratic powers. The next section ("Is Sexual Consent Meaningless?") then canvasses the provocative and regularly misinterpreted counterargument, championed by Catharine MacKinnon and others, that consent is of limited or no legal (or moral) utility in a world saturated by sex inequality. These antithetical objections to newfound political investments in consent differ from mine, and the contrasts anchor and clarify this book's arguments. I restate these objections because they are likely more familiar to readers, and I wish to forge a rather different path away from consent.

IS CONSENT THE END OF LIBERAL DEMOCRACY?

From the spring of 2011 onward, colleges and universities overhauled their sexual misconduct policies and procedures. These reforms were initiated by student activists and student survivors of sexual violence who aimed to hold academic institutions accountable for their failures to redress sexual violence under the sex nondiscrimination guarantee of Title IX of the Education Amendments of 1972 (Gassó 2011).[3] Contemporaneously, the Obama administration enumerated and expanded universities' Title IX compliance obligations (Assistant Secretary, Office for Civil Rights 2011; see also American Council on Education 2014). While the federal directives address disciplinary procedures, standards of proof, and reporting requirements, inter alia, they do not, as of this writing, mandate the adoption of a specific consent definition into sexual misconduct codes. Nevertheless, it is this reform—encoding or redefining consent to be "affirmative," as a performance of positive agreement rather than as the absence of refusal—which has garnered the most media attention and public criticism. In addition, some states have enacted laws that require their public universities to adopt an affirmative consent standard (along with certain disciplinary procedures); over the past few years, the American Law Institute (ALI) has debated whether to similarly redefine the consent standard for sexual assault in the Model Penal Code (Flannery 2016; McArthur 2016).[4]

Harvard law professor Janet Halley is one of the most vocal critics of the potential MPC revisions, affirmative consent, and, more generally, Title IX–based reforms to university sexual misconduct policies and procedures. "The campaign for affirmative consent requirements," she warns, "is distinctively rightist" (Halley 2015; see also Gruber 2015). Among her many concerns: an affirmative consent standard authorizes broader administrative and statutory intervention that "will often be intensely repressive and sex-negative"; feminists are "seeking social control through punitive and repressive deployments of state power [and] are criminalizing as a first rather than a last resort to achieving social change"; an affirmative consent standard potentially invites women to claim as rape sex they enthusiastically desired but later regretted; the standard reinstalls gender norms of women as emotional and weak and men as sexually predatory and (yet) responsible for absorbing all risk; to the extent that affirmative consent policies will result in greater surveillance and punishment, populations already targeted by the criminal justice system—black men, for example—will disproportionately suffer under these new regimes (see also Gruber 2015, 692). Finally, the most panic-inducing consequence of affirmative consent for Halley is that the standard culminates in the criminalization of *undesired* sex. It is not merely forced sex, sex under threats of force, or even nonconsensual sex that will qualify as a criminal sex offense. Now, or soon, affirmative consent standards will shift the threshold from force to nonconsent, to affirmative consent, all the way to *wantedness,* which for Halley represents nothing short of totalitarianism (or "governance feminism" gone ballistic): "A requirement of positive consent will deliver the boon many feminists are seeking: sex that women have that is dysphoric to them at the time will be punishable" (Halley 2015; 2006, 20–22; see also Gersen and Suk 2016, 923).

Halley is not alone in her outspoken dissent. Her fellow Harvard law professors Jacob Gersen and Jeannie Suk (2016) argue that we are now "living in a new sex bureaucracy," in which the federal government and nongovernmental organizations—chief among them institutions of higher education—are enacting and enforcing ever-expanding regulatory policies and procedures over sex. Insidiously enfolded into this "bureaucratic sex creep," they warn, is the regulation of "ordinary sex" itself (883, 885). By broadening definitions of, and requiring more robust administrative responses to, sexual violence, sexual harassment, and sex discrimination, "the bureaucracy" is regulating and attempting to renorm ordinary sex, which the authors define as "voluntary adult sexual conduct that does not harm others" (885). Gersen and Suk share Halley's concern about state overreach and about entrusting more and more power to institutions to solve social problems and to govern our everyday lives (913–18). They express an additional concern that the expansion of "ordinary sex" to regulatory capture *as* sexual misconduct inadvertently trivializes actual sexual violence and harassment (886–87).

For Gersen and Suk, newly revised affirmative consent standards of campus sexual misconduct codes exemplify acutely and extend invasively such regulatory oversight to ordinary sex. By redefining consent to entail "enthusiasm, excitement, creativity, and desire," colleges and universities are reregulating norms of sex full throttle, likewise punishing students who fail to meet the companionate, "marriage-like" sex ideals of university bureaucrats (930–31). The authors list Gordon College, Elon University, University of Wyoming, and Georgia Southern

University (925–26, 928–30), among others, as drafting especially unreachable and moralized definitions of consent. For example, Georgia Southern defines consent as "a voluntary, sober, imaginative, enthusiastic, creative, wanted, informed, mutual, honest, and verbal agreement." (However, this revised "definition" tells only part of the story of consent and campus sex norms; I will return to these supposedly wild and crazy expansions of consent definitions anon.)

Trumpeting a similar note, Yale law professor Jed Rubenfeld (2014) laments in the *New York Times* that his university's definition of sexual consent reclassifies ordinary sex as rape: "Under this definition [of sexual consent] a person who voluntarily gets undressed, gets into bed and has sex with someone, without clearly communicating either yes or no, can later say—correctly—that he or she was raped. This is not a law school hypothetical. The unambiguous consent standard requires this conclusion." In her polemic against the transformation of campus sexual misconduct codes and policies propelled by the federal expansion of Title IX's regulatory reach, cultural critic and Northwestern professor Laura Kipnis (2017b) opines that "sexual consent can now be retroactively withdrawn (with official sanction) years later, based on changing feelings or residual ambivalence, or new circumstances. Please note that this makes anyone who's ever had sex a potential rapist" (91).

On the one hand, Halley, Gersen and Suk, Rubenfeld, Kipnis, and several others are right to shine light on these fast-paced, sometimes half-baked developments that can seem motivated more by threat of liability than by sex nondiscrimination. And students, like the rest of us, risk disempowering and depoliticizing themselves by surrendering social agitation and democratic deliberation to third-party declarative fiat. Take, for example, the Northwestern University students who demanded that Laura Kipnis be sanctioned, rather than debated, for her writings about sex between professors and students (Kipnis 2015).

On the other hand, this scholarly sex panic about our campus sex panic seems, at times, even more panicky than the alleged panic. For even as Kipnis writes, "I don't mean to be hyperbolic," she nevertheless terrifies her readers by claiming that on campus, via campus codes, "virtually all sex is fast approaching rape" (2017b, 121). This is hyperbolic.

Let's take the sex terror alert level down a few degrees. Contra Kipnis, sexual consent *cannot* "now be retroactively withdrawn (with official sanction) years later" (2017b, 91). Kipnis is reporting on a relationship that soured between a graduate student and a philosophy professor at Northwestern; the student subsequently accused the professor of initiating an inappropriate relationship with her and, on one occasion, having sex with her without her consent. The accusations triggered a Title IX investigation of the professor, who was eventually forced out of the university (the student subsequently filed a Title IX complaint against Kipnis herself for writing about the incident; Kipnis 2015).

But this is the important part: the student claimed to have *not consented* to sex with the professor on one drunken night, not that she consented and retracted that consent. Based on conflicting evidence, Title IX administrators concluded that they could not determine whether the sex was nonconsensual and found the professor in violation of university policy on other (shaky) grounds (Kipnis 2017b, 114). There are many ways in which the Title IX officers and other stakeholders at Northwestern bungled and perhaps manipulated this case. But even according to Kipnis's own account, Northwestern adopted no policy whereby consent to sex could be retroactively withdrawn. The student simply said she never consented! If she is lying, that is a question of fact. The student might have "flip-flopped" on consent, but the university in no way ratified the flip-flop. Codifications of affirmative consent do not weaponize sexual regret.

As I have written with a colleague elsewhere, Jed Rubenfeld's imagined scenario—whereby a man who has sex with a woman who "voluntarily" gets undressed and into bed with him has committed "rape" under Yale's new definition of consent—is not simply far-fetched but nigh impossible (Boyd and Fischel 2014). First, Yale's consent standard, like nearly all university and college consent standards, does not require a verbal *yes* for the subsequent sex to be permissible, so the woman in the scenario need not "clearly communicat[e] either *yes* or *no*," at least not verbally (Rubenfeld 2014).[5] Second, whatever the woman "voluntarily" does will likely adequately meet the affirmative element of affirmative consent. Third, Rubenfeld misleadingly refers to such conduct as "rape" and to university sexual misconduct hearings as "rape trials." Halley also slips into the language of "crime," "criminalization," and "carceral" in reference to university policies and procedures (Halley 2015). To be clear, the severest forms of punishment for violating a college's sexual misconduct policy is suspension or expulsion, not imprisonment. While Gersen and Suk convincingly document that the sex bureaucracy "operates largely apart from criminal enforcement [. . .] [though] its actions are inseparable from criminal overtones and implications" (2016, 891), it is one matter to look like a duck ("overtones and implications") and another matter to be a duck (throwing hapless fraternity brothers into prison).

Professors Gersen and Suk rightly raise alarms that some of the sex norms that university administrations and student groups are promoting are both suspiciously traditional (for example, campus administrative literature extolling the values of a "more caring, responsive, respectful love life" [929; quoting a brochure from the Dean of Students Office, University of Wyoming]) and convoluted (campus literature that describes nonsober sex, rather than *intoxicated* sex, as nonconsensual and therefore assaultive; 926).[6] Yet I am also inclined to agree with Susan Appleton and Susan Stiritz (2016) that there is no such thing as pre-regulated, "ordinary sex" on college campuses; that sex is always already shot through with norms; and that in the United States, those norms are often informed by sex education curricula that are homo- and erotophobic, are medically inaccurate, and reinforce traditional, restrictive norms of femininity and masculinity. Looked at panoramically, Title IX–based initiatives to facilitate more informed and more egalitarian campus sexual cultures are (or could be) correctives to prior modes of sex regulation and sex superintendence that are largely indefensible (Appleton and Stiritz 2016).

As for the apparently absurd university definitions of sexual consent that incorporate elements such as enthusiasm, sobriety, respect, and verbal agreement, Gersen and Suk are correct that University of Wyoming, Gordon College, Elon University, and Georgia Southern University include these rather lofty, rather dubious notions of consent in their student life brochures or in their Annual Security Reports (ASRs) to the federal government. However, these are not the definitions of consent in the respective institutions' actual sexual misconduct policies. At the University of Wyoming, the policy defines consent, in part, as "a freely and affirmatively communicated willingness to participate in particular sexual activity or behavior, expressed either by words or clear, unambiguous actions." Gordon College defines consent, in part, as "the clear, knowing, and voluntary agreement to engage in a specific sexual activity during a sexual encounter." Elon defines consent, in part, as "voluntary, intentional agreement to engage in a particular sexual activity." And Georgia Southern defines consent, in part, as "words or actions that show a knowing and voluntary willingness to engage in mutually agreed-upon sexual activity." The policy also states that silence alone will not meet the consent standard.[7]

I contacted the deans and other Title IX coordinators at these institutions via email; they confirmed that their schools use their policies' definition of consent, and not the ASR–sexual violence prevention manuals' definition of consent, in their adjudication of sexual misconduct.[8]

Finally, despite the thoroughness and incisiveness with which Professor Halley criticizes the American Law Institute and the State of California for potentially injecting an element of desire into their respective definitions of sexual consent, I do not see it. California, along with a few other states, has legislated that its colleges and universities adopt a standard of consent requiring "affirmative, conscious, and voluntary agreement to engage in sexual activity."[9] Given that the standard is an expressive one, a person could very well be reluctant, ambivalent, or even uninterested in sex, yet the sex will not be rendered assaultive (or rendered in violation of a school's misconduct policy) so long as the person in some way *performs something*—some behavior, some cue, some token of willingness—beyond frozenness or silence (Westen 2004, 65–93). So desire is not an element of consent; communicated willingness is. Halley continually refers rhetorically to the woman who "passionately desired [sex] at the time" but later successfully accuses her partner of rape or sexual misconduct (Halley 2015). The accusation will be found valid, presumably, because even though the woman passionately desired the sex, she made no bodily, verbal, or otherwise communicative indication of her passion. So the woman lies on the bed absolutely motionless and expressionless, passionately desiring and passionately enjoying sex with her partner, and then later accuses him of rape. This seems somewhat implausible.

None of my criticisms of these criticisms are full takedowns, since some of the federal regulatory and university administrative trends in the governance of sexual misconduct are worrisome, not least of which are the secretive hearings with sometimes-arbitrary rules that threaten due process rights of defendants (Kipnis 2017a; New 2016). But it strikes me that the main problems regarding sexual violence, harassment, and discrimination are that incidents still go largely unreported; that women are still largely disbelieved; that student defendants are rarely expelled for violating their universities' sexual misconduct policies; that police, prosecutors, and medical examiners routinely neglect victim complaints or discourage rape victims from pursuing charges; that arrest rates, conviction rates, and sentencing terms for sex offenses are still so thoroughly racialized (Corrigan 2013; Hefling 2014; Kingkade 2014); and that sexual violence, harassment, and discrimination are epidemic (Gavey 2005, 50–75; but see Gruber 2016, 1031–39). Contra Halley, we can protest the racialization of criminal justice enforcement while still making the consent standard for sexual assault one degree more than silent acquiescence (Schulhofer 2015, 677–78). In a racist criminal justice system, all criminal laws may be enforced discriminatorily. Yet this does not mean we abrogate our responsibility to make better laws and policies. It is neither utopic nor irresponsible to advocate for better laws and policies while also protesting racist enforcement and our current system of mass incarceration (Schulhofer 2015, 679).

And even accounting for legitimate concerns over state and university overreach, affirmative consent is just not the bad guy. The bureaucratic buildup, the due process concerns regarding university misconduct hearings, the stringencies and negative externalities of federal reporting mandates—all of these phenomena can be debated and redressed without skewering affirmative consent.

IS SEXUAL CONSENT MEANINGLESS?

If sex is normally something men do to women, the issue is less whether there was force and more whether consent is a meaningful concept.

—Catharine MacKinnon (1983, 650)

Sex women want is never described by them or anyone else as consensual. No one says, "We had a great hot night, she (or I or we) consented."

—Catharine MacKinnon (2016, 450)

Consent is a pathetic standard of equal sex for a free people.

—Catharine MacKinnon (2016, 465)

The practice of consent shows you care about the desires and the boundaries of each other. [. . .] Sex with consent is sexy.

—Poster for Consent Is Sexy campaign (2011)[10]

The three statements above from renowned feminist law professor Catharine MacKinnon and the messages conveyed in the Consent Is Sexy poster are 110 percent incompatible. So which are right?

MacKinnon is a lot more right. But while her interventions are necessary as social critique, her alternative—excising consent altogether—falters as a reform of rape law.

The fourth epigraph above is from a poster of the Consent Is Sexy campaign, one of many promotional items the organization distributes to anti–sexual violence groups across college and universities.[11] The image in figure 1 is a screen grab from a training video released by the

FIGURE 1. Screen grab from Thames Valley Police training video *Tea and Consent*. Blue Seat Studios.

Thames Valley Police in England (Blue Seat Studios 2015). Titled *Tea and Consent*, the video went viral and was circulated widely, even by *Harry Potter* author J. K. Rowling (O'Regan 2016). By analogizing consent to drinking tea with consent to having sex, the video is a clever send-up of men's presumptively willed ignorance ("Unconscious people don't want tea"; "If they say 'no thank you,' then don't make them tea. At all. Just don't make them tea"). The video ends with a public service announcement that is simple, straightforward, and, as I shall argue, (politically) stupid: "Whether it's tea or sex, consent is everything."

Both the Consent Is Sexy campaign and the *Tea and Consent* video have been criticized and lampooned (see, for example, Young Turks 2014; Young 2015). I will not rehash all of those criticisms and satires; but as I hope to have already convinced you, sex with consent is just not always sexy. Literalized as an injunction to verbally request permission for a particular sexual act (*Can I place my finger in your vagina?*), "ask her first" is usually and decidedly unsexy.[12] And the more I read the brochures, posters, and other paraphernalia of the Consent Is Sexy campaign, the more I am convinced that its slogan makes little sense. People, places, things, and fantasies can be sexy; it is hard to discern how the fact of agreement to sex is the top candidate for sexiness. A blowjob with consent might be very sexy indeed, but not summarily *because* it was consensual. A blowjob without consent is not unsexy; it is just sexual assault.

In fact, the most plausible grammatical meaning of "Consent is sexy" is hortatory: *Give consent because consent is sexy!* For example, if jockstraps and Axe deodorant are sexy, I suppose I should wear more jockstraps and apply more Axe. Under this interpretation, the campaign is pressuring people to consent to sex because consenting is allegedly sexy, the new black. This surely cannot be the objective of the campaign (Graybill 2017, 176).

And consent is *absolutely not everything* "whether it comes to tea or sex." Consent does not give you any information about the heat of the tea, whether the tea is black, green, or herbal, whether the tea is Rishi or some tasteless bag of Lipton. Nor does consent to the present tea-drinking moment tell us anything at all about the tea drinker's past experiences with tea. Does she know about the many options available to her? Does she know there is more in the tea universe than the tasteless Lipton bag, or is her imagination limited by Lipton-only tea education? Does she know that she can create her own tea, experiment with combinations of loose leaves, and forgo the prepackaged bag altogether? I am going to assume you can make the analogic jump from tea to sex yourself.

But in that case, is Catharine MacKinnon right? If consent is neither "sexy" nor "everything," is it also not much of anything at all?

In her earlier work from the 1980s, MacKinnon's criticism of the consent standard in rape was a broadside against patriarchy, not a blueprint for redefining rape law. Her point was that, in a world saturated by sex inequality compounded by other inequalities, liberalism's unit of analysis—the individual who does or does not contract or consent to x (here the x is *sex*)—cannot possibly take stock of structures and socialization that condition and constrain human exchanges, sexual or otherwise (MacKinnon 1989, 45–48, 164–65). Against a gendered division of labor that diminishes women's options and mobility, against jurors' and judges' sexist interpretations of women's behavior (their resistance as part of "normal" sex, for example), and against heterosexuality as a system of eroticized male dominance and female submission, MacKinnon asserted, consent looks less like a remedy for sexual assault and more like its alibi (1983, 648–50; 1989, 174–75). If women's choices are so constrained, if women are enculturated to be passive and to please others, then their "consent" is not nearly as morally transformative as the good liberal would like (MacKinnon 1989, 177–78; see also Gavey 2005, 155–64). MacKinnon's point back then, though, as I read her, was this: Sex inequality exists. In a host of ways, sex inequality undermines the voluntariness of women's sexual choices that we might otherwise read as consent.

Given the ubiquity of the misattribution, it bears repeating over and over and over that *Catharine MacKinnon never said or wrote that all heterosexual sex is rape* (see also Cahill 2016, 759n3; Oberman 2001,

823–24; Roberts 1993, 369–70). Rather, MacKinnon is commenting that only in the fantasy world of liberal legal equality is the line between rape and sex so cut-and-dried, a line clearly demarcated by the presence or absence of consent. In the real world structured by sex inequality and regressive gender norms, we must much more deeply question the voluntariness of all allegedly voluntary sex and the supreme transformative power we assign to consent. MacKinnon is not alone in her observation that women's consent in no way guarantees women's freedom or equality, let alone their pleasure (see also Pateman 1980; West 2000).

Twenty-five years later, MacKinnon converted her searing social commentary into a proposal for rape law reform, and here things fall apart (2016; see also Halley 2006, 43–50). She argues that consent should be stricken altogether from the legal definition of rape. Her arguments against the consent standard—and against an *affirmative* consent standard—are familiar ones: consent, like affirmative consent, can be forced, intimidated, and manipulated; consent inquiries focus on the woman's feelings and behaviors rather than the man's actions; consent, as a metric for women's freedom of choice, is incapable of targeting the inequality that forces the choice (MacKinnon 2016, 442–43, 454–56, 463–65). Instead, MacKinnon argues for expanding the legal definition of *force* to include social and professional inequalities and, in turn, redefining rape as

> a physical invasion of a sexual nature under circumstances of threat or use of force, fraud, coercion, abduction, or of the abuse of power, trust, or a position of dependency or vulnerability.
> [. . .] Psychological, economic, and other hierarchical forms of force— including age, mental and physical disability, and other inequalities, including sex, gender, race, class, and caste when deployed as forms of force or coercion in the sexual setting, that is, when used to compel sex in a specific interaction. [. . .] As in the international context of war and genocide, for a criminal conviction, *it would be necessary to show the exploitation of inequalities—their direct use—not merely the fact that they contextually existed.* (2016, 474; emphasis added)

Anticipating the objection, MacKinnon is careful to explain that she is not proscribing sex across all inequalities outright, but only sex in which the inequality is leveraged for sex. I will revisit sex across vertical status relationships in chapter 2, but I want to suggest that MacKinnon's qualification does not do much qualifying. For what exactly does it mean for gender to be deployed as a form of force? Or for class to be so deployed? MacKinnon does not spell it out for us, but she gives some indications: she would prohibit all forms of commercial sex, whether in pornography or as prostitution (2016, 447–48, 454; see also MacKinnon 1985; 1993). It seems likely that she would also prohibit most or all forms of sadomasochistic sex (2016, 461–62; see also MacKinnon 2007b, 264, 269–70). And given her reflections on the "welcomeness" standard of sexual harassment law, it seems too that she is willing to criminalize consensual sex that women agree to but do not want, by the very fact that such an agreement is secured through something akin to gender as deployed force (2016, 450–51). MacKinnon writes:

> When a sexual incursion is not equal, no amount of consent makes it equal, hence redeems it from being violative. Call it sexual assault. This statement does not end here. If sex is equal between partners who socially are not, it is mutuality, reciprocity, respect, trust, desire—as well as sometimes fly-to-the-moon hope and a shared determination to slip the bonds of convention and swim upstream together—not one-sided acquiescence or ritualized obeisance or an exchange of sex for other treasure that makes it intimate, interactive, moving, communicative, warm, personal, loving. (476)

I am not entirely sure what she is arguing in this passage, but I think that if sex occurs between people who are socially unequal—paradigmatically men and women, for MacKinnon—it is presumptively sexual assault. The sex is *not* sexual assault if it is equal, but then what makes equal sex equal across inequality is "mutuality, reciprocity, respect," and so on. This is a dumbfounding conclusion. Despite MacKinnon's preemptive strike against those who might charge her with inviting gross state overreach (2016, 477), I do not see any other result from this line of argument. Any sex that women agree to with men for purposes other than "mutuality, reciprocity [. . .] desire" would make the sex rape and the men rapists. Consider—and apologies for perpetrating gender stereotypes—the sorority sister who willingly sleeps with the football quarterback in order to tell the story to her friends but is not all that into the sex and maybe even finds it unpleasant. Consider the wife who agrees to mediocre or even subpar sex with her husband not because she respects him but because she feels obligated, or maybe she wants to have a child. Consider, à la *Teen Vogue,* the teenage girl who tries anal sex at the suggestion of her boyfriend, dislikes it, but tells him, *un*enthusiastically, "it's OK" as he dutifully and periodically checks in with her throughout the regrettable encounter. We should work trenchantly to change the cultural norms that compel the sorority sister and the wife and the teenage girl into blah or less-than-blah sex. But to imprison the quarterback and the husband and the adolescent boy for rape is worse than absurd; it is unconscionably unfair to the men and offensively disrespectful of the women's choices.

The proposal's prospects are grim even if I have read MacKinnon wrongly. For if we suppose the above scenarios are not instances of rape—that is, if we suppose the inequality between the men and women in these scenarios do *not* constitute force as MacKinnon expansively redefines the concept—then acquaintance rape is left untouched by her suggested reform. Because if consent is removed entirely as an element of the crime of rape, then what crime has occurred if the sorority sister, wife, and teenage girl all say "no"—*or say nothing*—to their partners, who then proceed to have sex with them anyway? The wrong is not best conceived or legally defined as a wrong of force, but as a rights or autonomy violation, indicated by nonconsent (saying "no") or the absence of affirmative consent (saying nothing).

For the reasons raised by MacKinnon and many others, consent is a pretty crappy legal standard for permissible sex, as both a practical and philosophical matter. But it is also the *least* crappy standard from the menu of options (desire, consent, force; see Schulhofer 2015). Insofar as an affirmative consent standard requires neither enthusiasm nor mutuality nor desire, but rather an *indication of agreement beyond silence and frozenness,* then we should, I believe, adopt such a standard into the criminal law of sexual assault, despite Janet Halley's concerns from one direction and Catharine MacKinnon's opposing concerns from the other (Schulhofer 2015, 669).

In law, then, let's not screw consent. The argument of this book is, as I have already proposed, that we should screw consent most everywhere else: in life, activism, and political organizing. In other words, the sex inequality problems MacKinnon exposes—sexual intimidation and coercion, norms of male dominance and female submissiveness, collective disregard for women's sexual agency and desires—are best addressed not by eliminating the consent standard from rape law or abandoning efforts to redefine consent affirmatively, but through social transformation: political debate, public health initiatives, educational interventions, artistic productions, and creative collaboration across student groups and community organizations. There are also other problems of our sexual culture not fully explainable by sex inequality (sexual shame, for example, as well as medically inaccurate sex education curricula and some variants of erotophobia), but if all you have is a sex equality hammer, every problem looks like a sex inequality nail (Halley 2006, 31–35; G. Rubin 1993 [1984]). Of course, such debates, initiatives, and collaborations are already occurring, but too many of these interventions are conceptually, semantically, politically, and ultimately foolishly rooted in consent. The language of law is attractive because it is definitive, but its bluntness blunts bigger and better thinking and politicking around sex and sexual violence. *Screw Consent* asks: Even if consent really could do all the work MacKinnon says it cannot do, would that be good enough? Even under imagined conditions of perfect sex equality, might we nonetheless demand more—much more— from our sexual ethics and our sexual culture than redefining consent by beefing it up (Gavey 2005, 218)?

SCREW CONSENT, POLITICALLY

The idea is to identify, through group communication and brain-storming, what defines good and healthy sex. Our goal is to develop a shared idea of consent that encompasses self-advocacy, respect, and mutual fulfillment—and not to treat it like a checkbox.

—Amelia Marran-Baden (2017)

Anything less than voluntary, sober, enthusiastic, verbal, non-coerced, continual, active, and honest consent is Sexual Assault.

—STOP Violence Program, Dean of Students Office,
University of Wyoming

If you engage in a sexual behavior with a partner who is reluctant or unsure, it is sexual assault.

—STOP Violence Program, Dean of Students Office,
University of Wyoming

In her *New York Times* op-ed (2017), Middlebury College graduate Amelia Marran-Baden laments the clunkiness of campus programming around sex and sexual violence. Because, as Marran-Baden explains, "communication and education" are the "roots of the problem [of unwanted sex and sexual violence]," simply drilling into students that *no* means no or *yes* means yes does next to nothing to facilitate better sex and better sexual culture. Having students repeat a school's consent policy does not help those students learn to communicate with their partners, to navigate drugs and alcohol, or to negotiate fears of rejection and inadequacy.

What is so fascinating and so telling about her op-ed is that even as Marran-Baden bemoans the inadequacy of college consent workshops and the silliness of consent apps for social media, she cannot help but try to resuscitate consent, to make it stand for all the values good sexual citizens ought to hold. Marran-Baden finds herself in a consent cul-de-sac.

She complains that media representations of sexual encounters "generally fail to include any language of consent *at all*" and protests that universities' affirmative consent definitions "overloo[k] emotional intimacy and vulnerability." She cofounded the Consent Project at Middlebury, which aims to redefine consent to entail "self-advocacy, respect [. . .] and not to treat it like a checkbox" (2017).

I am all about resignifying language, but at some point we are in worlds and words of nonsense. For it is one matter, for example, to rework *he* and *she* and *man* and *woman,* or to repurpose nouns and pronouns in our cultural lexicon to allow for a range of gender identifications, stylizations, and expressions. It is another matter to redefine *cow* to mean "cup" or *consent* to mean "awesomest sex ever." While we may legitimately debate the proper criteria for sexual consent to be valid in law, on campus, and in life, it verges on absurdity to redefine consent to entail respect, desire, fulfillment, and enthusiasm. Consent *is* a checkbox.[13] A feminist, democratically hedonic sexual culture—by which I mean a culture that facilitates and more equitably distributes its possibilities for pleasure and intimacy—requires a whole lot more than the check of consent (see also Cahill 2016, 755). Student activists and all others campaigning against sexual violence should undoubtedly advocate for sex that is fulfilling, respectful, and participated in enthusiastically by all parties. But it is politically mistaken and phenomenologically dangerous to stuff those defensible values into the small, legalistic box of consent.

Why? Politically, because consent restrictively narrows the spatial and temporal parameters of discussion. If we are talking about the presence or absence of consent, we are by definition talking only about a sexual encounter between two or more persons in the immediate present, right there and then. Consent talk fundamentally cannot address drinking and hookup culture on campus; fraternity and sorority culture and their concomitant cultures of sexual pressure; impoverished sexual education; people's sexual skill set or lack thereof; the routinized violence of homosociality; (consented to but sexually abusive) hazing; or better ways to communicate in the sexual encounter itself in order to enhance possibilities for pleasure and decrease possibilities for discomfort or regret. All right, I have made the analogic jump for you: as with tea, consent is not everything when it comes to sex. Put most broadly, if we wish to facilitate a feminist, more democratically hedonic, better-informed sexual culture of mutuality, respect, and women's self-advocacy, then let's focus on ways to facilitate mutuality, respect, and women's self-advocacy, rather than simply renaming those values *consent* (see also Westen 2004, 3). I have no doubt that Marran-Baden (2017) and her fellow activists are undertaking necessary conversations about "pleasure, anatomy, and masculinity," but then why call the campaign the Consent Project? How about the Pleasure Project? Or the Reciprocity Project? My fear is that by packaging our substantive and wide-ranging sexual values into the procedural and winnowing talk of consent, we are sacrificing a far more capacious project that could zoom out of sex and zoom in on sexual culture (see also Graybill 2017, 176). What values, norms, and practices in our culture facilitate mutually fulfilling, creative, nonrote, nonblah sex? What values, norms, and practices in our culture enable unpleasant, unwanted, or even assaultive sex?

Phenomenologically, the problem goes deep too. For if consent is our benchmark of permissible sex, and if consent is culturally redefined—even if not institutionally recodified—as entailing mutuality, enthusiasm, sobriety, creativity, and so on, then sex without enthusiasm, or nonsober sex, will be increasingly understood, and increasingly felt and experienced, as sexual assault. This slippage is literalized by the University of Wyoming Dean of Students Office brochure that informs its students that sex without enthusiasm is "Sexual Assault," capital S, capital A. One could also imagine a scenario in which a person affirmatively agreed to sex but nevertheless felt "reluctant" or "unsure." The brochure names this sex sexual assault too (Halley's governance feminism nightmare).

My concern is less about codification. The University of Wyoming's definition of consent in its sexual misconduct policy is more mundane and straightforward than in the dean's brochure. One cannot be found in violation of the sexual misconduct policy for having sex with someone who positively agreed to sex but felt ambivalent; one can also not be found in violation of the policy for having sex with someone who consented positively but not enthusiastically. Still, we should be troubled by the way the Dean of Students Office brochure (and I take the brochure to be a dramatic yet representative symbol for the circulating pedagogies of the Consent Moment) is inculcating its students to experience and feel sex. Perhaps I sound as panicky and cranky as the critics I consider earlier, but I worry that the more we equate consent with desire, pleasure, or enthusiasm, the more students will feel themselves as sexually assaulted when sex does not go well, or when it is not as rock star as they had hoped. Sex that is OK, regretted, unenthusiastic, and not pleasurable will be retroactively experienced as *assaultive* if nonregret, enthusiasm, pleasure, and better-than-OK are culturally conceptualized as necessary ingredients for consent. My point is neither to trivialize sex that is not assaultive but still bad, nor to accuse students of lying. To the contrary—I think students will be telling the truth of their experience because their felt experience is discursively conditioned (Gavey 2005, 232; Marcus 1992; Scott 1991). And we ought to take quite seriously, as a target of social reform, sex that is pressured into, unpleasant, and unenthusiastic. But that effort will undoubtedly backfire (and lead to lawsuits) if we call all that unpleasant and unenthusiastic but agreed-to sex sexual assault because we make consent more than it can or should be. Whereas scholars such as Professors Suk and Gersen argue that such definitional expansion of consent trivializes "actual" rape, I am suggesting that by calling all that bad sex rape we are (a) potentially generating and amplifying people's psychological and sensorial injuries and (b) missing political opportunities and underutilizing political resources to remedy bad, sometimes really bad, sex (see also Cahill 2016, 758; Conly 2004; Gavey 2005, 136–65).

As it currently circulates among activists, students, and university administrators, consent talk splits the sexual world, rhetorically and perhaps experientially, into two realms: sex that is enthusiastic, mutually desired, fantastic, and thereby consensual and sex that is unenthusiastic, maybe a bit drunken, ambivalently desired, thereby nonconsensual, and thereby classed as sexual assault. Lost in this unforgiving binary are better ways to talk about and redress sex that is not good yet not assaultive (which, let's face it, is a lot of sex). For one way to politicize bad sex is to call it rape; the badness of the sex then retroactively vitiates consent. The cost is pretty high, phenomenologically. The other way to politicize bad sex is to ask: *Why are we consenting to it?* Or: *What went wrong and how can we as a society make sex better or less bad more of the time?*

Here is a pipedream: I would like to see campus programs titled "The Consent Project" or "Project Consent" or the "Communication and Consent Educators Program," and campaigns like Consent Is Sexy and #Consentiseverything, delete *consent* from their names altogether and strike most references to consent in their promotional literature.[14] Such programs and campaigns might reasonably copy-and-paste the university's definition of sexual consent, as well as the home state's definition of sexual consent, for general-information purposes; they might also include a sentence that reads something like "Consent is a legal concept; good sex takes more than acquiescence or agreement." But other than that, screw it. Bad semantics lead to muddled thinking and enervated politics. Programs promoting more feminist, more democratically hedonic sexual cultures should focus not on stuffing their values into consent but on defending and debating the values themselves.

Or perhaps it is not a pipedream. When I emailed the Dean of Students Office at the University Wyoming to inquire about the different definitions of consent in its brochure and its sexual misconduct policy, a coordinator from the university's sexual violence prevention program responded that the brochure was outdated and that, because of my email, she removed the brochure from the dean of students website. My point is not to congratulate myself but to suggest that we need to engage with and respectfully challenge one another within, across, and outside universities about the sexual ethical values we hold and advocate; we need to think and debate, too, about whether and to what degree those values are compatible or incompatible with contemporary valorizations of consent.

The sexual violence prevention coordinator from the University of Wyoming and the assistant dean of students at Elon University replied to my inquiries about their operative definitions of consent in oddly similar ways. Both explained to me that the consent standard of the university policy (affirmative—voluntary, freely given, and so forth) differs from "best practices for consent" promoted by administrators and peer educators. In other words, there is a thinner consent for policy standards and a thicker consent for advocacy and education. Their responses reveal consent's overwhelming magnetism for thinking about sex. Why is it so hard for us to think about good sex and better sexual communication beyond the concept of consent? Why must we "educate on broader definitions of consent [. . .] than are normally recognized in state law or university disciplinary processes," and what does that even mean?[15] Would not that thicker-consent education just lead to confusion if the thinner definitions are the ones that count for anything? Do students really need to be educated that much about whether or not their partners are agreeing to sex with them? Should we prioritize "best practices for *consent*," or should we prioritize instead "best practices for *sex*" whereby we facilitate sexual literacy, access to sexual information, and access to sexual health resources, and whereby we critically interrogate sexual pressure, gender norms, drinking culture, media representations of sex, and the like?

What are we sacrificing when we tether sexual politics over and over to consent? What values remain un- or underarticulated?

TURNING THE SCREWS

Each chapter of this book, a book that is one part polemic and two parts exercises in more measured provocations, turns a different screw on consent. By interrogating sex on the social margins—sexual practices that are atypical, nonnormative, or just weird—*Screw Consent* takes aim, indirectly but effectively I hope, at sex imagined at the center of our moral universe: "ordinary" sex between consenting, usually heterosexual, adult humans. And by investigating comparatively unexamined forms of sexual misconduct and sexual assault, I wish to show how consent talk can often obscure, rather than clarify, what is wrong about wrongful sex. Indeed, neither consent as a legal concept nor consent talk as political advocacy effectively removes the biggest (material, cultural, epistemological, and ideological) impediments to realizing a more flourishing, more feminist sexual culture. This is not to say that this book will singlehandedly usher in a feminist sex-positive utopia. Rather, it is to say that we activists, progressives, and scholars urging a capacious, more adventurous, more imaginative, more informed, less phobic, less misogynistic, less racist, less ableist, and less rote sexual culture should probably screw consent and mobilize instead other concepts and correlating modes of thought.

Screw Consent levels three consent criticisms across its first four chapters. For easy reference, I file these three criticisms under *insufficiency, scope,* and *inappositeness*. As each criticism of consent unfolds, competing concepts and values—for example, human flourishing, nonsuffering, nonexploitation, feminist consciousness—rise to the surface. Some of those values are argued for, while others are simply intimated or asserted. Two such values, *autonomy* and *access,* are more fully presented, parsed, and defended in "Cripping Consent," the book's fifth chapter. To adumbrate briefly: I offer a feminist reconstruction of sexual autonomy that, contrary to competing notions of the term, prioritizes the *capability* for sexual choice over sexual choices themselves. Sexual autonomy is defined and refined throughout this book as the *capability to co-determine sexual relationships*. And I propound a notion of access developed from disability studies that aims to democratize and deconcentrate opportunities and experiences of intimacy and pleasure.

The first two chapters look at sexual scenarios in which consent is *insufficient*. In chapter 1, I argue that consent is insufficient to adjudicate some kinds of *sexual conduct*. In chapter 2, I argue that consent is insufficient for adjudicating sex across some differences in *relationship status*. The *insufficiency* criticism is thus split into two types: insufficiency as to conduct and insufficiency as to status.

The first chapter, "Kink and Cannibals, or Why We Should Probably Ban American Football," marshals the sensational "German cannibal" case—involving a man who consensually and erotically dismembered, ate, and killed another man—to make the point that consent is not and should not be a green light for any activity whatsoever, even if that activity is sexual, erotic, or intimate somehow or to someone. Some human practices on or with other humans, even if those practices are superduper and affirmatively, enthusiastically consented to, should be impermissible because those practices are incompatible with humans' well-being and -doing in the world and incompatible with humans' capability to co-determine their sexual relationships, their sexual autonomy. Kinky sex practitioners, activists, and scholars often argue that if consent legitimates the violence of physical contact sports like hockey and football, so too should consent authorize rougher forms of sadomasochistic sex. I argue that the analogy is more convincing in the opposite direction: rather than extending the consent defense to rougher, more pain-inducing kinds of kinky sex, we should eliminate the consent defense for American football, and we should probably ban the sport as it is currently practiced, marketed, and corporatized. While nearly all varieties of kinky sex ought to be legally permitted, as most kinky sex neither permanently nor gravely impedes people's ability to do and be in the world, consent is not at all sufficient to make the case for kink. At the end of the chapter I parry with scholars who have proposed that the degree of *physical injury* or the violation of human *dignity*, or both, might serve as the necessary side-constraints to consent's authorizing power. Neither the dignity nor the physical injury threshold is an adequate corrective to the insufficiency of consent.

Chapter 2 turns to sex across differences in relational status. The focus is on the status part, not the sex. Put perhaps grandiosely, whereas the first chapter's arguments are largely driven by philosophical consideration of the meaning and moral value of human life, the second chapter's arguments are largely driven by empirics. Chapter 2 codes relationship patterns in roughly six hundred U.S. criminal sexual assault cases and catalogs status sex laws across all fifty states. The term *status sex laws* refers to statutes that categorically prohibit sex between people if they are in a specified relationship to each other (for example, parent-child or teacher-student). Chapter 2, "The Trouble with Mothers' Boyfriends, or Against Uncles," contends that status sex laws are too often premised upon biology or blood (for example, prohibitions against sex between adult siblings, or between biologically related uncles and nieces), when they should instead more consistently proscribe sex within relationships of trust, authority, and dependence (for example, between a minor and her parent's intimate partner, or between a nephew and his non–biologically related aunt). Power matters over blood. But not all power differences compromise sex in the same way, and so the chapter distinguishes between those kinds of status differences in which sex might be good, hot, consensual, and kosher, and those kinds of status difference in which sex—however good, hot, or consensual—is still a really bad idea and should probably be prohibited.

"The Trouble with Transgender 'Rapists,'" chapter 3, takes as its point of departure a handful of criminal cases from the United States, England, and Israel in which transgender men or butch women were convicted of some form of sexual assault for allegedly deceiving their female partners that they were men (this chapter builds on the insights of A. Gross 2009; 2015; and Sharpe 2014; 2015). While I maintain that these cases were ruled wrongly—that the gender identifications of the defendants, whether or not disclosed to their partners, do not vitiate sexual consent—I also concede that the cases dramatize a serious conceptual and legal problem for the consent standard of modern rape law (Rubenfeld 2013a). Once we jump on the consent bandwagon, how far do we ride it? Or, what do we consent to when we consent to sex? What is consent's *scope*? In other words, if what we care about when we care about consent is the right of person A to choose the conditions under which she engages in sexual activity, then surely we care if person B withholds, alters, or straight-up lies about information to (unduly?) influence person A's choice. But what kinds of deceptions and nondisclosures, if any, undermine consent? There is, I suggest, a principled way to cabin the scope of consent such that we respect people's sexual choices without making each and every kind of lie ("I'm Canadian") or embellishment ("I give the best massages") to procure sex against the law.

Unlike the first two chapters, which screw as in "jettison" consent, this chapter screws as in "tightens" consent.[16] Rather than abandon consent in order to amplify other kinds of values and problems we could or should suture to sex, "The Trouble with Transgender 'Rapists'" maps alternative definitional parameters of consent to better allocate sexual risks and responsibilities. I conclude the chapter by asserting that some yes-or-no questions cannot and should not be answerable as truth claims under law (for example, *Are you a man?*), and thus the defendant's response, whatever it is, cannot possibly vitiate sexual consent.

The fourth chapter, the most speculative, is shortest by pages and longest by title: "Horses and Corpses: Notes on the Wrongness of Sex with Children, the Inappositeness of Consent, and the Weirdness of Heterosomething Masculinity." In the state of Washington, several men regularly convened to be anally penetrated by horses. In Michigan, after three men tried (and failed) to exhume a human, female, and apparently quite attractive corpse so one of the men could penetrate it, the men were convicted of attempted sexual assault.[17] I discuss these strange scenarios to puncture the good liberal's posture. The good liberal defaults to consent when faced with these scenarios: *sex with horses must be wrong because horses cannot consent; sex with human corpses must be wrong because human corpses cannot consent.* But consent is startlingly (if obviously, after but a moment of contemplation) inapposite for adjudicating or rendering the moral permissibility of sex with either horses or corpses. Horses and corpses are not the kinds of things to which a consent inquiry reasonably applies, because consent is a human construct for governing human relations. We do not, because we really cannot, ask if the dog "consents" to play fetch or roll over, though we can and should ask about animal welfare, cruelty, and suffering.

The meditations on sex, horses, and corpses lead to unsettling conclusions about child sexual abuse. The modern notion of the "child" presupposes adult superintendence, precisely because children are not creatures who are capable of consent. But if children cannot consent to anything (like attending preschool or getting vaccinated), why should it matter that they cannot consent to sex? Sex between adults and young children is wrong and rightfully unlawful, but not primarily, I argue, because children cannot consent.

The final point of the chapter concerns men—the men who wished to be penetrated by horses and the men who wished to penetrate a corpse. I surmise that perhaps what these men sought in their sex was not gendered dominance but in fact a break from the normative strictures of gendered dominance—a break from being heterosexual "men" under the ruthlessly competitive and precarious conditions of late modernity. That speculation could very well be wrong but in any case opens up a point of entry for elaborating the aspirations of the book's final chapter and conclusion: to generate conceptual coordinates for a more accessible, more egalitarian, more feminist, and ultimately more democratically hedonic sexual culture.

The fifth chapter, "Cripping Consent: Autonomy and Access," explicates a Connecticut case of alleged sexual assault committed against a significantly physically and cognitively disabled woman.[18] The facts and fallout of the case facilitate an analysis of sex and sexual ethics that applies, synthesizes, and also qualifies the three core criticisms of consent (insufficiency, scope, and inappositeness). The examination of the case shores up several ways consent fails to deliver sexual justice. My coauthor for this chapter, Hilary O'Connell, a friend and former student, and I propose legal remedies and social reforms that would better facilitate sexual and intimate possibilities not only for the alleged victim in the Connecticut case and people similarly disabled, but also, if more speculatively, for people positioned across the spectrum of ability. The legal remedies are grounded in a feminist reconstruction of sexual *autonomy* that rejects the equation of autonomy with consent. The social reforms are grounded in a disability studies reconstruction of *access* that promotes institutional arrangements facilitating people's equal participation in politics, education, employment, and sex. To a large degree, the reconstruction of sexual autonomy retroactively justifies legal reforms introduced earlier in the book, while the reconstruction of access portends broader transformations outlined in the chapter's final pages.

What would it mean if, utilizing the social model of disability, we created "ramps" to access sexual culture (Shakespeare 2006)? As a person in a wheelchair utilizes a ramp to access her or his school or workplace, how might we, metaphorically, build ramps for people to access a more feminist, more democratically hedonic sexual culture? How do we make pleasures, experiments, and adventures in sex more safely accessible to more people? The ramp metaphor is not without its problems (for example, its potential overreliance on a notion of disability as physical rather than cognitive and its presumption that all human problems and impairments are resolvable through social rearrangements), problems also addressed in the chapter.

While O'Connell and I advocate and elaborate autonomy and access as abstractions more finely attuned to an egalitarian, feminist, hedonic, and nonoppressive sexual culture, our goal, and the measure of this book's success, is not so much that you adopt our preferred principles for regulating and thinking about sex but that you avow and articulate the principles you hold and promote, principles that in good deliberative and politically liberal fashion are always revisable and improvable with new information and new experiences.

The conclusion, "#MeFirst—Undemocratic Hedonism," offers a brief and highly partial (in both senses of the term) analysis of the post-2017 searing, public exposures of powerful men who have committed sexual assault, harassment, and misconduct. Such exposures, gathered under the sign and movement #MeToo, have rocked the nation and the world. When I started writing this book, the sexual misconduct du jour was on campus; as I finish it, we have shifted our attention back to sexual misconduct in the workplace and in Hollywood, perpetuated by celebrities, politicians, and other elites.

I propose in the final pages of the book that thinking in terms of autonomy and access, and not in terms of consent, might reframe some of the central ethical and political questions #MeToo raises. For, while some have argued that nonconsent is the common denominator of #MeToo's wrongful sex, and others have argued that (potential) sex discrimination is the common denominator, I suggest that neither nonconsent nor discrimination identifies the core wrong of #MeToo's wrongful sex. Instead, the pervasive problem underlining so many of the incidents that constellate #MeToo is men's sense of sexual entitlement, their leveraging positions of power to exact sexual gratification, and the consequent undemocratic, asymmetric distribution of pleasure. These problems, and not the problem of nonconsent, form the connective tissue across #MeToo stories and scandals. Querying how and why powerful men constrain (indexically) women's autonomy and access, rather than presuming all such sex nonconsensual, is more generative for our feminist politics. When nonconsent is proffered as the thread that ties together #MeToo moments, skeptics once again predictably sound alarms that we are hastily lumping all regretted, regrettable, or bad sex as rape. Some contend this conflation belittles rape and infantilizes women. I think the conflation belittles bad sex, and misdiagnoses as assaultive sex men's sense of sexual entitlement and superordination. If the problem is misdiagnosed, therewith the proposed solutions.

CODA: IS SEX SPECIAL?

I will confess now that the book does not have a definitive answer to the question of whether sex is special. I teach an undergraduate seminar titled "Theory and Politics of Sexual Consent," from which many of the ideas in this book first percolated and then matured, thanks to challenging discussions with bright, creative students. Invariably, no matter what the topic is for class on any given day—feminist legal theory, kink, bestiality, age-of-consent laws, Marxism, the social contract—we ultimately arrive at the question, Is sex special? or more precisely, Why is sex special? since its specialness across space and time seems undeniable, even if sex is not always special for the same reasons and even if sex is not special to each and every person. Assisted by a wide variety of theories and theorists, we arrive at several hypotheses: sex is special because it is how babies are made (usually); because it activates, as it represses, our primary attachments to Mom and Dad; because it is phenomenologically distinct from any other human activity; because we say it is special; because medical and legal experts have material and ideological stakes in promoting sex's specialness; because it connects us to one another profoundly (see, for example, Alcoff 1996, 127–28; Foucault 1990 [1976]; Freud 2000 [1905], 94–95; Lorde 2007 [1984], 53–59). As a corollary: Why is sexual violence special? Some suggestions from class (and from our class's texts): because we say it is; because law isolates it from other kinds of violence; because it reinstalls sex inequality; because it is distinctly invasive of the body; because it is distinctly violative of a person's selfhood or right of self-determination; because it results in distinctively damaging psychological (and often physical) injuries and trauma; because it distinctly disables people from being and doing in the world; or maybe because sex is special (see, for example, Cahill 2001; du Toit 2009; MacKinnon 2016; Marcus 1992; McGregor 2005, 221–26).

My students and I never come to a definitive answer, but asking the questions—about the specialness of both sex and sexual violence—and posing some speculative answers, prods us, as I hope this book will prod you, to think about whether and when sex and sexual violence should be special. Throughout this book, I draw comparisons to consent in the context of sexual activities with consent in the context of nonsexual activities to question both the moral utility of consent and the presumptive specialness of sex. Unlike Foucault, I do not support the position that "when one punishes rape one should be punishing physical violence and nothing but that [. . .] there is no difference, in principle, between sticking one's fist into someone's face or one's penis into their sex" (Foucault 1988, 200; see also Cahill 2001, 143–66; Franke 2002, 308). Whether the psychological, phenomenological, corporeal, affective, and sociological differences between a punch in the face and a penis forced into a vagina are differences "in principle" or "in practice" is beside the point and probably impossible to answer anyhow. The point is: there are differences, and those differences warrant different (if sometimes imbricated) social responses and legal remedies.

But Foucault's provocation is not without its benefits. Just as your car radio fuzzes out in a tunnel, so our thinking sometimes fuzzes out when it gets too close to sex. Comparisons to our values, norms, and practices regarding nonsex can help clarify or amend our values, norms, and practices regarding sex, since those values, norms and practices sometimes get stuck in sex's Velcro of nonthought or sloughed in sex's accretion of crappy customs. Are there times when we exceptionalize sex but should not, and are there times when we do not exceptionalize sex but should? And how might such cultural calculations and legal rules impact the transformative force of consent?

In chapters 1 and 4, respectively, I argue that progressive defenses of kink and laws against bestiality unjustifiably exceptionalize sex. If we do not think a person's consent is always sufficient to legitimate, say, heroin use or medically unnecessary limb removal, then we ought to be more cautious in supposing that consent ought to legitimate any sexual activity whatsoever, like the eroticized removal of one partner's penis. And if we are to outlaw human sex with animals, we had better outlaw all sorts of farming, agricultural, and husbandry practices that cause animals to suffer (and why isn't gelding a horse considered sexual assault if being penetrated by one is?).

In chapters 2 and 3, respectively, I argue that we might make sex a little more special than we do. In proposing that we categorically outlaw sex between a parent's intimate partner and the minor child of that parent, *regardless of consent,* I am suggesting that sex is a bit more special than, say, basketball, car washing, or any other nonsexual activity. It should not be a crime for a parent's intimate partner to ask the parent's child to perform any number of activities or to perform those activities with the child. But sex should not be on the list of acceptable requests or activities. And in proposing that we render as a legal wrong (but not a crime) the deliberate violation of an explicit conditional to procure sex ("I will have sex with you if and only if you are unmarried"), I am likewise elevating the normative import of sexual autonomy over other kinds of autonomy. (For example, the deliberate contravention of the conditional "I will drive you to the train station if and only if you are unmarried" is a weaker candidate for tortious liability.) Yet I also deflate the primacy of the penis, making it less special. When one consents to sexual penetration, I argue in the third chapter, one ought to have no prima facie right that the contravention of a normative expectation (for example, that one's partner comes equipped from birth with a fleshy, functional penis) is legally actionable.

I do not explicitly lay out a logical, philosophical, or moral principle to justify my seesawing between arguing for the specialness of sex on one hand and its ordinariness on the other. But that seesawing productively aligns with the conceptual and policy interventions of disability studies scholars and disability rights activists discussed in chapter 5. This affinity begins to attest to the political necessity of nimbly thinking about sex—making the case for its specialness sometimes and its ordinariness at other times. Disability scholarship has documented, devastatingly, all that goes wrong when disability is made "special"; for the most part, scholars and activists of disability have worked tirelessly to normalize disability, to deinstitutionalize people with disability, to accommodate persons with disabilities so they can participate as fully in civic and cultural life as people who are temporarily of able mind and body. We might think of these efforts as making disability less special (Clare 2017). At the same time, accommodating persons with certain kinds of disabilities requires expensive, labor-intensive, or otherwise "special" interventions. Not all people with disabilities—and this is especially true of people with cognitive impairments—can be fully integrated into everyday life, in which case special accommodations are required to promote their well-being (but not always their "participatory parity"; Bérubé 2016, 198, citing Fraser 1996; see also Bérubé 2010). And, finally, there is something special about the spectrum of human ability itself and about the genetic diversity of humans, and there are many, many things special about the contributions and perspectives persons with disabilities bring to the world, a fact that augurs for preservation and promotion, rather than the necessary constriction or even elimination, of the spectrum of abilities.

As with disability, so with sex, and so with their intersection—cocultivating sexual cultures for persons with disabilities (see Siebers 2012). What explains the back-and-forth between segregating sex, like disability, for special consideration and integrating sex, like disability, into ordinary everyday life is an abiding commitment to human flourishing, erotic or otherwise (see generally Halwani 2007). Which values, norms, and practices, and which institutional combination of exceptionalizing and de-exceptionalizing sex, enable people to freely and effectively codetermine their intimate and sexual relationships? What social, political, educational, and legal arrangements facilitate more equitable, less gender-asymmetric, less hierarchical access to a democratically hedonic sexual culture for people across the spectrum of ability?

These are the questions we think we are asking when we ask about consent or when we nobly redefine consent as kumbaya. But consent is a term of law, necessary and insufficient, and we should let the law have it. What is the sexual culture to which we aspire, and how do we get there? I offer some tentative answers near the end of the book, but my hope is that each screw of consent encourages you to come up with, and then advocate for, better answers of your own.

CHAPTER 1

Kink and Cannibals

*or Why We Should Probably Ban
American Football*

Fetishists fetishize consent. Practitioners and sympathetic scholars routinely defend and celebrate kinky sex—BDSM[1]—for the moral primacy it places upon consent. Certainly BDSM is praised for other reasons too—for eroticizing otherwise flaccid publics, for contravening stale norms of "harmonic" intimacy, for helping practitioners work through earlier traumatic experiences, and for theatricalizing and thereby subverting hierarchical social relations (e.g., Bauer 2014, 3; Califia 1994 [1980], 172–74; Henkin 2007). But nearly all advocacy for BDSM starts with consent as moral square one. Whether conceptualized as a "contract," a "safe word," or something far more communicatively cumbersome, consent not only exonerates but also extols BDSM sex. This is consent unbound.

It is time to tie it up.

As the first of two chapters describing the *insufficiency* of consent for adjudicating sex, this one makes the following five arguments: (1) consent should not green-light any sexual conduct whatsoever simply because the conduct is sexual; (2) while BDSM defenders analogize kinky sex to physical contact sports in support of the former's legitimacy, the (dis)analogy in fact makes a stronger case for the illegitimacy of the latter, especially American football; (3) (yet) in sex, as in football, the sufficiency threshold for consent should not be, ipso facto, either the *seriousness* of any given physical injury or an affront to human *dignity*, as some critics propose; (4) we can begin to excavate alternative sufficiency thresholds to seriousness and dignity by turning to two contradictions within consent-centric, pro-BDSM literature; (5) these contradictions are resolved once consent is checked and once other abstractions—already articulated within the BDSM lexicon—are entrusted with more power. Not incidentally, these other abstractions—mutuality, communication, care for others, power exchange, and so on—sound with a feminist commitment of sexual *autonomy* and a feminist reconstruction of sexual *access*.

CHEWING PENIS

On March 9, 2001, two German men in their forties, Armin Meiwes and Bernd Brandes, together attempted to dine on Brandes's fried penis. Meiwes and Brandes had met online earlier that month, after Meiwes had posted an advertisement soliciting men who wished to be eaten, to which Brandes eagerly responded. Brandes traveled by train to Meiwes's farmhouse, whereupon the two men had sex before Brandes consumed copious quantities of alcohol and sleeping pills, apparently in anticipation of the ensuing pain of having his penis removed. Meiwes cut off Brandes's penis after he failed to bite it off, frying the penis when it proved too tough to eat raw. Now charred and inedible, Meiwes fed what was left of Brandes's member to the dog. Brandes spent the next several hours in a warm bath bleeding out before Meiwes stabbed and killed him with a kitchen knife. Meiwes cut Brandes into pieces, stored some of the remains in the freezer, and buried the skull and bones of the deceased in his backyard. In the months following, Meiwes would periodically dine on Brandes flesh with his "best cutlery" and a glass of red wine (Harding 2003).

Scandalizing this scandal further, Meiwes "had recorded every bloody detail of the slaying on video," a video in which Brandes evidently and continually consents to his dismemberment and death (although there is some question about the validity of consent given Brandes's blood loss and intoxication) (Barcroft TV 2016). Following a tip-off, police went to Meiwes's farmhouse and discovered the frozen flesh and bones of Brandes, as well as the video.

In a German criminal court, Meiwes was convicted of manslaughter, not murder; Brandes's voluntariness—his consent—in part mitigated Meiwes's culpability (Harding 2004). However, on appeal Meiwes was convicted of murder and sentenced to prison for life. The court held that consent could not be a defense to murder (Fickling 2006).

Obviously, "chewing penis" is neither the only nor chiefly objectionable activity that went down that eventful night, though I imagine the subheading grabbed your attention. Yet the incident—explosively reported alike in popular media (e.g., Eckardt 2004; Bovsun 2015) and in academic journals (e.g., Bergelson 2007, 166–67; Y. Lee 2007, 2982–88)—flags three dilemmas: the first on the limits of consent, the second on the normative significance of bodily injury, and the third on the multiple meanings of penis removal (and death). In truth, these three dilemmas are but shaves off the first: the insufficiency of consent, however valorized and sexified, for adjudicating sexual conduct between or among (the legal fiction of rational, competent, adult) human beings.

The fetishists' fetishizing of consent looks like this: as consent transforms what would be rape into "sex" (Hurd 2005, 504; Baker 2009, 97), so consent transforms sex with violence, scenes of hierarchy, role-playing, or other forms of explicit power exchange into kink (Weinberg 2016, 15).

For example, in his ethnography of what he terms "dyke + queer BDSM" practitioners, Robin Bauer (2014) reports that "the one feature that all interview partners agreed was crucial for an activity to count as BDSM [was] consent" (13). Bauer quotes well-known practitioners who insist, against charges of sadomasochistic sex as violence, that "what we are doing is consensual. Period" (Moser and Madeson 1996, 71, quoted in Bauer 2014, 75).

For another example, in her visual and discursive analysis of kink and black female sexuality, Ariane Cruz (2016), even as she demagnetizes consent from its presumptive normativity, nonetheless reports that "black women BDSMers suggest that [. . .] consent is not only possible but also pleasurable and affectively empowering" (45).[2]

For a third, acute example of consent fetish, consider the words of well-known kink practitioner and advocate Carol Truscott (1991): "Consensual sadomasochism has nothing to do with violence. Consensual sadomasochism is about *safely* enacting sexual fantasies with a *consenting* partner. Violence is the epitome of nonconsensuality" (30).

And for a fourth and final example of consent's staying power over kink community and politics, visit the National Coalition for Sexual Freedom's (NCSF's) "Consent Counts" project site.[3] Founded in 1997, NCSF is a nationwide kink support and advocacy coalition that has, over the past few years, initiated its Consent Counts project, which "seeks to decriminalize consensual BDSM which does not result in the infliction of serious bodily injury" (NCSF 2013). Toward that effort,

NCSF has filed amicus briefs in cases involving allegedly consensual kink, has petitioned state legislatures, and has lobbied the American Law Institute to recommend that BDSM conduct be permitted a consent defense under the revised Model Penal Code (more on the Model Penal Code below). "It's all about consent," the coalition's website asserts, "and the law should reflect that" (NCSF n.d.).

Let us assume, in light of these four examples, that Bernd Brandes consented with sound mind to the removal of his penis and his death at the hands of Armin Meiwes. Let us assume too that neither intoxicants nor blood loss corroded Brandes's consent, for "sooner or later we are doomed to encounter a mentally competent person who would wish to be killed or injured" (Bergelson 2007, 186; see also Baker 2009, 103–4). Whether conceptualized as a moral concept or a legal construct, *consent* is unhelpful for indicting this cannibalistic erotic encounter, an encounter that strikes me as, without question, morally and legally indictable, unless one adopts the most stringent libertarian posture (to be fair, NCSF argues for consent as a defense to kink that "does not result in serious bodily injury," a qualifier that I will argue in the third section is necessary yet overinclusive and underinclusive; NCSF 2015). The German Cannibal case readily reveals that consent cannot be dispositive; it cannot be sufficient (Westen 2004, 129). The case also reveals that a definitional core of BDSM is readily confused as an ethical core (Hanna 2001, 240). For if we are disinclined to green-light non-eroticized but consensual activity involving gross or even fatal injuries, why should sex make all the difference? If I ask my friend to push me off a skyscraper, most would agree that she should not do so, and that if she did so, my asking to be pushed might mitigate but not eliminate any responsibility on her part (Bergelson 2007, 236; Hanna 2001, 241). Are we really willing to say that if pushing me off the building aroused me (or her), the push (and death) would be morally kosher (Baker 2009, 97–98; McGregor 2005, 243)? Why should "sex"—or sexualizing, really—be so transformative? It should not, even accounting for the specialness sex and intimacy find in many people's lives (and in the U.S. Constitution; see *Lawrence v. Texas* [2003]; cf. Spindelman 2003). Indeed, courts in the United States and elsewhere have generally agreed on this point when ruling on cases involving BDSM sex (or rather, cases involving consent as a defense to alleged BDSM sex). In Anglo-American jurisdictions, defendants are usually charged with some form of assault (not sexual assault), for which consent is typically not recognized as a defense (Haley 2014, 636–40; NCSF 2015).

Some critics contend that prosecuting BDSM as assault rather than sexual assault delegitimizes BDSM sex as sex (e.g., Haley 2014, 640–41; Kaplan 2014, 121–22). On this reading, it is not that the legal classification of BDSM as assault reflects the assaultive social reality of BDSM sex but that the legal classification of BDSM as assault purposively discards the sexual social reality of BDSM sex.

Other critics have pointed out that judicial findings of harm (under allegedly consensual circumstances) are thinly guised pretexts for eroto- and homophobia (Khan 2014, 225–303). This judicial sleight of hand is nowhere more infamously on display than in the "Spanner" case in the United Kingdom, in which several men were convicted on various counts of assault for engaging in rough, kinky sex with a younger, submissive man (*R. v. Brown* [1994]). The graphically described conduct (for example, sterilized fishhooks inserted into the submissive's penis) is discomfiting, but the injuries sustained were neither permanent nor incapacitating postcoitus (Egan 2006, 1615, 1629). Moreover, despite gestural concern for the welfare of the submissive (who refused to testify against the defendants), the justices' statements drip with derision, homophobia, and AIDS panic.[4] Adding heteronormative insult to queer injury, a defendant was held not guilty of similar conduct (for example, branding the alleged victim's buttocks) three years later, in large degree because the victim was a woman and the defendant's wife (*R. v. Wilson* [1996]; Khan 2014, 237–42). In US jurisdictions, kink advocates point to cases in which defendants have been charged, and some convicted, for assault despite the fact that the BDSM activity did not reach the "serious bodily injury" threshold of the criminal statute. "In one case—particularly notorious in the BDSM community—a woman was prosecuted for assault for consensually spanking another woman with a wooden spoon" (NCSF 2015). The harm of an activity (nipple clamping, for example) is moralistically overstated as "serious" in order to classify it as assaultive (Kaplan 2014, 122; NCSF 2015).

I recount these sex-positive objections to concede that my seemingly simple normative claim—*consent, on its own, should not morally or legally green-light any eroticized activity whatsoever, however injurious or impeding*—is proposed not in a social vacuum but against a sexual regulatory landscape historically hostile to sexual minorities. Yet bad cases make for bad normative propositions.[5] Law professor Cheryl Hanna (2001) points out that the Spanner case is an outlier, "sensational and rare" (263). In most cases in the United States and Canada, the facts follow this pattern: the defendant—almost always male—alleges the conduct in question to have been rough sex that the victim—almost always female—consented to ("asked for"). "In the vast majority of cases that make it into the criminal justice system, consent is questionable at best" (Hanna 2001, 248). In these cases of likely rape, prosecutors charge defendants with assault, not sexual assault, effectively bypassing the he said–she said dispute that women typically lose (Hanna 2001, 269–70; see also *State v. Gaspar* [2009]).[6] One might take issue with this prosecutorial reach-around, and one might concede that phobia underwrites too much judicial reasoning about sex, but Hanna's observation reveals that the paradigmatic "BDSM case" that makes its way to appellate courts is not kinky-consensual-sex-that-judges-and-juries-are-repulsed-by but rather rape-that-men-claim-as-rough-sex (see also McGregor 2005, 245; Westen 2004, 71–74). In any case, however we come down on these judicial opinions and prosecutorial practices, the central conceptual point I wish to press remains unchallenged: consent, on its own, is insufficient to exonerate any and all forms of sexualized conduct.

One could claim that I am caricaturing the BDSM position, as there are other tools in the kink toolbox besides consent with which to scrutinize erotic cannibalism and erotic murder. BDSM communities have long been in the business of moral advertising to countervail dominant misperceptions and misrepresentations of kink. BDSM's most widely recognized and longest-running public campaign is SSC, which stands for "safe, sane, and consensual" (d. stein n.d.; Langdridge and Barker 2007).[7] Again, if we assume *arguendo* that Brandes was sane, we are nonetheless left with *safe* as an abstraction to reach for that might militate against consensually consuming and killing one's partner. Yet is not a foundational premise of kinky sex its libidinized dangerousness? Surely much if not most avowedly BDSM sex is more about power exchange and its eroticization than about brute infliction of serious injury (Newmahr 2011, 161). To that end, flogging and spanking, bondage, role play, and even knife and breath play are put in the service of eroticizing a relationship rather than, simply, severely physically or psychologically endangering or injuring a person: "There is so much more to pain scenes than simply the application of a pain stimulus during and/or for sexual arousal" (Langdridge 2007, 87; see also Egan 2006, 1616). However, this leaves unchanged the fact that the erotic charge of much BDSM is dialed up by transgressing a norm of "safeness," however symbolically or to whatever degree. Isn't "safe BDSM" just sex? Indeed, part of what motivated the renovation from "SSC" to "RACK"—risk-aware consensual kink—is the acknowledgment that kinky folks play with and thereby eroticize the boundaries of safeness ("If we want to limit

BDSM to what's safe, we can't do anything more extreme than flogging somebody with a wet noodle"; Switch 2002). *Risk-aware* more precisely references what *safe* was meant to: practitioners know what they are doing and choose to do so. In that sense, *safe* is a redundancy on *consent*—it is "safe" because it is "consensual." On its face, though, RACK offers no reason to hold cannibalistic homicidal sex impermissible. Brandes and Meiwes were aware of the risks; or, more accurately, there are no fatal risks when what is sought is fatality. Perhaps they were unaware of the chewiness of uncooked penis.

In the past five years, several BDSM scholars-cum-practitioners advanced their preferred ethical model to both SSC and RACK: the "4Cs"—caring, communication, consent, and caution (Williams et al. 2014). This model fares no better with Brandes and Meiwes. Meiwes may very well have caringly, communicatively, consensually, and cautiously eaten and murdered Brandes.

Notice, finally, that the only shared concept across the three ethical models—SSC, RACK, the 4Cs—is *consent*. Among BDSM practitioners and advocates, consent is of primary, nearly summary ethical import, and it is insufficient if we think there are reasons either to prohibit or penalize consensual erotic cannibalism and erotic murder.

Maybe the problem of cannibalistic homicidal sex is what may seem obvious to readers: the degree of physical injury, here dismemberment and death (NCSF 2015). This is the second of three dilemmas previously listed (the normative significance of bodily injury), flagged for now and addressed in the following two sections. But the third dilemma, on the many meanings of penis removal (and death), begins to trouble the obviousness of the nth-degree physical injury boundary, by which we might imagine a specified threshold of "serious bodily injury," somewhere past spanking but before death, that renders sex impermissible and consent insufficient.[8]

It cannot suffice that nth-degree serious physical injury, by itself, is the limiting case for consent's transformative power. Consider gender-affirming surgery that entails the removal of the penis and testes, or a mastectomy. However much one might question the medicalization of gender or the genital essentialism of some transgender narratives (Spade 2003), it would seem cruel—and indefensible—to deny a patient's gender-affirming surgery on the grounds that consent does not authorize nth-degree physical injury.

Lisa Downing (2004) takes the position opposite to mine regarding erotic homicide. She argues that if we are on board with physician-assisted suicide, we have no principled grounds to oppose autassassinaphilia, the desire to be killed by a sexual partner (10). Instead, such opposition is erotophobic prejudice masquerading as principle. Downing is mistaken and the mistake is a function of the analogy. Take the better analogy, one suggested by a student of mine and referenced previously in simplified form: the nonsuffering, non–terminally ill person who has had a bad day and asks his friend to push him off a skyscraper.[9] Our reluctance to push our friend or to sanction consensual pushing off a skyscraper reveals that our refusal to sign on to autassassinaphilic sex, even as we might hesitantly endorse physician-assisted suicide, may have less to do with our aversion to sex than our compassion for the imagined subject of physician-assisted suicide. In other words, both the transgender person seeking gender-affirming surgery and the terminally ill patient seeking medical assistance to end his or her life have "good reasons" for consenting to nth-degree physical injury, reasons which intimate that nth-degree physical injury should not by itself side-constrain consent's transformative force (Bergelson 2007, 224–36). The transgender case and the physician-assisted suicide case suggest that what renders consent insufficient in matters of sex is not simply physical injury alone but, rather, a moral calculation that balances statutory, subjective, and human welfare interests, a calculation I sketch out later in the chapter.

First, though, let us look at American football. For the legally (and culturally) accepted permissibility of physical contact sports is the ubiquitous argument-by-analogy in defense of BDSM sex. The analogy fails, but instructively. For rather than shoring up the goods of kinky sex, the (dis)analogy spotlights the wrongs of American football. Moreover, such wrongs are neither only nor exhaustively wrongs of *serious physical injury* (i.e., brain damage and chronic traumatic encephalopathy) but wrongs of unfairly impeding boys' and young men's capabilities to be and do in the world. And once the "kink" of consensual kinky sex starts to do *that*—starts to nontrivially impair people's capabilities to be and do in the world—then consensual sex *is* more like American football, and should, like American football, probably be prohibited.

FOOTBALL IS NOT SEX

The analogy between BDSM and contact sports espoused both by criminal defendants and kink advocates to legitimate consent as a defense to rough sex is well worn (e.g., Pa 2001, 64–65; Bergelson 2007, 193–93; Kaplan

2014, 123–25; cf. Hanna 2001; Egan 2006).[10] In the United States, part of the reason the analogy is so popular is that the Model Penal Code (MPC) permits consent as a defense to "serious bodily injury" if such injury is incurred in "lawful athletic contest or competitive sport or other concerted activity not forbidden by law" (MPC §211(2)(b)).[11] States have adopted variants of this clause while refusing to permit consent as a defense to assault charges arising from alleged BDSM sex. "If a person is allowed to consent to harm for the sake of sports," goes the analogic argument, "he should arguably also be allowed to consent to harm for the sake of this metaphysical experience [sex]" (Haley 2014, 644).

Against what we might call the sex-positive tide, or the kink lobby if there were one,[12] Cheryl Hanna, in "Sex Is Not a Sport: Consent and Violence in Criminal Law" (2001), warns us not to jump on the sex-is-like-contact-sports bandwagon. For Hanna, the critical difference between contact sports and sex is that the former is distinguished by "rules and regulations and referees," whereas the latter's violence is potentially unbounded (2001, 290; BDSMers and advocates rebut this claim: see, e.g., Truscott 1991, 19; Pa 2001, 77–78). Moreover, for Hanna, the rules of contact sport have "evolved to control [violence]" among equals, mostly men, whereas rough sex, Hanna observes, is more often rough for women; this sex smells like violence among differently sexed non-equals, or patriarchy (254, 269–70). So Hanna drives a wedge between contact sport and sex, applauding consent's "moral magic" in sport but distrusting its application to kinky sex (285–86, 290; Hurd 1996 ["moral magic"]).

Crucially, Hanna largely leaves out American football in her comparisons to BDSM sex, and for good reason. For once we admit football into the comparison, the sports side of the analogy, more than the sex side, is thrown into ethical crisis.

I am not a football fan, and I rarely played the game growing up. I view one game a year, *the* game, usually in a gay bar, sipping stupidly colored martinis, awaiting the multimillion-dollar commercials and glittery pop star at halftime. This is to say I am not the best candidate to convince readers about the moral questionability—probably moral wrongness, ultimately—of American football as it is currently practiced, preached, and corporatized. But my point is less to convince you that football is wrong than to suggest, first, that the football–kinky sex analogy augurs less for permitting kinky sex than for prohibiting or more stringently regulating and reorganizing American football; and second, that the reasons for which football are impermissible—reasons that ultimately have less to do with physical bodily injury per se than with impediments to *autonomy* and *access*—ought to migrate into our thinking about and adjudicating of sex.

Football and kinky sex are alike because in both cases people consent to physical violence committed upon them (Weinberg 2016, 4–5), though physical violence is *not* as intrinsic to kink as it is to football, the Spanner counterclaim notwithstanding.[13] "All the fancy strategy eventually gives way to the essential question: Which side hits hardest?" (Almond 2014, 135). As famed linebacker Ray Lewis puts it, "The long runs, the touchdowns and all that, that's the glamour. But the game is about taking a man down, physically and mentally" (quoted in Almond 2014, 135). Football and kink are alike in other, more anthropological ways as well—for example, common to both are special costumes, intimate rituals, and the libidinal pleasures of surrender and sacrifice—but consent is the commonality at issue in the defense of BDSM (Almond 2014; Foley 1990, 126–28; Newmahr 2011, 137).

Enumerated briefly below are four ways football is problematically *unlike* most kink (and unlike nearly all other contact sports, in degree if not in kind), the list compiled mainly from journalist Steve Almond's piercingly persuasive *Against Football: One Fan's Reluctant Manifesto* (2014).

- **American football objectifies or otherwise degrades black boys and men.**

Football is a nostrum for poorer, predominantly African American communities, a nostrum sold to black high school boys and their families as a way out of destitution and into the high life. Yet since only "1 out 500 [high school] players" "wind[s] up in the pros," Steve Almond argues provocatively that the allure of football, like the allure of crack cocaine, is a distraction "from the systemic inequalities that keep such boys locked in a cycle of poverty and incarceration" (2014, 106). In this sense, football is an object of cruel optimism (Berlant 2011). Attritional for too many of its players, football sustains the racialized inequities it promises to overcome.

Almond asks more controversial questions still. "What is the relationship between our nation's racial history and our lust for football?" "What does it mean that football fever tends to run so hot in those states where slavery was legal and Jim Crow died hardest?" (2014, 106) "Does football provide white Americans a continued sense of dominion over African-American men?" (112) I acknowledge both the technical beauty of the game and the racial diversity of its fans and players, but it is hard to deny that the franchise is built upon mostly white team owners purchasing mostly black bodies so mostly white fans can watch those bodies bulldoze one another, all of which is underwritten by corporate advertisements (Almond 2014, 112; Jefferson 2010; on the racialized history and ongoing racial stratification of player positions, see, e.g., Rhoden 2011).

Undoubtedly, some BDSM scenes stage or reenact racialized slave scripts, and much BDSM gets its libidinal charge, avowedly or not, from racial inequality (B. Weiss 2011, 194–201; Cruz 2016, 29–73); yet racial subordination is baked into the profitability of American football. "Watching young African-Americans in tight pants engage in mock combat has become our most profitable form of entertainment" (Almond 2014, 110–11). Indeed it is not absurd to suggest, as Almond does, that football contributes significantly to white Americans' racist worldviews and, in particular, to the fatal stereotyping of black men as animalistic and aggressive (186–87; see also Shor 2014).

- **American football subscribes boys and men to the most unforgiving masculinity norms.**

Football "prizes physical dominance"; trains, socializes, and desensitizes boys and men to physical dominance; and discourages empathy, sensitivity, and other forms of emotional connection (Almond 2014, 97–99). Attendant to the habituation of dominance, what lubricates and extends that dominance is a casualization of racism, misogyny, and homophobia that constitutes (or, less polemically, may constitute) the psychic stuff of the successful football player (94). In turn, football masculinity, which is to say players' sense of self-worth (and monetary worth), is indexed through successful subscription to a norm of domination and brutality.

Such violence commingles spectacularly with hypersexualized comradeship, a homosociality in overdrive, built upon shared enterprises of hurting one another, "get[ting] more bitches," and humiliating and quashing alleged signs of femininity in one another (Jonathan Martin, quoted in Almond 2014, 95; on this score, BDSM is more promising than football by, for example, sometimes eroticizing men's femininity). "No other sport defines masculinity in such radical terms, as both violent and physically intimate," Almond writes. "The brutality of the game is what allows for such intimacy. Men purchase the rights, through their valor, to love other men without experiencing shame" (93).

When football men dominate and practice the same acts of violence in everyday life for which they are celebrated on the field, when the cultivation of aggression and obliteration overflows off the stadium and off screen, the players (or the victims, or both) are shunned and demonized, though the players are hardly ever convicted of a crime (Almond 2014, 100; Withers 2015). This is not to say we should excuse Ray Rice for knocking out his fiancée, or Josh Brown for assaulting his wife; it is to ask: Where did Rice and Brown learn that beating up others was a masculine form of problem-solving? (Almond 2014, 99; see also Schulman 2016, 15–17) Football corroborates that lesson whether or not it is the first to teach it. And despite hardening policies against players who have committed domestic violence or sexual assault, it is at least worth pondering why, "relative to the income level (top 1 percent) and poverty rate (0 percent) of NFL players, the domestic violence arrest rate is downright extraordinary" (Morris 2014).

Not to mention, American football assigns *women* to the narrowest of femininity norms too: women "can either dance around on the sidelines as a half-naked sex object or sit in the stands cheering on [their] man" (Almond 2014, 89).

· **Football is predatorily capitalistic and exploitive.**

The NFL "is the epitome of crony capitalism, a corporate oligarchy that has absorbed or crushed all potential competitors, that routinely extorts municipal and state governments, and openly flouts its tax obligations" (Almond 2014, 73). Taxpayers "have funded 70 percent of the construction costs of the stadiums in which NFL teams play," while team owners collect the lion's share of profit (Almond 2014, 76; see also Easterbrook 2013): "Consider the economic impact if taxpayers were to receive 70 percent of the profits generated by those facilities [$7 billion]. [. . .] Think about how much social *good* $7 billion would do in cities such as Detroit and Cleveland and St. Louis, where bright new stadiums rise above crumbling schools, closed factories, and condemned homes" (Almond 2014, 76).

One could speciously analogize the financial dealings of the NFL that perpetuate social inequalities to BDSM as a late modern "paradigmatic consumer sexuality" (M. Weiss 2011, 104). Some BDSM subcultures, especially coastal ones, are increasingly organized around, and gather meaning from, the purchase and proper use of expensive toys and paraphernalia (slings, rope, dungeon equipment), thus creating financial barriers to entry. BDSM comes to look like other modes of conspicuous consumption that make the rich look sexy and good sex more accessible for the rich. *Fifty Shades*'s Christian Grey pays to play; his wealth makes him desirable and is its own object of desire (James 2011; C. Smith 2015; M. Weiss 2011, 104).[14]

But a prohibitively expensive erotic pastime is worlds apart from the NFL, a multibillion-dollar corporation that until 2015 held nonprofit status and was tax exempt, an arrangement that, as Almond artfully puts it, allows "so much money to be siphoned from the public till and funneled directly into the private koi ponds of the nation's wealthiest families" (2014, 77).[15] Commodity kink is also worlds apart from college teams and their multimillion-dollar expenses, offloaded onto taxpayers and students. "Only a small share of the nation's college football programs turn a profit at all," and those profits go not toward financial aid and university services but to football (127). The NFL and NCAA football generate and widen economic and educational disparities (Almond 2014, 124–25). Kink does not.

· **Football diminishes boys' and men's ability to be and do in the world.**[16]

The cultural will-to-football "reinforce[s] the idea that violence [is] a source of power and path to destiny" (Almond 2014, 106). Football is the most popular organized sport among high school boys. It is also the sport in which they suffer the worst and most frequent injuries. While "high school players are nearly twice as likely to incur a concussion as their college counterparts," itself a shocking statistic, it is also important to recognize that the recurring collisions of football lead to damaged brain function of teenage players, whether or not the players are concussed (117).[17] According to a Purdue University medical researcher, "You have the classic stereotype of the dumb jock and I think the real issue is that's not how they start out" (quoted in Almond 2014, 117–18). One is not born, but rather becomes, a dumb jock (de Beauvoir 2010 [1949]).

In the college league, players practice forty to sixty hours a week and are not paid for their labor (Almond 2014, 124). The NCAA is even more defensive and unaccountable than the NFL regarding brain trauma and death resulting from play (129). Meanwhile, "up to a third of Division I football players never graduate" (125), and this must in part be attributed to the time commitment the team demands.

As has become well known in recent years, football players are disproportionately impacted by chronic traumatic encephalopathy (CTE), a degenerative brain disease (Bennet et al. 2005; Laskas 2009). CTE is more likely to occur in people who suffer multiple concussions and collisions to the head, though the "precise incidence of CTE after repetitive head injury is unknown" (McKee et al. 2009, 709). CTE symptoms include "cognitive impairment, impulsive behavior, depression, memory loss, difficulty planning or carrying out tasks, emotional instability, substance abuse, and suicidal thoughts, according to the Mayo Clinic" (Howard 2017). In 2016 the NFL finally acknowledged that its players are more susceptible to brain diseases than the general population (J. Martin 2016). NFL-hired actuaries estimate that "30 percent of [NFL] retired players [will] suffer 'long-term cognitive ailments'" (Almond 2014, 180; Belson 2014). And since nearly 70 percent of the NFL players are black, and since black men are more likely to be in high-collision positions, "football's concussion problem is also clearly a racial problem" (Moore 2015).

Fans underwrite the "Football Industrial Complex" and its diminishment of men's capacities to do and be in the world (Almond 2014, 181). As Almond starkly observes, when Ray Rice knocked out his fiancée, Janay Palmer, "millions of American watched replays of this neurological event and reacted with horror and outrage." Yet, "every weekend, the brains inside numerous NFL players [are] rendered insensate by fellow players. Millions of Americans watched replays of these neurological events, as well, and reacted with fascination and sometimes glee" (185).

Insofar as one objective of football is to take out other players, injure them, and prevent them from further participation, football diminishes the lives of both the injurer and the injured. As for the injured: brain and other injuries corrode or extinguish a wide range of human capabilities, not least of which are the abilities to speak and remember. As for the injurer: surely weaponizing humans so relentlessly, fostering their capacity for violence, entails a foreclosure (if not always) of other modes of relating to the human and nonhuman word.

Notice these enumerated wrongs of football mix brain injury, concussions, and CTE with other sorts of harms to players, such as a relentless conditioning to violence at the cost of pursuing other goals, such as education. I want to recognize the seriousness of brain and other injuries without aggrandizing those injuries or centralizing physicality. As evidenced above and discussed in more political theoretic terms below, physical injury—what amounts to "serious" injury under the criminal law of assault in Anglo-American jurisprudence—is but one of the multiple ways American football—and not, typically, BDSM sex—unjustly diminishes people's ability to do and be in the world.

Footballers all *consent*, or maybe they do, and consent is what is supposed to morally and legally exonerate the game. Just ask President Obama: "I would not let my son play football. At this point there's a little bit of caveat emptor. These guys, they know what they're doing" (quoted in Almond 2014, 169). Did they? Do they? What are the other viable options for upward mobility for children in the neighborhood? Yet perhaps what is most striking about reading Steve Almond's *Against Football* are the telling ways the author uses *consent* to name, rather than remedy, the harms of football. Consider: "The notion that [NCAA players have] enrolled in college to learn more about the world of ideas is a fraud we all *consent* to so we can watch them compete on Saturday" (125; emphasis added). "So the question isn't just *why* we dig the violence, but what it means and what it does to us [. . .] we are buying into a value system, making a tacit agreement that winning matters more than someone getting hurt. We *consent* to this premise over and over until we no longer really have to *consent*. The psychic structures within us *consent*. Football [. . .] enforces conformity and desensitizes us to violence" (142; emphasis added).

Of course, the actual reason that the consensual violence of football is permitted whereas the consensual violence of some sex is proscribed is that only one of these activities generates astronomical profit for white men. We can keep telling ourselves that the difference between a knocked-out football player and Janay Palmer, Ray Rice's fiancée, is the difference between consent and nonconsent, refereed group activity and an unrefereed intimate relationship. But should we unequivocally permit, let alone promote, the counterfactual in which Janay asked, as part of a kink scene, to be knocked out? What if Janay were Jamal? What if, as part of the kink scene, Ray and Jamal wore jockstraps and tights and knocked each other out on artificial turf instead of in a sling (see fig. 2)? In 1985 an Iowa appeals court held that "whatever rights the defendant may enjoy regarding private sexual activity, when such activity results in the whipping or beating of another resulting in bodily injury, such rights are outweighed

FIGURE 2. Consensual diminishment. Photographer, Keith Johnston. Courtesy of Pixabay.

by the State's interest in protecting its citizens' health, safety, and moral welfare" (*State v. Collier* [1985], 307). To my mind, raising football as the counterexample that exposes the lie of erotophobia gets at only half of the ethical quandary. The other half of the quandary is best addressed by finishing the (rather poorly constructed) sentence: ". . . when such activity results in the whipping or beating of another resulting [*sic*] in bodily injury, such rights are outweighed by the State's interest in protecting its citizens' health, safety, and moral welfare, [*unless those bodies are disproportionately black, and the beatings are for mostly white entertainment and mostly white profit.*]" Under critical race rather than queer theoretic lights, the "sport" exception to assault statutes in US jurisprudence effects racialized disposability more than sex negativity. Which bodies matter?

Because American football disproportionately objectifies or otherwise degrades black men and boys; because American football subscribes men and boys to the most unforgiving, narrowest, and violent forms of masculinity; because the current corporatization of American football exacerbates social, economic, and educational inequalities; and because American football diminishes boys' and men's abilities to be and do in the world on account of both physical and nonphysical damage, we should probably ban the sport.[18]

THE CORPORANORMATIVITY OF SERIOUSNESS AND THE DUBIOUSNESS OF DIGNITY

The analogy drawn by criminal defendants and kink advocates between BDSM and football rests on the assumption that both activities entail consensual physical violence. Above, I showed that physical injury is but one of many wrongs of American football and that the physicality of the injury is not so much at issue as is the kind of capability diminishment (speech, memory, psychological well-being, affiliation) to which the injury eventuates (Nussbaum 2001; 2006). This is why, perhaps obviously, repeated injuries to the head are more morally disconcerting than broken bones. Below, I consider the limitations of legally (and culturally) equating "serious" injury with *physical* injury in adjudications of allegedly consensual BDSM sex. Another criminally kinky gay couple—this time in Nebraska, not Germany—enter the analysis, as do our two patients from earlier—the transgender patient undergoing gender-affirming surgery and the patient undergoing physician-assisted suicide. In the last part of this section, I question "dignity" as an alternative for or supplement to "seriousness" in order to adjudicate BDSM.

The Corporanormativity of Seriousness

In Anglo-American criminal law, serious bodily injury has historically been a definitional component of assault. "Courts in the United States, England, and Canada," Hanna (2001) observes, "have consistently maintained that one cannot consent to any activity which could cause serious bodily injury or death [. . .] with a few exceptions, voluntary participation in organized sports being the most common" (242). But the primacy of physicality appears not just in assault law. Consider police and prosecutors' unwillingness to pursue a rape complaint, let alone the difficulty of securing a rape conviction, in the absence of bruising or other visible injuries.[19] And under tort law, "damages based on emotional distress alone are notoriously rare. Negligent infliction of emotional distress (NIED) torts nearly always require accompanying *physical harms* as well" (Brodksy 2017, 200; emphasis added). One can also track the elevation of bodily injury as "real" injury, for instance, to critical race theorists' arguments for restrictions on hate speech. To make the case that hate speech harms, critical race theory (CRT) scholars have argued that "racist hate messages [. . .] *hit the gut* of those in the target group" (Matsuda 1989, 2332; emphasis added). One of the better-known CRT volumes is tellingly titled, *Words That Wound: Critical Race Theory, Assaultive Speech, and the First Amendment* (Matsuda 1993). The primacy of physicality, of the body, stems from John Locke's (2003 [1689]) notion of property-in-the-person, or the body as proprietary (even though, for Locke, our bodies are made not by us but by God).

But back to kink: nearly all legal scholars and BDSM practitioners advocating a consent defense to kinky sex make an exception for "serious bodily injury," provided judges and juries do not ratchet up temporary, nongrievous injuries as serious in order to convict kinky defendants for assault (e.g., Bergelson 2007, 179; Egan 2006, 1615–16; Haley 2014, 652–54; NCSF 2015).[20]

I call these modes of thought and argument corporanormative, because the privileging of the body and bodily injury obscures other kinds of wrongs that might be entailed under consensual activity (e.g., encaging or enslaving someone over a nontrivial amount of time) while also inflating the body as the primary site of injustice.[21] If my lover carves his name into my back, it is hard to make the case that this is not *serious* in some corporeal, permanent way; but it is not therefore necessarily injurious, or actionably injurious, if procedural cautions have been taken. It seems to me that we should be more concerned with repeated blows to the head than with carving a name into a back, for the former impedes one's ability to do and be and the world; the latter hurts for a bit, and leaves a mark. Both head hitting and (not too deep) back carving cause "serious physical injury," but head hitting causes more than that, and it is the more-than-that (capability diminishment) which escapes corporanormative analysis and which, as I am arguing, is of graver moral concern and may warrant state intervention.

Cheryl Hanna's proscription (2001) on BDSM adopts the corporanormative position: "The law should not allow consensual violence that results in *actual serious* physical injury outside of highly regulated contexts" (248; emphasis in original). She repeats: "The criminal law protects a civilized society from actual physical violence" (288). However, her argument concludes: "To suggest that anyone should have the right to *control*, beat, or brutalize another and escape culpability under a theory of sexual consent violates our deepest notions of freedom, human rights, and civility" (289; emphasis added). I agree to an extent, but noteworthy is how "control" slips into this list of consent firewalls at the very end of an argument about beating and brutalizing. One can be controlled, however, without being beaten or brutalized, and one can be beaten or brutalized without being controlled. What I find objectionable about certain consensual sex practices has more to do with undue control than grievous injury (Pettit 2013, 58–59). Physical injuries are problematic more because they unduly control the subject than because they alter the body—hence, a noncorporanormative accounting of corporeal injury.

To flesh out the kinds of noncorporeal threats to flourishing I am pointing toward, consider another extraordinary case of gay kink gone awry (or exactly as planned, depending on your perspective).

In 2001, nine months after Meiwes dismembered, killed, and consumed Brandes, Roger Van, in the basement of his flower shop in Nebraska, shaved, gagged, whipped, branded, and anally penetrated J.C.G., locking him in a cell between thrashings. For his effortful beatings, Van was convicted of sexual assault, assault, false imprisonment, and terroristic threats, and sentenced to prison for sixteen to twenty-nine years (*State v. Van* [2004]).

Over the course of the earlier fall months, J.C.G., residing in Houston, Texas, and Van exchanged "300 e-mails" in which J.C.G. complained that in his current master-slave BDSM relationship, "he felt that he was not getting enough structure, pain, and discipline" (*State v. Van* [2004], 609). J.C.G. told Van "he wanted to become a total slave" for him. Both men came to agree about their ensuing relationship: it was to be "defined and understood [. . .] to be without limits, to have no safe word, and to be permanent." "During their e-mail correspondence, J.G.C. *specifically told Van that he may try to escape, but that Van should never allow him to do so and should keep him restrained.* [. . .] J.G.C. indicated that he wanted to be flogged, whipped, beaten, restrained, gagged, shaved, tattooed, pierced, blindfolded, injected with saline, and locked in a cell" (609; emphasis added).

J.G.C. staged his own abduction and fled Houston and his relationship for a four-by-six-foot cell in the basement of Van's floral shop. A day after his arrival, J.G.C. apparently changed his mind: he did not want to be Van's total submissive, he did not want to be caged and abused, and he did not want to be in Nebraska—all concerns he expressed to Van. Van, now perplexed, "reviewed the e-mail correspondence [. . .] to confirm that J.G.C. had instructed Van not to allow J.G.C. to leave, even if he requested to leave" (610). Van refused the request, alternately beating, penetrating, and caging J.G.C. for the next few days. Another submissive of Van, one of Van's employees, gave more credence to J.G.C. at time present than time past and secretly helped J.G.C. escape the cell, putting him on a bus back to Houston. J.G.C.'s father encouraged J.G.C. to press charges against Van. Van appealed the trial jury's conviction on several grounds, all of which were dismissed by the state supreme court. With regard to the *assault* charges, the Nebraska Supreme Court found that *Lawrence v. Texas*, the US Supreme Court decision holding sodomy laws unconstitutional, does not extend a consent defense to physical abuse (613–14). As for the *sexual* assault charges, the court upheld the trial jury's verdict that anal penetration occurred without J.G.C.'s consent, despite J.G.C.'s earlier emails (*I consent at an earlier time to your disregarding my consent at a later time*). J.G.C. had "testified that he did not consent to this act, but did not resist either verbally or physically because of the threats which Van had made previously" (612).

In their respective considerations of *State v. Van* (and BDSM more generally), Margo Kaplan and Daniel Haley focus—corporanormatively— on questions of physical force and consent. For Kaplan (2014), *Van* is a case of sexual violence without consent: "Defendant continued activity after consent was withdrawn entirely" (135n234). Haley (2014) aligns *Van* with BDSM writ large, thus making it a case of not-so-violent sexualized violence with consent (645–46). In other words, Kaplan renders the conduct "entirely" nonconsensual when the consent question is equivocal at best, allowing her to bypass the substantive question of when, if ever, certain conduct, however consensual, is nonetheless impermissible. Haley skips over the details of *Van,* allowing him to argue that the court moralistically refused to extend *Lawrence*'s reach to kinky but noninjurious sex.[22]

But what neither Kaplan nor Haley consider is the *false imprisonment* charge against Van, and the false imprisonment. Being caged in a four-by-six-foot cell for a week with occasional outings for a beat-down is not as spectacular, not as lurid to the reader, as having one's scrotum injected with saline or being branded on the leg; but imprisonment is, from a human capabilities perspective, as objectionable, if not more so.

Notice that according to many a college sexual misconduct code, Van's behavior is nothing short of exemplary. Van is the ideal sexual citizen: he secured the "affirmative consent" of J.G.C.—written out explicitly over e-mail—consulted with J.G.C., then double-checked the written statement of affirmative consent. Of course, the not-so-small catch is that J.G.C. had affirmatively consented to the disregard of his later withdrawal of affirmative consent. I will not wade into the philosophical waters about whether or to what degree, abstracted out from any particular content, person A's permission at time 1 for person B to disregard A's resistance at time 2 should have moral or legal force (Wertheimer 2003, 120–21, 159–69). Happily we need not get so abstract, for I am arguing that however consensual, nonconsensual, or ambivalently consensual, imprisoning someone in a basement cage indefinitely, or for an extended period of time, is wrong.

Of her BDSM interviewees, sociologist Jill Weinberg (2016) observes: "Practitioners challenge a series of norms around gender, race, age, but no one expressly says *consensual BDSM is a way to resignify, or reappropriate, hierarchies.* Instead, consent serves as a tool for individuals to *temporarily* experience domination or subordination" (106; emphasis added). I cite Weinberg for two reasons. First, because my account so far risks caricaturing BDSMers as unthinking, uncritical mouthpieces for the transformative force of consent, when surely they are not. For Weinberg's BDSMers, consent does not transvalue or eliminate hierarchy; consent kneads hierarchy into an erotic resource. But, second, I cite Weinberg because of her reference to duration: "temporarily experience." This, I think, is crucial to BDSM's moral and perhaps legal legitimacy: "The act of consent provides space to play with power *for the short term*" (2016, 115; emphasis added). I am not condemning unilaterally long-term master-slave contracts (legally unenforceable anyhow), in part because they seem fantastical, themselves erotic objects, and in part because the fact of a master-slave contract tells us nothing about the

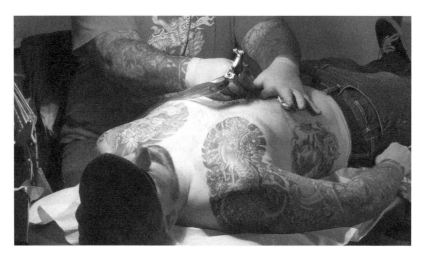

FIGURE 3. Corporanormativity: is tattooing assault? Photographer, Mario Schmidt. Courtesy of Pixabay.

content of that contract (so perhaps I am wading into these philosophical waters a tad). That a young woman is required to physically exercise several days a week (James 2011) or wear pink on Wednesdays (Waters 2004) does not constitute a particularly troublesome contractual condition, depending on the retaliation for a breach. That someone is placed in a cage in a windowless basement for an undetermined amount of time as part of a sexual contract—in which it is stipulated that the encaged cannot revoke his initial consent to the agreement, and in which he cannot extricate himself from the cage—is unacceptable. And it is unacceptable regardless of whether the encaged sustains "serious bodily injuries." Certainly, there are already legal tools that make this sort of scenario actionable (false imprisonment; the Thirteenth Amendment to the U.S. Constitution),[23] but my point is less about constructing statutes or doctrine than about ways of framing (sexual) injury and violation, even in the presence of consent.

My first concern, then, with permitting BDSM sex a consent defense except in the case of "serious bodily injury" is that if we adopt the definition of "serious bodily injury" as codified in many statutes and the Model Penal Code (with its inclusion of "permanent disfigurement"), we criminalize branding, scarring, and other kinds of kink that, to be highly technical, are just not that big a deal—or at least not that big a deal from a capabilities approach that prioritizes human flourishing (Nussbaum 2001; 2006).

My second concern is that we may fail to see how other kinds of non–physically injurious kink practices—however infrequently performed—unduly inhibit human functioning and flourishing. I am admittedly unsure after what duration of time (days? weeks?) the consensual, eroticized, windowless caging of another should not be legally permissible, but I think this is the better, noncorporanormative question to ask about the ethics of kink.[24]

My third and final concern is that exempting "serious bodily injury" from a consent defense leaves both our transgender patient seeking gender-affirming surgery and our patient seeking physician-assisted suicide without remedy, as a matter of logic if not as a matter of law. (More precisely, the serious bodily injury exemption morally indicts the doctors of such patients, whom by analogy we would consider the dominants or tops.) Indeed, Roger Van challenged Nebraska's assault laws along these very lines, arguing that, "in their literal application, [the state's assault statutes] would criminalize such things as surgeries, tattoos, and body piercings" (*State v. Van*, 615).[25] In other words, if the argument against football were simply and absolutely that *competent adults should not suffer nth-degree physical injury, regardless of their consent, and regardless of other outcome variables,* we would be hard-pressed to legitimate gender-affirming surgeries and physician-assisted suicides, along with many other medical practices (e.g., cosmetic surgery).

Kelly Egan (2006) proposes just such a serious physical injury exemption while arguing for the legalization of BDSM by analogy to body modification. Noting that body modification is largely unregulated, she argues that similar conduct in an erotic context should be legally permitted, since "sexual relationships are also vital to self-expression and personal autonomy" (1639). However, Egan, like other BDSM-friendly scholars, makes explicit that "consent should not be available as a defense in cases involving serious physical injury" (1640). A seemingly sexually progressive stance, but observe that the proposal makes a strong case for *banning* gender-affirming surgery (and physician-assisted suicide), and a stronger one still for banning kink practices like branding and scarification.[26] That is, even for practices that are "vital to self-expression and personal autonomy"—such as choosing one's genitals (and the conditions of one's death)—Egan's proposition might contravene a consent defense. This is the problem with corporanormativity: primacy of body and bodily violation at the expense of other values and moral concerns.

I tentatively propose a spin on Egan's solution: perhaps consent ought to be a defense to serious bodily injury provided the injury neither violates one's autonomy nor impedes one's access to the world, and provided we define autonomy not simply as personal choice but as a capability to exercise choice, to co-determine the contours of one's relationships, and to be and do in the world. This sort of exemption allows for gender-affirming surgery (which might even be reinterpreted as promoting autonomy, human capability, and access to the world) while disallowing for Bernd Brandes to be eaten and killed. It may also allow for a terminally ill or grievously suffering patient to seek and commit suicide—thus co-determining her or his life trajectory rather than its being determined by illness and pain—while disallowing less considered, capricious death wishes (cf. Baker 2009, 118–20; 2014). The exemption probably excludes American football as currently practiced and corporately organized.

You may not be convinced that my "autonomy and access" counterproposal (sketched out and very sketchy here) does the morally distinguishing work I would like it to do. Certainly, though, we need modes of analysis and adjudication less tethered to corporanormativity.

The Dubiousness of Dignity

What about *dignity* as that alternative mode of analysis and adjudicative metric? Since philosophical discussions of dignity tend to extol the humanity, rather than corporeality, of humans, dignity appears as a promising side-constraint to the authorizing power of consent. Might dignity, the inherent worth of humans qua humans, do a better job of reigning in consent's reach than, or in addition to, serious physical injury? I am dubious.

In "The Right to Be Hurt: Testing the Boundaries of Consent" (2007), law professor Vera Bergelson tackles the same conundrum I do in this chapter: drawing justifiable limits on consent as a defense to (violent, sexualized) conduct. Where I seesaw between moral and legal parameters of consent and focus on sex, Bergelson concentrates on the law and focuses on violence or otherwise injurious activity. She argues that violations of one's rights are not sufficient to circumscribe the limits of permissible hurtful conduct. Bergelson reaches for *dignity* as the additional side-constraint that authorizes legitimate third-party (state) intervention: "A wrongful interference with one's interests includes not only violation of one's autonomy [side-constraint 1], but also violation of one's dignity [side-constraint 2]" (170).[27] Bergelson also opens her investigation with the German Cannibal case (166–67), opining, "No matter how respectfully Armin Meiwes treated his victim, cannibalism *by its very terms* denies people equal moral worth and thus assaults the victim's dignity" (217).

I agree with Bergelson that (erotically, consensually) eating and killing another person should in nearly all, if not all, instances be impermissible, yet I disagree with Bergelson that such impermissibility rests on dignitarian grounds. Rather, the core moral wrong of the sexualized consuming and killing of another, even with consent, is that it sets back (in this case, eliminates) one's ability to do and be in the world. Another word for that doing and being might be *autonomy*. Whereas Bergelson adds dignity to autonomy as a limiting principle of hurtful conduct, I gesture instead toward an expansive definition of autonomy to delimit the scope of permissible harmful conduct. To explain my disagreement with Bergelson and why it matters for sex and sexual ethics, I briefly synopsize Bergelson's argument, point to an alternate reading of her position that supports mine, and conclude with a counterfactual of the German Cannibal case.

Bergelson's regulatory schema for hurtful consensual conduct embarks from a distinction between "offenses in which the act becomes wrongful due to lack of consent from offenses in which the very conduct constitutes a prima facie norm violation" (2007, 213). For Bergelson, sex is an example of an act that becomes wrongful only in the absence of consent. Interestingly, acts like sex are not too morally or legally complicated for Bergelson, since consent does all the necessary transformative work. Activities like killing and maiming, however, are examples of conduct that are "bad per se," for which consent may or may not exculpate the responsibility of the perpetrator (210). Consent always mitigates responsibility: killing, maiming, asphyxiating, and so forth are less blameworthy if the killed, maimed, or asphyxiated person agreed to or sought out the activity than if he or she did not (222, 245). But some kinds of "bad," norm-violating activity ought to be fully exonerated by consent, proposes Bergelson; specifically, activity that neither sets back a person's interests nor violates her dignity. To flip the conditional: if consented-to activity both sets back a person's interests and violates his dignity, it should be rendered impermissible (219–20).

Bergelson does not define dignity, but the word as she uses it has a Kantian flavor: recognizing the humanity of humans, respecting the moral worth of their personhood, treating them as an end, not instrumentalizing them for one's own satisfaction. And it is because *dignity* is subject to such subjective interpretation and thus potential overreach (shall we criminalize fisting? piss play? anal sex?) that Bergelson adds the side-constraint *interest*—a side-constraint not included in the beginning of her article. Like dignity, interest is not explicitly defined, but refers to abstractions such as property, healthiness, and longevity (214n288). So Bergelson's second accounting of the wrongness of erotic cannibalism looks like this: "By killing Brandes, Meiwes [. . .] not only defeated the most essential interest of Brandes (his interest in continued living), but also used Brandes as an object [. . .] and thus disregarded his dignity" (221).

Here is where Bergelson and I part ways, for once she has introduced "essential interests" (221), "welfare interests" (222), and "long-term interests"(226) into the juridico-ethical mix, it is no longer clear to me what transformative work dignity does or should do. And to the extent that what these stipulated "interests" more or less track is a person's ability to flourish, to do and be in the world, could we not also call these interests *autonomy*, as the ongoing capability to co-determine one's life course?

It seems neither legally nor even morally objectionable to permit, for example, consensual piss play—arguably undignified treatment of another without a corresponding setback to essential, welfare, or long-term interests. Since piss play reaches only the indignity prong of Bergelson's two-prong test, it passes muster (for Bergelson and for me). But what about conduct that meets only the other prong, *essential interest*? Suppose Meiwes had not degraded and cannibalized Brandes before extinguishing him. Suppose Meiwes and Brandes had loving, vanilla, not too thrusting, painless anal sex with lots of lubrication. Then suppose as part of the agreed-to erotic encounter, Meiwes, upon climax, shot the otherwise healthy Brandes in the head and instantly killed him. Ending someone's life like this is morally reprehensible and should be legally impermissible, however dignified the foreplay. Bergelson's dignity prong is unnecessary. One might object that the taking of a life, with certain exceptions for consensual "mercy killings" (what I described above as physician-assisted suicide), is always a dignity violation, but then that merely synonymizes indignities with setbacks to essential interests (226).[28] Yet if our one-prong test is a dignity test, and not a welfare interest test, we render too much conduct impermissible (e.g., piss play). While what constitutes welfare, essential, and long-term interests is surely contestable, it seems as if the range of conduct that may debatably violate human *interest* is far narrower than the range of conduct that may debatably violate human *dignity* (Haley 2014, 651). "Racc play," "Nazi play," and other extreme scenes of domination and submissions that trope on historical atrocities are some of the most taboo, but apparently some of the hottest, scenes of kink (Weinberg 2016, 106). Surely one could make the case that these scenes involve indignity, but I do not see why indignities should bring kink within closer reach of criminal law.

Neither consent nor serious bodily injury nor dignity can explain in full why some mutually consensual, agreed-to injurious behavior ought to be prohibited. Yet some such behavior should indeed be prohibited. Protecting one's long-term interests to do and be in the world, one's capability to make, and make again, decisions for one-self and one's relationships, is the best (or least bad) rationale for proscribing some forms of consensual violence.[29]

I end this section on a cautionary note about the dangers, dubiousness, and smuggled-in antisex moralism that recourse to "dignity" invites (see also Baranetsky 2013; Siegel 2008). Like Professor Bergelson, law professor Dennis Baker (2009) proposes that dignity ought to supplement consent—what he terms "personal autonomy"—as a threshold for criminalizing human conduct (98). Yet, unlike Bergelson, Baker would incriminate the sadomasochistic gay men of *R. v. Brown,* who, recall, caused no permanent injuries to the submissive partners (101). Moreover, he would criminalize all (or nearly all[30]) unprotected sex between HIV-positive and HIV-negative people, whether or not the HIV-positive person discloses his or her status, whether or not the HIV-positive person is on anti-retroviral medication, and whether or not the sero-discordant couple is in a long-term relationship (109–10). Why? Because of dignity.

Baker's argument is confused: initially, he states he is willing to criminalize consensual conduct only if such conduct violates human dignity *and* causes "serious physical harm or death," presupposing that there are dignity violations that do not cause physical harm and death (99); he later argues that the degree of a dignity violation correlates directly with the degree of physical harm inflicted (116, 118); still later he drops the "serious physical harm" constraint entirely in order to criminalize (likely) all BDSM sex (117–18, 120) and (likely) all unprotected sero-discordant sex (114); nor does he ever consider the potential dignity violation in categorically prohibiting people from pursuing the intimacies of their choice. What lubricates these slippages and what camouflages these omissions is the empty signifier that is *dignity,* which is ultimately not much more than a prop to moralize against the sex Baker does not like.

However, Baker's concept of dignity is more or less equivalent to my reconstruction of autonomy, and so Baker's argument supports my conclusions, not his. Following Kant, Baker wedges a gap between human choice and human dignity: "Respecting personal autonomy is fundamentally different from respecting human beings as ends in themselves (rational autonomy: dignity)" (2009, 98). For Baker, personal autonomy = choice = consent, whereas rational autonomy = dignity = respecting humanity. So Baker's criminal law would be as attuned to violations of humanity as it is to violations of human choice. But what is humanity and how might it be violated? "A person alienates her humanity if she rids herself of the *capacity of choice*. Maintaining humanity is about retaining a *sufficient degree of your freedom and powers to set and pursue your own purposes*" (112; emphasis added). This is a subtle distinction with an enormous difference: personal autonomy = choice; humanity = *capacity* of choice. The latter is how I understand *autonomy,* as a capability for making choices (an elaboration for this feminist reconstruction of autonomy can be found in chapter 5 of this book). Whether we call it dignity, autonomy, or broccoli, the principle of capacity of choice—as outlined by Baker himself—simply does not allow for sweeping criminalization of kinky and sero-discordant sex. Temporarily nailing a man's scrotum to a board does not incapacitate choice any more than does a mandatory faculty meeting at my university (*R. v. Brown,* 246).

TWO BDSM CONTRADICTIONS

I have so far argued that *consent* should not green-light any and all (sexual, athletic) activity between or among humans (on interspecies sex, see chapter 4), but I have also argued that neither *serious physical injury* nor *dignity* are defensible side-limits to consent's warrants. The arguments have been mostly about unforeseen consequences: look what happens if we permit any consensual conduct whatsoever; but look what happens if we criminalize all consensual conduct that involves permanent body modification; and look too how the conceptual malleability of dignity risks erotophobic criminalization.

If the above arguments, then, are about *external* consequences, this brief section points to two *internal* contradictions within BDSM advocacy and literature. I exposit these consent contradictions less to criticize BDSM than to show, in the final, equally brief section of this chapter, that kink advocates and scholars already hold within their own lexicon better concepts than consent (or bodily injury or dignity) to categorize good sex, bad sex, and impermissible sex.

The first BDSM consent contradiction: the capacious redefinition of consent offered by some BDSM practitioners and advocates can run *against* the wishes—the consent—of a participant.

Nowhere is this contradiction more apparent than in the ethical parameters for BDSM sex issued by D.J. Williams and his fellow BDSM scholars and practitioners (Williams et al. 2014). Williams and colleagues renovate the safe, sane, and consensual and risk-aware kink models into the 4Cs of caring, communication, consent, and caution. The authors schematize consent as three-layered: "surface consent," "scene consent," and "deep consent." *Surface consent* refers to the subject's agreement or refusal to a sex act; *scene consent* refers to prior negotiations outlining the BDSM exchange and its limits; *deep consent* is, as far as I can tell, paternalism, and is where the contradiction lies. "We are talking about something beyond just a bottom's ability to use a safeword or gesture," the authors explain. "For instance, when a bottom is crying and sobbing and in obvious distress and perhaps full into some kind of subspace [. . .] we might wonder to what extent the scene is affecting the thinking of the bottom and affecting the bottom's mental capacity. [. . .] In addition, *even if the bottom is still able to think, the bottom may not actually know whether he or she is consenting. In such cases, it seems like the question of consent is something that almost has to be considered after the fact*" (Williams et al. 2014; emphasis added).[31]

Deep consent, then, is not a layer of consent, but a contradiction of consent. The authors are suggesting an act of imaginative substitution as ethical obligation for the dominant: *pretend yourself as the future self of the sub you are flogging; cease kink play if the future sub self you conjure, and now ventriloquize, would withdraw consent.* This future perfect ventriloquy—*in the name of consent*—runs roughshod over subjective desire. The dominant is expected to disregard the submissive's prior or present demand based on the likelihood of future regret. This credo is parallel to what "several dominants" in Jill Weinberg's "study said[,] that if they learned about a woman's history of sexual abuse they would reconsider performing a scene with her" (2016, 113). When one such dominant was "bullwhipping the crap out of this young girl," and "she kept asking to be whipped harder," he "ended the scene" because "she looked bad." The dominant later learned from the girl that "she was molested as a kid and liked being whipped for punishing herself for not telling her mom that her dad was doing it to her and her brother" (quoted in Weinberg 2016, 112). According to Williams et al., this dominant practiced "deep consent."

What is "deep" about deep consent, what privileges this consent over *surface* consent, is its refusal to abide a submissive's initiative or interest as a token of consent. I do not mean to suggest that the definition of consent must be static, unchangeable, and entirely juridical. Weinberg demonstrates persuasively how BDSMers retool consent to be ongoing, affirmative, and contextually dependent, for example (2016, 55). But it is one matter to substitute consent as a token of acquiescence with consent as an ongoing process and quite another to substitute consent as a token of acquiescence with consent *as surmising the best interests of your partner, contrary to her or his expressed preferences.* The latter substitution cannot be reasonably interpreted as mere redefinition; it is paternalism.

The second BDSM consent contradiction: while consent sits at the heart of BDSM's political campaigns and ethnographic expositions, some kink is libidinized by nonconsent.

By *nonconsent* I do not mean, in this instance, a scene of staged violence or rape where the sub says "no" and the dom forces or penetrates the sub "against" her or his will, but the resistance is scripted at the outset (see, e.g., B. Weiss 2011, 20–22). These scenes of nonconsent draw on the same erotic reservoir as nonconsensual scenes, but they are not identical. I am referring instead to what Staci Newmahr (2011) describes in her BDSM ethnography as "edgeplay." *Edgeplay* refers to kink scenes that avowedly put pressure on the political and ethical boundaries set by BDSM subcultures, and the "most serious of the boundaries with which to play [. . .] is not the line between life and death, but the edge between consent and nonconsent" (149). These are encounters in which a sub's withdrawal of consent ("scene consent," in the vernacular of Williams et al. [2014]) is disregarded, or the sub's ability to refuse is preempted (by becoming unconscious, for example, or by being bound and gagged), or in which partners mutually agree to not coin a safe word to terminate the play, as was the case with Roger Van and J.G.C. While Newmahr notes that "edgeplayers occupy a marginal role in the scene," she also observes that such practitioners "enjoy the notoriety of outlaws. Their names are spoken with an uneasy mix of reverence and disapproval. [. . .] [T]hey have little difficulty finding play partners" (2011, 147–48).

Similarly, Jill Weinberg (2016) learned from her BDSM interviewees that "there is room for non-consent within a scene," by which she refers not to incidents of withdrawing consent but to incidents in which a submissive's apparent disengagement from the scene (becoming silent or withdrawn, for example) does not function as an emergency break (57). Weinberg is attentive, too, to the eroticization of transgressing the very consent boundary BDSM subculture extols. A "younger gentleman" reported to Weinberg about a recognized dominant in the community that "he's known for going far. People all over the country seek him out for that" (quoted in Weinberg 2016, 81). The dominant in question had just publicly cut a woman's thigh with a knife, after the woman requested that the scene end.

Williams and colleagues (2014) note: "Some of us play on the safe side of consent, and some of us like to dangle over the cliff. Some of us go so far as to secretly long for our consent to be violated mid-scene in the hope that our retrospective analysis will lead us to conclude that at some deeper and more meaningful level, we really did consent." What if that deeper and more meaningful level is chimeric? What if there is just dangling over the cliff?

While BDSMers praise consent on websites and in informational literature, and while consent does the heaviest, most public ethical lifting to separate kink from violence, at least some BDSMers are attracted to BDSM because it promises the possibility of sex without liberal propriety, with nonsovereignty, without consent. BDSMers "see a value in having their limits tested" (Weinberg 2016, 80), even their consent limits. This is a rather profound contradiction.

TWO BDSM CONTRADICTIONS PARTIALLY RESOLVED

If "'consent' is considered the 'first law' of S/M sex," it is by no means the only law, and certainly not the core of its ethical (or erotic) value (Pa 2001, 61; see also d. stein n.d.). Once we reconceptualize sexual *autonomy* as the capability to co-determine sexual relations, and once we take seriously the moral and phenomenological import of granting sexual subjects *access* to experience and exploration, we can partially resolve the two BDSM contradictions. If we ground the goodness of BDSM sex not simply in terms of *consent* but in terms of *autonomy* and *access*, it becomes more sensible why the dominant disregards the submissive's willingness to kinky conduct that is ill-advised (contradiction 1, partially resolved by recourse to autonomy), and why we might want to approve, however cautiously, kinky sex that edges toward the nonconsensual (contradiction 2, partially resolved by recourse to access).

Partially resolving the first contradiction (autonomy overriding consent). Staci Newmahr describes two separate "needle play" scenes in a BDSM club (2011, 152–53). In the first, a heterosexual couple familiar to the kink community seclude themselves in a well-lit area away from the other players. The man sticks many needles into the back of the woman, evidently in pain. He is wearing gloves and a cloth is laid down to catch the drops of blood. Onlookers express concern, but the purveyors of the club permit the scene to continue.

In the second scene, the club is quite crowded. The needle players are unknown to the community. They do not set themselves off from foot traffic, nobody is wearing gloves, the area is poorly lit, and there is no towel to absorb the blood of the bottom. The club purveyors ask the players to cease play. They refuse and so are ejected from the club.

The difference between these two scenes is not consent, for the "needled" in each case clearly consented. Newmahr does not relay the reasons the club owners kicked out the second set of players but let us speculate that the differences between the scenes—familiarity, precautions, preparedness, attentiveness to the bottom and to onlookers—signal to the club owners that the needled in the first scene is not at great risk of either unanticipated or serious injuries, or both, injuries that could very well debilitate her future participation in kink (or in life, for that matter); the needled bottom of the second scene is at great risk of debilitating injury, as the tops are either reckless or inexperienced or both. Now perhaps the BDSM club owners were thinking simply about liability or reputation when they kicked out the needlers but the upshot is the same. Kink members police their own when conduct threatens a player's ability to continue play (or to do and be in the world).

Partially resolving the second contradiction (access through nonconsent). Newmahr's kink players who play on the edge seek access to feeling: feeling trust, feeling pain and fear, feeling risk, and even feeling petrified (2011, 151, 154, 158). Paradoxically, the transgression of consent grants special clearance to these feelings and intensities. But—and this is key—these sorts of scenes are legitimated *as* scenes in the kink community, rather than as abuse or bad planning, only if the players are experienced and familiar and only if appropriate precautions have been taken regarding setup, toys, conditions, aftercare,[32] and so forth (153). Because, and not despite the fact that, Newmahr's "edgeplayers" play on so many ethical edges (conscious-unconscious, temporary-permanent, consent-nonconsent), "they are considered extremely skilled and safe (as tops) and particularly tough and strong (as bottoms)" (148).

In other words, some antecedent degree of trust and social consensus is already operating behind nonconsensual or not-so-consenting edgeplay. Things can still go wrong, of course, but Newmahr witnesses a stark contrast between scenes in which consent is deliberately and collaboratively contravened (e.g., the suspension of a safe word) and scenes in which consent is casually or capriciously disregarded (2011, 149–50). The former scene is controversial in Newmahr's kink community but at least ethically defensible; the latter is abusive at worst and sloppy at best. The contrast is one between, as an interviewee of Newmahr put it, "intense bad things" and "sexy bad things" (quoted in Newmahr

2011, 151). It is the contrast between your accessing new sensations and new worlds, and having those sensations and worlds stolen from or closed off to you.

To emphasize once more, there is a critical difference between jointly determining to play without a safe word, or jointly agreeing that the top flout a safe word, and a top arbitrarily flouting a safe word. As one kink player warns, if "you ignore safewords, like flat out ignore them, you're done. Might as well be dead" (quoted in Weinberg 2016, 77). Insofar as the penalty for disregarding safe words is excommunication from the kink community, such a penalty reiterates that respecting safe words, as signs of consent, is not the good stuff of BDSM, but the baseline for entry into and residence in the subculture, a subculture whose values and priorities are of course so much richer than the promotion of sex that is merely consensual.

"Probably the single most important reason people continue to do S/M once they've started is that it gets us 'high,' brings ecstasy, causes a sense of loss of self and of being one with our partner and with the universe" (Truscott 1991, 22). Otherworldliness, the dissolution of psychological and physical boundaries, "exuberant intimacy" unmoored from tiresome dictates of gender, vanilla sex, and the monogamous couple form (Bauer 2014, 107–43, 194–238): this seems to be some of the good stuff of BDSM to which its practitioners seek access.

If Williams and his colleagues "like to dangle over the cliff" (2014), what saves them is not a latent, more meaningful *consent* hiding under manifest resistance; rather, it is the antecedent knowledge, avowed or not, that their partners will not send them plummeting. Such cliffhangers seek access to the sensorial rush of life endangerment, perhaps only reachable *without* the escape valve of a safe word, and with full entrustment over to another. Yet what is sought is the thrill of death, or a brush with death, not death. Or, if death is what is sought, it is not kink, or at least not ethical kink.

BDSM is more like being dangled off a cliff; American football is more like being dropped off a cliff.

CHAPTER 2

The Trouble with Mothers' Boyfriends

or Against Uncles

In 1996, in the state of Georgia, Anthony San Juan Powell was charged with rape and "aggravated sodomy" against his wife's seventeen-year-old niece, Quashana (*Powell v. Georgia* [1998]; Huffer 2013, 109). Georgia defines "aggravated sodomy" as "any sexual act involving the sex organs of one person and the mouth or anus of another" that is "committed with force and against the will" of the victim (*Powell* [1998], 20). According to Powell the sexual activity was consensual; according to Quashana it was not. At trial the niece testified that she "was crying" as Powell performed oral sex with her, even though "she never said the word 'no'" (Huffer 2013, 109, 111). The jury dismissed the charges of rape and aggravated sodomy against Powell but convicted him of "simple sodomy," that is, for supposedly consensual cunnilingus.

Powell appealed his conviction to the Georgia Supreme Court, arguing that the state sodomy statute violated his right to privacy. His appeal was famously successful. On November 24, 1998, the court invalidated Georgia's sodomy law, the very same law the United States Supreme Court had upheld as constitutional twelve years earlier in *Bowers v. Hardwick* (1986). In 2003, in *Lawrence v. Texas,* the Court invalidated state sodomy laws nationwide. *Lawrence* cites *Powell* as precedent for its ruling, and *Powell,* like *Lawrence,* is now memorialized as a gay rights case paving the way toward greater sexual justice (Huffer 2013, 97; see also Sack 1998).

We should be wary of this "queer victory" cautions philosopher Lynne Huffer, given that it is brokered on "feminist defeat": gays' privacy is enshrined by discrediting a young woman, her "crying" converted to "consent" (2013, 113). The invalidation of sodomy statutes, while endorsed by Huffer, nonetheless robs sexual assault victims, typically girls and women (but historically boys—see Robertson 2010), of a legal tool to bypass juries' and judges' rape biases (women lie, women consent, women did not resist enough, resistance counts as consent, and so forth). In this sense, sodomy law prohibits forced oral and anal sex that defendants claim to be consensual just as assault law prohibits rape that defendants claim to be BDSM (see the last chapter). Sodomy law and assault law bypass consent and the he said–she said dilemma.

I am sympathetic to Huffer's admonition although I am critical on some of the finer points (see Fischel 2017). Here, however, I wish to take up a criticism contiguous to Huffer's. For if Huffer asks, *If consent is an available defense to Anthony Powell for having sex with his teenage niece, then might sodomy law function as a "fallback measure" to juries' sexism?* (110), I want to ask, *Why is a consent defense available to Anthony Powell at all?* Should consent be an available defense to family members and intimate partners of family members superordinated in vertical status relationships over complainants, especially if the complainant is a minor?

Had Quashana been fifteen, not seventeen, Powell could not have claimed his niece consented, given the state's age of consent law.[1] But what difference does a two-year age difference make when the complainant is still a financially dependent minor and the perpetrator is her uncle, in a position of authority and trust?

Georgia prohibits sex between uncles or aunts and nieces or nephews if the persons are related by blood. Since the court referred to Quashana as Powell's wife's niece, we can infer that Quashana and Powell are not blood-related. But what difference does blood make? Should the sex crime be classified as incest—a crime for which both parties would or could be accountable, like "simple" sodomy—or as some form of sexual assault—an abuse of authority for which Powell should be accountable?

In 2012 the Connecticut Supreme Court overturned Richard Fourtin's conviction for sexually assaulting his girlfriend's daughter. The girlfriend's daughter, referred to as L.K. in court documents, is nonverbal, uses a wheelchair, and was diagnosed with cerebral palsy and hydrocephalus. L.K. depends on others for her eating, bathing, and welfare needs, as well as for her general ability to move about in the world. Like L.K.'s mother, Fourtin provided care to L.K. (*State v. Fourtin* [2012],

677; *State v. Fourtin* [2009], 263). I discuss in more detail this quite complicated case in the book's concluding chapter, but for now the following is relevant: Fourtin's conviction was overturned on the grounds that L.K. was not so "physically helpless" that she was unable to consent to sex with her mother's boyfriend. Fourtin was charged under a law that prohibits engaging in sexual activity with someone who is "physically helpless," which by precedent and judicial interpretation refers to victims who are unconscious, comatose, or the like. It is not that the appellate and state supreme courts demanded L.K. resist; it is rather that because she is the kind of being capable of demonstrating resistance (and she had a history of physically, if nonverbally, expressing refusal to nonsexual activities), Fourtin was likely prosecuted under the "wrong statute" (*State v. Fourtin* [2012], 689n20).

But there was no "right statute" under which to prosecute Fourtin either.[2] Unlike Anthony Powell, Richard Fourtin did not put up a consent defense, but he could have, and if he had, he probably would have won. For in Connecticut, sexual assault retains a force requirement, but Fourtin did not need to use force against L.K. because she was immobilized by her disabilities. L.K. was thus caught between sex crime statutes: helpless enough that the force requirement is irrelevant but not so helpless that the court considers her unable to refuse sex.

In Connecticut there was (and still is) no sound legal remedy available to L.K. to exercise against Fourtin and her sexual assault, but there could be. Connecticut proscribes sex between teachers and students; coaches and students; and psychotherapists and their current as well as former patients.[3] Some of these status proscriptions are conditioned by the ages of, and age differences between, the parties. But if we are willing to prohibit psychotherapists from having sex with their patients why not prohibit people from having sex with the children of their intimate partners, such as mothers' boyfriends? *Fourtin* is perhaps less straightforward than *Powell*; L.K. was twenty-five years old at the time of the alleged assault, not seventeen like Quashana. And I am skeptical of any decontextualized attempts, however well intentioned, to anchor a person with cognitive disabilities to a specific chronological age (e.g., "She has the mind of a three-year-old"). Still, given L.K.'s substantial dependence on her caretakers, her inability to move in the world without help from others, and the vertical, familial-like relationship superordinating Fourtin and subordinating L.K., it is likely that the benefits of categorically proscribing this sex outweigh the costs. Note, too, that such a legal remedy does not ban L.K. from any chosen sexual activity whatsoever (as would declaring her too "physically helpless" for any sexual activity); it would just prohibit sex with certain persons in vertical relations of trust or authority.

"STATUS SEX" AND THE INSUFFICIENCY OF CONSENT

In the previous chapter I suggest, utilizing cases of kink, cannibalism, and football, that consent is insufficient, on its own, to render any erotic activity whatsoever permissible—in other words, that consent is insufficient as to sexual *conduct*. Demonstrated in this chapter is that consent is insufficient for permitting sex within certain *status* relations.

In the following chapter I argue that the "trouble" with transgender "rapists"—that is, with transgender men being convicted of sex offenses for "deceiving" their partners about their gender—is that they are not rapists, and should not be rendered so by the law. The defendants' gender identifications, stylizations, and expressions should not be understood to corrupt the sexual consent of their partners.

In this chapter, by contrast, I argue that the trouble with mothers' boyfriends is that they are rapists. Less provocatively, mothers' boyfriends and other people superordinated in positions of authority over their victims—but not related to those victims by law or blood—disproportionately perpetuate sexual assault. Sex in these kinds of nonbiological, not otherwise legally recognized vertical status relations are generally not prohibited by state laws. Some sex in some of these vertical relationships, I am proposing, ought to be proscribed, *whether or not the person subordinated in the relationship consents* (though force, coercion, or nonvoluntariness might aggravate the crime). If that sounds draconian let me put it this way: just as consent is not a defense to having sex with an eleven-year-old or a defense for eating and murdering someone for pleasure, consent should not be a defense for sex between a minor and the intimate partner of the minor's parent. Consent should not have been an available defense for Anthony Powell; nor, probably, should it have been an available defense for Richard Fourtin had he reached for it.

The first section of this chapter examines two sex crime datasets (newly compiled for this book) in order to advocate for more carefully and more defensibly tailored regulations of what we could call *status sex*. The first dataset tracks vertical status relationship patterns in sexual assault cases across three states. The data reveal that perpetrators of rape and sexual assault are quite often in nonbiological, not otherwise legally recognized positions of authority over their victims. The second dataset is a fifty-state survey of status-based sexual assault statutes. The data reveal that states do not universally proscribe "status sex" in the kinds of relations that the first dataset demonstrates to be common sources of and shelters for sexual assault.

State status sex laws are (still, if waningly) grounded in traditional morality and concerns surrounding consanguinity (blood relations). In the chapter's second section (following the lead of other political philosophers and legal scholars), I propose instead that status-sex laws should target abuses of authority, as do parallel laws in the United Kingdom and Canada (Eskridge 1995, 66–67). We should be more concerned with sex in vertical status relations, whether or not between biologically and legally related partners, than with sex in horizontal status relations, however consanguineous (or, in a word, "icky"). A relic of pre-*Lawrence* morality, let's excise "incest" from the books (Sunstein 2004, 1064–65; *Lawrence v. Texas* [2003], 590; Justice Antonin Scalia is grinning "I told you so" from his grave).

The problem comes down to line drawing as it so often does: which vertical relations are too vertical to permit sex? If we disallow a consent defense for Anthony Powell, must we commit to criminalizing sex between employers and employees? Professors and undergraduate or graduate students? Financially asymmetric spouses? Should we have thrown Bill Clinton in prison for having sex with his younger intern, Monica Lewinsky?

The third and last section of this chapter addresses three concerns of state overreach. First, where do we draw the line on proscribing sex in vertical relations of authority, trust, and dependence? For example, should US presidents be legally banned from sex with their interns or employees (the Bill Clinton problem)? Second, would prohibiting sex across vertical relations beyond nuclear familial lines disproportionately impact people in nontraditional kinship arrangements (the race problem)? Third (a more general, composite version of the first two concerns), does expanding the ambit of criminalizable or at least regulable sex in certain status relations feed the bloating carceral state and thereby detract from a more creative and capacious sexual justice politics (the governance feminism problem)?

GETTING VERTICAL

The question motivating the collection of these sex crime and sex law datasets (presented fully in appendices A and B) arose from my first encounter with the *Fourtin* case discussed above (Fischel and O'Connell

2015). How often, I wondered, are mothers' boyfriends defendants in sexual assault cases? Of course, what I really wanted to know is *whether mothers' boyfriends are overrepresented among the universe of sexual assault perpetrators,* yet the first question is a smaller, more manageable, imperfect but reasonable proxy for the second.

My (awesome) research assistant Jenny Friedland and I looked at relationship patterns across perpetrators and victims of sexual assault cases that reached the appellate level in three states: Wisconsin, Connecticut, and Michigan.[4] We coded 595 cases reported between 2010 and 2016: 200 randomly sampled cases from Wisconsin and Michigan each, and all 195 cases from Connecticut available on LexisNexis.[5] The following subsection, "Perpetrator Patterns," summarizes key findings from the three states.

We looked at these three states in part because they define sexual assault quite differently from one another. Michigan was the first state in the union to undertake modern rape law reform, in the 1970s, excising the word *rape* from its criminal code and instead enumerating graduated degrees of "criminal sexual conduct," largely determined by "force," "coercion," and "position of authority" (Caringella 2009, 13–21). Nonconsent is not an element of any degree of Michigan's criminal sexual conduct statutes, and "force" and "coercion" are defined more broadly in comparison to other states. Also in comparison to other states, Michigan proscribes sex across the greatest number of status relations. Rather expansively, the law declares "a person [. . .] guilty of criminal sexual conduct" when he or she "is in a position of authority over the victim and use[s] this authority to coerce the victim to submit."[6] Connecticut retains a force or "threat of use of force" element for nearly all of its sexual assault statutes, but "force" is defined more narrowly than in Michigan and less attention is given to sex across status differences.[7] Wisconsin, meanwhile, took the consent route. The state defines its varying degrees of sexual assault as "sexual contact or sexual intercourse [. . .] without consent," in turn defining consent as "words or overt actions [. . .] indicating a freely given agreement." Wisconsin is one of very few states that define consent as affirmative, rather than as the absence of refusal.[8] Given the varying ways these states criminalize sexual misconduct, we wanted to see how commonly mothers' boyfriends and others in positions of authority and trust are defendants in sexual assault cases, and to what extent the state laws provide remedy.

And what of the other forty-seven states? In addition to the data collected on perpetrator-victim relations in Connecticut, Wisconsin, and

Michigan, Jenny Friedland and another (awesome) research assistant, Jim Huang, conducted a fifty-state survey cataloging ways in which the nation does and does not proscribe sex across certain status relations. The subsection "Status Sex Prohibitions" summarizes key findings from the survey. Before going to press, a third (awesome) research assistant, law student Emma Stone, double-checked our compilation.

Perpetrator Patterns

How often are mothers' boyfriends and others in positions of authority and trust defendants in sexual assault cases? Do state laws regulate this sex(ual misconduct)?

In Wisconsin, across 200 of the appellate sexual assault cases decided between 2010 and 2016, at least two-thirds of all victims (153 out of 230) were minors, and at least two-thirds of the victims (likely more) were female.[9] In nearly half the cases, the relationship between the perpetrators and his victim(s) was unstated in the appellate decision.[10] Among the 120 perpetrator-victim relationships specified in these cases (110 relationships were unspecified), at least 49 (but likely more[11]) involved vertical status difference (parents, stepparents, other caretakers, or the like). Of those, father-child relationships are the second-most common (4.8% of all 230 perpetrator-victim relationships); *the most common vertical status relationship in the Wisconsin appellate sexual assault cases is between mothers' boyfriends or intimate partners and the child of the mother/other partner* (5.2% of all perpetrator-victim relationships). Stepfather-stepchild, uncle-niece (or -nephew), and grandfather-grandchild relationships constitute 2.6, 2.2, and 1.3 percent of sexual assault perpetrator-victim relationships, respectively. If we assume these patterns hold across the approximately 800 sexual assault appellate cases reported during this time period, then roughly *42 of the relationships in these 800 cases are of mothers' boyfriends or intimate partners and the child of the mother/other partner,* and that is just in the cases that have been appealed (thus excluding, obviously, jury trial convictions not appealed and excluding, even more obviously, unreported, unprosecuted, or pled-out sexual assaults). We could likewise expect about 38 relationships in these appellate cases to involve fathers and daughters (or sons) and another 18 to involve uncles and nieces (or nephews).

In Connecticut, across all 195 of the reported appellate sexual assault cases decided between 2010 and 2016, at least two-thirds of all victims (148 out of 222) were minors, and at least three-fourths of victims (but

TABLE 1   COMMON VERTICAL RELATIONSHIP PATTERNS IN SEXUAL ASSAULT
CASES, WISCONSIN, 2010–2016

	% of total	
	No.	(*n* = 230)
Mother's boyfriend or intimate partner	12	5.2
Father	11	4.8
Stepfather	6	2.6
Uncle	5	2.2
Grandfather	3	1.3

TABLE 2   COMMON VERTICAL RELATIONSHIP PATTERNS IN SEXUAL ASSAULT
CASES, CONNECTICUT, 2010–2016

	% of total	
	No.	(*n* = 222)
Father	28	12.6
Mother's boyfriend or intimate partner	19	8.6
Uncle	8	3.6
Stepfather	7	3.2
Grandfather	5	2.3

likely more) were female. Just over 80 of the relationships specified
(41%) comfortably classify as entailing vertical status differences
between the perpetrator and his victim(s).[12] Of those, father-child is the
most prevalent (12.6% of all perpetrator-victim relationships), *followed
by mother's boyfriend or intimate partner and child of the mother/other
partner* (8.6% of all perpetrator-victim relationships). Stepfather-stepchild, uncle-niece (or -nephew), and grandfather-grandchild relationships make up 3.2, 3.6, and 2.3 percent of sexual assault perpetrator-
victim relationships, respectively.

In Michigan, across 200 of the appellate sexual assault cases decided
between 2010 and 2016, at least 70 percent of all victims (154 out of
230) were minors, and at least 85 percent of victims (but likely more)
were female. Minimally, 67 of the relationships (33.5%) comfortably
classify as entailing vertical status difference between a perpetrator and
his victim(s).[13] Of those, father-child is the most prevalent (7.8% of all
perpetrator-victim relationships), *followed by mother's boyfriend or*

TABLE 3   COMMON VERTICAL RELATIONSHIP PATTERNS IN SEXUAL ASSAULT
CASES, MICHIGAN, 2010–2016

		% of total
	No.	($n = 230$)
Father	18	7.8
Mother's boyfriend or intimate partner	11	4.8
Stepfather	11	4.8
Grandfather	8	3.5
Uncle	6	2.6

intimate partner and child of the mother/other partner, as well as step-father-stepchild (11 relationships from each category across cases, representing a combined 9.6% of all perpetrator-victim relationships). Uncle-niece (or -nephew) and grandfather-grandchild make up 2.6 and 3.5 percent of all sexual assault perpetrator-victim relationships, respectively. If we assume these patterns hold across the approximately 1,400 sexual assault appellate cases reported during this period, then roughly *67 perpetrators of the relationships in these 1,400 cases are of mothers' boyfriends or intimate partners and the child of the mother/other partner,* and just in this highly limited pool of appellate rulings. We could likewise expect about 109 relationships in these appellate cases to involve fathers-daughters (or -sons), another 36 to involve uncles-nieces (or -nephews), and another 49 to involve grandfathers-grandchildren.

In all three states cases of "stranger rape" are overrepresented, given the existing data that point to family members and acquaintances as the most common perpetrators of sexual assault (National Institute of Justice 2010). The overrepresentation is unsurprising. Sexual assault is underreported, more so when the perpetrator is known to the victim (though the gap in reporting rates between stranger and nonstranger rape has narrowed over time; see Baumer 2004). Police, prosecutors, and other authorities are meanwhile more likely to pursue charges of sexual violence committed with force and by strangers (Corrigan 2013, 65–116). Therefore, it is even more significant that in all three states, 30 to 40 percent of the relationships in sexual assault cases that reach the appellate level involve vertical status differences. We can justifiably assume that these numbers are the tip of the iceberg. Consider how many daughters and sons, stepdaughters and stepsons, grandchildren, nieces and nephews, and children of the perpetrator's partner have no one to whom to report the assault. Indeed, these victims' comparative isolation from medical and legal services and their limited exit options (if they have any) are precisely what makes sex in such vertical, age-discrepant relations so troublesome.

Sexual assault within vertical status relations is not an exception but a prevalent pattern. And it is not just fathers but uncles, grandfathers, and mothers' boyfriends who leverage the verticality of close, supervisory, or dependent relationships to commit sexual assault, typically but not exclusively against girls.

Status Sex Prohibitions

Does the law protect subordinated (mostly) minors from sex with (mostly) adults superordinated by trust, authority, or dependence? Yes and no. All states codify a range of age of consent laws. In most states the age of consent is sixteen, though the majority of states also include age span provisions; for example, sex between a sixteen-year-old and an adult of any age (or another teenager) may be permissible, but sex with a fourteen- or fifteen-year-old may be permissible only if the older partner is nineteen or younger. Some states retain a higher age of consent explicitly for relations of trust, authority, and dependence. The age of consent for the general population might be sixteen, but the student-athlete must be eighteen, say, before his coach is permitted to have sex with him (Lowder 2011; Phipps 2003, 441–45).[14]

To the extent that the vertical relationship sexual assault cases in Connecticut, Wisconsin, and Michigan involved victims below the states' legal age of consent, there is some remedy. However, roughly one-third of the sexual assault cases from each state involved adult victims, and surely some of those victims were subordinated in vertical status relations to the perpetrators (doctors' patients, caretakers' clients, and the like). So too, teenagers and young adults above the state's age of consent but financially dependent and still living with their parents or guardians remain unprotected (like seventeen-year-old Quashana), at least by age of consent statutes. Finally, there is a normative issue. The problem I am pointing to is that sex across vertical status relations is also often sex across age difference, but the problem is neither age nor age difference alone. To prosecute a thirty-five-year-old man for sex with the fourteen-year-old daughter of his girlfriend on the grounds of age and age difference misses (part of) the point. The legal wrong should be, chiefly, sex procured through leveraging (his) superordination and (her) isolation and dependence (Buchhandler-Raphael 2011, 199–200; Green 2017,

26–27; Hörnle 2014, 87). The guy who goes home with the girl he met at a bar and mistakenly believes her to be "legal" (or even if he knows she is not) is less blameworthy than the mother's boyfriend, but blameworthy for separate but contiguous reasons. Moreover, consensual sex between a seventeen-year-old and an actual, not just legal, adult stranger with no other status difference or dependence seems neither morally nor legally problematic. But allegedly consensual sex between a seventeen-year-old and a legal stranger who is actually a guardian or partner of a guardian seems both morally and legally problematic, since it is a relationship in which "consent might not easily be refused" (*Lawrence* 2003, 578), a point to which I return later.

Beyond age and age spans, then, how and when does the law criminalize or otherwise regulate sex across status relationships, vertical or otherwise?

Neither Connecticut nor Wisconsin categorically proscribes sex between minors and the intimate partners of the minors' parents or guardians (for short, a "mother's boyfriend clause"). Michigan stipulates what looks like a mother's boyfriend clause. The state bans sex between a minor aged thirteen to fifteen and another actor if "the actor is a member of the same household as the victim" or if the "actor is in a position of authority over the victim and used this authority to coerce the victim to submit." But this begs the question I asked above: why does protection stop on the minor's sixteenth birthday? "Member of the same household" is a good proxy for dependent relations in which "consent might not easily be refused," but not all superordinated persons (mothers' boyfriends, stepparents, and so forth) live in the same house as the victim. And in a small subset of vertical relations—namely, minors and the intimate partners of their parents or guardians—it seems unnecessary that the person in the position of authority "us[e] this authority to coerce the victim." Superordination makes this sex suspect enough, whether or not the mother's boyfriend coerces the sex (say, by explicitly threatening to leave the victim's parent or to stop financially supporting the family, or both).[15]

All in all, eighteen states (36%) have laws that could reasonably be construed—in the broadest interpretation of statutory language—to prohibit sex between minors and the intimate partners of their parents or guardians. North Carolina, for example, bars "a defendant who has assumed the position of a parent in the home of a minor victim" from sex with the minor. Mississippi disallows sex between a minor and an adult if the adult is cohabiting with the minor's parent.[16] Several states

TABLE 4 SEX PROSCRIBED IN VERTICAL RELATIONS

State	Parent	Stepparent	Intimate partner of parent	Sibling	Biological aunt or uncle	Nonbiological aunt or uncle	Teacher & Student	Teacher & Student Age Specifications	Psychotherapist
CT	Y[i]	Y[ii]	N	N	N	N	Y[iii]	No age specifications	N[iv]
MI	Y[v]	Y[vi]	Y[vii]	Y[viii]	Y[ix]	Y[x]	Y[xi]	Student is 13–17[xii]	Y[xiii]
WI	Y***[xiv]	Y[xv]	N	Y*[xvi]	Y[xvii]	N	Y[xviii]	Student is over 15	Y[xix]

KEY: Y = yes; N = no.

NOTE: For a survey of proscribed sex in vertical relations across all fifty states, and for a full table key, see appendix B.

[i] Connecticut General Statute §§53a-71a. The law stipulates that the perpetrator "is such person's [the victim's] guardian or otherwise responsible for the general supervision of such person's welfare."

[ii] Connecticut General Statute §53a-71a.

[iii] Connecticut General Statutes §§53a-71, 53a-65.

[iv] Connecticut General Statutes §§53a-71, 53a-65, apply only if the victim is "a patient or former patient of the actor and the sexual intercourse occurs by means of therapeutic deception." Sex is therefore not categorically proscribed in such patient-actor relationships.

[v] Michigan Penal Code §750.520e.

[vi] Michigan Penal Code §750.520b; if victim is age 13–15.

[vii] Michigan Penal Code §750.520b; if victim is 13–15.

[viii] Michigan Penal Code §750.520e.

[ix] Michigan Penal Code §750.520e.

[x] Michigan Penal Code §750.520b; if victim is 13–15.

[xi] Michigan Penal Code §750.520b/e; if victim is 13–15/16–18, respectively.

[xii] Second degree sexual assault if victim is between 13–15; third/fourth degree sexual assault if victim is 16–17.

[xiii] Michigan Penal Code §750.520e.

[xiv] Wisconsin Codes §§944.06, 765.03; 948.06.

[xv] Wisconsin Code §948.06; if the victim is a minor.

[xvi] Wisconsin Codes §§944.06, 765.03.

[xvii] Wisconsin Codes §§944.06, 765.03.

[xviii] Wisconsin Code §948.095.

[xix] Wisconsin Code §940.22.

TABLE 5 PROSCRIBED SEX IN VERTICAL RELATIONS: SUMMARY FINDINGS OF FIFTY-STATE SURVEY

	Parent	Stepparent	Intimate partner of parent	Sibling	Biological aunt or uncle	Nonbiological aunt or uncle	Teacher & student	Teacher & student age specifications	Psychotherapist
No. of states	49	39	18	47	47	17	38	30	22
% of states	98	78	36	94	94	34	76	80*	44

NOTE: For a survey of proscribed sex in vertical relations across all fifty states, and for a table key, see appendix A.

*To capture the percentage of states with prohibitions on teacher-student relationships that also specify age, this percentage takes a denominator of 38, not 50.

criminalize sex between a minor and a person in a position of trust or authority over the minor; whether an intimate partner of a parent or a stepparent qualifies as a person in a position of trust or authority is a question of fact to be determined by a jury. Still, eighteen states is thirty-two states too few.

By comparison, nearly all the states of the union (forty-seven, or 94%) ban sex between aunts and uncles biologically related to their nephews and nieces. However, only seventeen states (34%) ban sex between uncles or aunts and nephews or nieces even if they are not biologically related. From a vertical-status perspective of power asymmetry and potential for coercion, rather than from the perspective of incest and the specter of deformed offspring, why should blood matter? If we are committed to protecting the sexual autonomy of the niece or nephew, protecting her or his capacity for sexual decision making, and providing her and him access to intimacies and erotic experiences that are *refusable*, then it is flatly beside the point whether the uncle is the brother or brother-in-law of the victim's parent. Likewise, as of this writing, nine states gender-specify proscribed sexual relations between uncles or aunts and nieces or nephews. Uncles may not have sex with their nieces but may with their nephews (if the nephew is over the state age of consent); aunts may have sex with their nieces in these states too. The same-sex sex exemptions are obviously not gay-friendly gestures (as if queers have peculiarly avuncular predilections), but reflect long-standing anxieties regarding family stability, normative proprietary and intimate relationships, and (more recently) genetic health of offspring (Bergelson 2013, 45–49; "Inbred Obscurity" 2006, 2469–72). Still, as with blood, so with gender.[17] The verticality of the relationship between aunts or uncles and nephews or nieces, rather than gender or blood (but perhaps not independent of age difference), should be the normative core of sex-status regulation.

At present, blood matters too much. All states but one (Rhode Island) criminalize sex between parents and children and all but three (Connecticut, Ohio, and Rhode Island) criminalize sex between siblings. Thirty-nine states (78%) prohibit sex between stepparents and stepchildren. Just over three-quarters of states disallow sex between students and teachers (and 80% of those states further specify age and age difference thresholds that render sex permissible, misdemeanant, or felonious). To look at the problem of sex and status difference apart from consanguinity and mostly apart from age,[18] I also asked my research assistants to catalog laws proscribing sex between psychotherapists and their patients. Twenty-two states (44%) disallow sex between psycho-therapists and current (and in some cases former) patients.

My argument, already intimated, will come as little surprise: there are better reasons—liberal, feminist, sexual autonomy–based—for barring sex between psychotherapists and their patients, sex between minors and the intimate partners of the minors' parents or guardians, and sex between teachers and students than for barring sex between, say, adult first cousins or even adult siblings. Nor is such a proposal unfounded: "consensual adult incest" is "not a crime in [France], Belgium, the Netherlands, Portugal, Spain, Russia, China, Japan, South Korea, Turkey, Côte d'Ivoire, Brazil, Argentina, and several other Latin American countries" (Singer 2014).

A focus on potentially coerced sex in vertical status relations, rather than on potentially consanguineous sex in horizontal status relations, augurs for repealing or much more narrowly tailoring laws criminalizing consensual adult incest while enacting or more widely regulating sex with teachers, mothers' boyfriends, and psychotherapists. Likewise, as I have argued elsewhere, sex between same- or similarly aged teenagers (horizontal relations) should be decriminalized, whereas sex across wide age spans (an imperfect but legitimate proxy for vertical differences in education, experience, and capability) is rightfully regulated and often proscribed (Fischel 2016, 85–130).

GETTING HORIZONTAL

Blood, Marriage, and Morality

Lawrence swept away any lingering bans on voluntary sex among adults in private.

—Gersen and Suk (2016, 888)

Jacob Gersen and Jeannie Suk's claim is not accurate but perhaps should be.[19]

Lawrence v. Texas is the landmark 2003 Supreme Court decision holding state anti-sodomy laws unconstitutional. Although the grandiose yet grammatically iffy language of the decision has spurred debate about the precise contours of the sexual liberty the Court established (Case 2003; Tribe 2004), it seems that, at minimum, states cannot criminalize private, consensual sex between or among adults on the grounds of morality alone; some other, better state interest must be at stake (Bergelson 2013, 53; "Inbred Obscurity" 2006, 2467). As law professors Gersen and Suk (2016) observe, *Lawrence* heralds an alternative, ascendant rationale for sex law other than the preservation of (marital) morality, a rationale already gestated by the sexual revolution and the feminist rape reform movement: "Immorality mostly left by the way-side, criminal sex offenses now fly under the banner of efforts at *anti-violence* and its cognate concept *antisubordination. Violence* and *subordination* are now the key concepts for illegal sex" (889; emphasis added). Indeed, sex laws are today more calibrated to routing subordination and violence than to preserving marriage and morality, and they are increasingly justified as such. Prostitution and age of consent laws, for example, are generally rationalized as harm-preventative rather than morality-preserving (888–89; see also Harcourt 1999).

Nevertheless, bans on "voluntary sex among adults in private" linger on and those bans often hinge on status distinctions. Fornication and adultery laws, for example, are based on marital status (or nonmarital status, as the case may be); some such laws have been challenged and are certainly prone to challenge in the wake of *Lawrence* (see, for example, *Martin v. Ziherl* [2005], in which the Virginia Supreme Court held the state's fornication statute unconstitutional; see also Sunstein 2004). For the purposes of this chapter, though, I now consider sex bans on the "ickiest" of horizontal status relations: adult siblings, cousins, and other incestuous couplings (or threesomes, foursomes, and so forth). Shoring up the reasons why we should not categorically prohibit sex in these horizontal status relationships illuminates the reasons we should categorically prohibit sex in certain vertical status relationships.

For example, in addition to all the sex Michigan proscribes across vertical relations, the state also criminalizes sex when "the actor is related to the victim by blood or affinity to the fourth degree" and the victim is "at least 13 but less than 16 years of age"—regardless of the presence of force, coercion, consent, or abuse of a position of authority. On its face, the law criminalizes sexual contact between teenage first cousins. In Florida, both sexual intercourse and marriage between siblings are felonies.[20]

These laws overreach. Consider the infrequent, sensational, but nevertheless true news stories of long-lost siblings or adult children and their parents who meet up and fall in love, before or while finding out they are biologically related. These folks should not be imprisoned, nor are their relationships necessarily endangering to themselves or any third parties (Bergelson 2013, 43–44; Hörnle 2014, 80).

Proscribing sex in horizontal status relations, and proscribing it so broadly, seems indefensible both constitutionally (in light of *Lawrence v. Texas*) and ethically. The state has no business—because it has no convincing rationale—for so sweepingly criminalizing sexual contact between first cousins or, for that matter, between adult siblings who did not previously know each other or did not grow up in the same household. The state ought not to impede, absent any qualifications, the first cousins' or adult siblings' sexual autonomy (even if we find such exercise of sexual autonomy unpleasant or even disgusting).

Admittedly, the case of decriminalizing sex between long-lost relatives is more palatable than permitting sex between adult siblings who grew up in the same household. Yet criminal law has no sweepingly categorical place here either.

Y. Carson Zhou (2016) enumerates and then knocks down several rationales the state might put up for so broadly criminalizing adult incestuous relationships: morality, family stability and child welfare, genetic health, and potential for coercion. "Morality," as we know, wades us into homophobic or otherwise polluted waters: gay sex—not to mention any nonmarital, nonprocreative sex—can be successfully criminalized by "morality" (227–30; see also Hörnle 2014, 99–101). For the state to endorse, with its police powers, such a comprehensive doctrine of the sexual good is simply intolerable from liberal and most feminist perspectives (Tralau 2013, 103–5; but see Spindelman 2003). As for rationales of family stability and child welfare, genetic health, and potential for coercion, Zhou's main attack on extant incest laws is that they are, to varying degrees, over- or underinclusive (see also Bergelson 2013). For example, "child welfare" would seem inapplicable to incestuous sex and incestuous coupling that involve neither the bearing nor the raising of children; "genetic health" cannot plausibly be a rationale for criminalizing sex between same-sex, distant, or infertile relatives; and the Supreme Court has otherwise recognized a broad constitutional right for persons to structure their intimate relations and families as they choose, unconstrained by the state (Zhou 2016, 230–39; see also Hörnle 2014, 93–94). Blended, polyamorous, and cohabiting families may be just as stable, or just as unstable, as any other family formation—dyadic, nuclear, or incestuous. (Zhou likewise argues that the potential-for-coercion rationale is also over- and underinclusive, a position for which I offer a corrective below.) Finally, Zhou proffers an additional, persuasive and quite startling rebuttal to the rationale of genetic health: if we find that categorically barring persons with cognitive disabilities from marrying and reproducing to be eugenicist and Nazi-like, then we ought to pause before making the genetic health argument against incestuous couplings (234–38; see also Green 2017, 20; Hörnle 2014, 95–97; Singer 2014; Tralau 2013, 98–100). What questionable assumptions are we making about a livable, good life? And ought those questionable assumptions trump people's rights to co-determine their intimate, sexual, and procreative relationships, whether those people have Down syndrome or hemophilia or are first cousins (Zhou 2016, 236)?

Whether we try to retrofit rationales of traditional morality, genetic health, family stability, or child welfare onto existing and overbroad incest laws, we cannot help but notice that these rationales may not pass the sniff test; they are pretextual—wholly or in part disingenuous—for the sex we think icky (Haidt 2001).

Ickiness is a bad basis for regulating sex (Singer 2014; Bergelson 2013, 55–59). As Justice Anthony Kennedy wrote in *Lawrence,* there is an "emerging awareness that liberty gives substantial protection to adult persons in deciding how to conduct their private lives in matters pertaining to sex [. . .] [P]etitioners are entitled to respect for their private lives. The State cannot demean their existence or control their destiny by making their private sexual conduct a crime" (2003, 578).

Justice Kennedy's sexual emancipation proclamations answer the worry expressed by Justice George H. Carley five years earlier in his dissent in *Powell,* the case concerning Anthony Powell and Quashana that opens this chapter: "Thankfully, the majority includes incest among those sexual acts which it will continue to permit the State to proscribe as criminal. However, the majority offers no analytical or conceptual distinction between the crimes of sodomy and incest when committed by consenting adults. Neither a public performance of the proscribed sexual act, an exchange of money nor the use of force is an element of either offense" (*Powell* 1998, 36).

Justice Carley's worry was well founded; and the worry anticipates the parade of horribles that Justice Scalia foresees on the post-*Lawrence* horizon (*Lawrence* 2003, 599; decriminalization of adult incest, for example), and the parade of horribles that Justice John Roberts foresees on the post-*Obergefell* horizon (2015, slip opinion at 20–21; constitutionalization of adult incestuous and plural marriages, for example). The *Lawrence* opinion (as with the *Obergefell* opinion) gives wide berth to sex (as it does to marriage) across horizontal status relationships. From the perspective of sexual autonomy, permitting such an array of intimacies, sex practices, and relationships does not herald the end of times; it is just the right thing to do.

Status, Dependence, and Abuses of Power

A normative basis for regulating sex better than the ickiness test is the potential for coercion within vertical status relationships. On this front, Justice Kennedy offers what is now a commonly cited qualification to the otherwise seemingly vast-sounding sexual autonomy right announced in *Lawrence*: "The present case does not involve minors. It does not involve persons who might be injured or coerced or *who are situated in relationships where consent might not easily be refused.* It does not involve public conduct or prostitution" (*Lawrence* 2003, 578; emphasis added).

Many feminist and liberal legal theorists wished *Lawrence had* extended its sex rights to teenagers, sex workers, and sex in public—or argue that it did (see, for example, Franke 2004; Garcia 2005; Wardenski 2005). For present purposes, however, let us draw more attention to those people "who are situated in relationships where consent might not easily be refused." This is Justice Kennedy's cabining of the Court majority's sex right (Zhou 2016, 239), but the cabining is left unspecified—which people, in which relationships, might not easily refuse consent? Might we distinguish between people situated in relationships in which consent might not be *that* easily refused, but still reasonably refusable, and people situated in relationships in which consent is all but impossible to refuse?

Y. C. Zhou (2016) does not seem to think so. Zhou argues that the anti-coercion rationale, like the other rationales listed above, is over- and underinclusive. It is overinclusive in that all sorts of incestuous relationships are neither coercive nor even likely coercive purely by formal structure alone; for example, the siblings previously unknown to one another who fall in love (240). This is a sensible criticism. But Zhou argues that the anti-coercion principle is underinclusive in that it "poses [. . .] tailoring difficulties for most state statutes" (240). Zhou raises the specter of criminalizing workplace relationships: "If the state has the power to punish incest because parent-child relationships are inherently coercive, then we must contemplate whether the state also has the authority to ban consensual office romances. The answer could be a simple—but troubling—yes" (240).

This seems a hasty conclusion—the question, Where do we draw the line? is typically posed rhetorically to expose the futility of line-drawing. But the law is just a pile of drawn lines. So the best answer to this question is not *We cannot draw lines,* but *We draw the line here* and *Here is why.* I further elaborate the reasons for my preferred lines (*Here is why*) in the first part of the following section (the Bill Clinton problem). For now I state simply that I draw the line here: sex between all minors and adults superordinated in positions of authority, trust, or dependence over those minors—including parents, adoptive parents, stepparents; intimate partners of parents; uncles and aunts by full blood, half blood, or no blood; teachers, coaches, and counselors—should be legally proscribed. I draw the line more or less where Canada and the United Kingdom draw theirs. (Not incidentally, both countries have adopted an affirmative consent standard in their sexual assault laws; see Schulhofer 2015, 673).

In Canada a person commits the offense of "sexual exploitation" if he or she "is in a position of trust or authority towards a young person, [or] is a person with whom the young person is in a relationship of dependency or who is in a relationship with a young person that is exploitative of the young person," and, "for a sexual purpose, touches, directly or indirectly, with a part of the body or with an object, any part of the body of the young person." The Canadian Criminal Code defines "young person" as someone between sixteen and eighteen years old (other sex laws criminalize sexual contact with younger minors). In Canada, then, consent is not a defense to sex between a minor and an adult in a position of authority (see also Westen 2004, 17–19). Moreover, the law also authorizes a judge to infer exploitation in such relationships based on the age of the younger person, the age difference between parties, "the evolution of the relationship," and the "degree of control or influence" of the older person over the younger. In other words, Canada does not enumerate a specific list of vertical status relationships in which sex is proscribed (father-child, coach-player, and so forth), but leaves the question open to judicial interpretation. Canada also criminalizes as sexual exploitation sexual contact between caretakers and their patients with disabilities, but here the contact must be nonconsensual.[21] Throughout Canada's criminal sexual assault statutes consent is defined affirmatively as "the voluntary agreement of the complainant to engage in the sexual activity in question." Based on this definition of consent Richard Fourtin would have likely been found guilty of sexual misconduct against L.K. (see chapter 5).[22]

Some of Canada's criminal sex laws overreach or are otherwise unjustified. For example, the country criminalizes as "incest" sexual intercourse between siblings and half-siblings (but the law at least stipulates a knowledge requirement, unlike many US state laws).[23] Persuaded by Zhou's and others' arguments, I am no longer certain that such broad prohibitions banning oral, anal, and vaginal sex between siblings of any age, regardless of fertility status or contraception use, has a place in criminal law. Canada also sets a higher age of consent (eighteen) for anal sex than for other kinds of sexual contact (sixteen).[24] This seems absurd or homophobic or both; it is difficult to defend the categorically different treatment of anal sex on either pro-sexual autonomy or anti-sexual abuse grounds. Nevertheless, the country's approach to regulating sex in vertical status relations is laudable. Designed to target abuses of power rather than simply consanguineous sex, these laws might serve as a model of sexual regulation for Canada's southern neighbor.

In the United Kingdom the 2003 Sexual Offences Act criminalized sex across a wide variety of vertical status relations under two headings: "Abuse of position of trust" and "Familial child sex offences." I will not reprint the act's multiple enumerations here, but suffice it to say that the laws' foci are age differences compounded by status differences; biology and blood matter less than issues like caretaking, service provisions, and dependence. For example, a person is in a position of trust over another if such "a person looks after persons under 18 if he is regularly involved in caring for, training, supervising or being in sole charge of such persons." And the proscriptions on sex between adults and minor "family members" define "family members" in similarly broad terms. For the purposes of the act, person A is a "family member" to person B if "A and B live in the same household, and A is regularly involved in caring for, training, supervising or being in sole charge of B." Moreover, the law makes explicit that "step-parent" also includes a "parent's partner," and that a "person is another's partner (whether they are of different sexes or the same sex) if they live together as partners in an enduring family relationship." In other words, the Sexual Offences Act contains a "no sex with mothers' boyfriends (or fathers' boyfriends)" clause.[25]

Perhaps I see a line between office romance and sex between stepparents and stepchildren (Canada's and the United Kingdom's line, give or take) where Zhou might not because my distinction is *not* premised upon the assumption that some vertical relationships are "inherently coercive." These vertical relationships are colloquially described as "inherently coercive" in regard to sex and consent, but the phrase seems to me a contradiction in terms. Coercion is about one actor acting in such a way as to make another actor act in another way. Coercion does not "inhere" in persons or in any particular relational configuration; it is exercised through acts—speech and conduct (Wertheimer 2003, 191–92). To bracket a relationship between an employee and an employer or between a stepchild and a stepparent as "inherently coercive" implies that there is zero possibility of voluntariness on the part of the subordinate. The stepdaughter, prisoner, or employee might truly, genuinely, even enthusiastically consent to sex with a stepfather, correctional officer, or employer; the consent may be truly, genuinely uncoerced. The distinction that matters (to me, and I hope to convince you) is not whether the relationship is "inherently coercive" but rather how likely, all other things being equal, the relationship is to be coercive, and how "easily," all other things being equal, consent can "be refused." Thus it is verticality and horizontality, rather than nonconsent and consent alone, that compromise sex across status relations (cf. "Inbred Obscurity" 2006).

All other things being equal, consent to sex can more easily be refused by an employee than by a minor stepchild or a prisoner (Hörnle 2014, 91). The difference is the line: all sex with minor stepchildren should be categorically proscribed, however wanted by the minor; not all sex between employers and employees should be legally proscribed, especially if wanted by the employee.

The more tricky relationships to adjudicate—the trickier line to trace—concerns intimate vertical status differences not compounded by age difference, such as cases of sex and romantic relationships between an adult child and her parent, or cases of sex between an adult dependent (perhaps cognitively disabled like L.K. from the *Fourtin* case) and her caretaker. Age thresholds and differences, of course, are already an imperfect proxy for the likelihood of coercion within certain vertical relationships, although they are probably the least-bad proxy. But the question of adult-adult sex across vertical status difference remains outstanding.

I am inclined to follow Stuart Green's proposal (2017):

> One possible compromise solution for the parent/child-type cases would be to treat such relationships as raising a rebuttable presumption of coercion, rather than as conclusive evidence under a regime of strict liability. Under such a regime, defendants would be permitted to present affirmative evidence that, despite their violating the letter of the law, their relationship was in fact characterized by genuine consent. This would not be a perfect solution: it would intrude into the privacy of some innocent defendants' lives and subject them to stigma that attends even unproved charges of this sort. But it would at least reduce the potentially over-inclusive effects of a strict liability regime. (26)

Green's proposal is made in light of the fact that adult child–parent incestuous relationships may have begun when the adult was a minor—

more dependent and more isolated—in which case the relationship may continue to be abusive, exploitive, or otherwise damaging to the child (25–27). I believe the same principle is sensibly applied to adult dependents of caretakers. Given all the ways the caretaker can leverage her or his authority to procure sex, and given the minimal or non-existent exit options of the dependent adult, a legal proscription defeated by evidence of mutual consent appears as the least-bad solution (see also Hörnle 2014, 89–92). In short, no amount of "consenting" on the part of the dependent minor stepchild should transform sexual assault into sex with her stepfather; some amount of "consenting" on the part of an adult probably should transform sexual assault into sex with her parent.

INCARCERATION NATION?

A proposal to expand state power over sex across a greater number of vertical status relations poses serious problems for progressives committed to social and sexual justice; namely, criminalizing nonnormative sex and its practitioners and bloating the already-bursting system of mass incarceration.[26] And the incarceration nation problem is more acute here than with chapter 1's argument (suggesting that we be more concerned with impediments to flourishing than with "serious physical injury" when it comes to human practices like sex or football) or with chapter 3's argument (suggesting that sex procured under the deliberate contravention of an explicit condition might be a tortious but probably not a criminal wrong). The problem can be subdivided into three smaller ones, each of which I address below: the *Bill Clinton problem,* or the question of whether we can circumscribe the regulation of sex in vertical status relations once we close the door to mothers' boyfriends; the *race problem,* or the question of disparate impact once we open the door to greater regulation and criminalization; and the *governance feminism problem,* or the question of shrinking and disfiguring a heretofore capacious feminist project down to the juridical enforcement of the norms we like.

The Bill Clinton Problem

Based on a proposal to criminalize mothers' boyfriends for sex with their partners' children, ought we to have criminalized sex between the former president and his then-twenty-three-year-old intern? Short answer: no.

I began to address the line-drawing question in the previous section but here I want to consider, more finely, ways in which employer-employee relations are and are not like more private, more intimate vertical relations.

First, as readers likely know, a great deal of sex and sexual conduct is already impermissible under civil law. Sexual harassment, as a form of sex discrimination, is prohibited in workplaces and academic institutions (*Meritor Savings Bank v. Vinson* [1986]). Sexual harassment includes both creating a hostile work environment (for example, by posting antigay or misogynist messages in the office where co-workers can see it) and quid pro quo statements (for example, "Sleep with me or I will demote you"). And while the Obama administration issued directives that gender- and sexual orientation–based bullying and sexual assault in schools and on campuses are forms of sexual harassment covered under Title IX, the Trump administration has thrown these directives into question (Gibbs and Quinlan 2017). Nevertheless, students, teachers, and employees have a legal remedy available to them against impositions of unwanted sex. Many stepchildren, non-blood-related nephews and nieces, and children of parents with non–legally recognized intimate partners (mothers' boyfriends) do not.

Second, however, perhaps some unwanted sex in workplace and educational settings *should* be considered a criminal, not just civil, wrong (consider how the football analogy, rather than helping the case for kink, might hurt the case for football). Law professor Michal Buchhandler-Raphael (2011, 152) makes a persuasive case that compelling sexual submission by leveraging institutional power is a categorically different wrong than, say, a co-worker calling someone a "bitch" or a "fag." Arguing that we cannot reliably turn to "consent" to render such sex wrong, for the employee may "consent" to the sex to avoid getting demoted or fired (155, 168), Buchhandler-Raphael instead asserts that we render this sex assaultive—a crime—by virtue of its being an "abuse of power." For Buchhandler-Raphael, sexual conduct is a criminal abuse of power if the sex is explicitly procured by leveraging institutional power, thus "placing victims in fear of professional and economic harm" (204).

Buchhandler-Raphael's interventions seem mostly right to me, although her proposals may be overinclusive, depending on how we understand "abuse of power," and are underinclusive, leaving sex in some vertical intimate relationships unprotected if unaccompanied by the manifest leveraging of power by the superordinate. The divergence of our approaches sharpens the distinction—the line—between sex across certain vertical relations, and whether and to what degree such sex should be penalized. Consider the following two scenarios, one in which a superordinated person leverages his power, and the other in which he does not:

1. A divisional academic dean, while asking out a tenure-track assistant professor, "reminds" the professor that he, the dean, oversees her, the professor's, tenure and promotion. The professor is not attracted to the dean, is in fact rather repulsed by the dean, but agrees to the date and the sex afterward.

2. A sixteen-year-old girl and her stepdad have sex. Both the girl and dad consent to this unforced, uncoerced sex affirmatively, verbally, and enthusiastically. They desire the sex, and each other, unequivocally and deeply. The stepdad is a generous lover devoted to his stepdaughter's pleasure.

Buchhandler-Raphael, if her "exploitation of power" is interpreted expansively (but not unreasonably), would criminalize sex in the first scenario but would immunize sex from criminal law in the second.[27] This seems backward. Sex in the second scenario, by my argument, should be a crime or at the very least a serious legal wrong. Sex in the first scenario should be a civil wrong for which there is a civil remedy, and the academic institution, under Title IX liability, ought to fire or otherwise penalize the dean and ensure the professor the merit-based decision on tenure and promotion to which she is entitled. The impingement on the professor's sexual autonomy, to my mind, is not so great that the dean should be incarcerated for his wrongdoing. To be clear, the dean acted wrongly, but the wrong committed is different in kind and not just degree from the wrong committed by the stepdad. If we are to draw lines, especially those distinguishing criminal from civil wrongdoing, I would draw the line above the stepdad and below the dean.

I return to those unspecified but fruitful words of Justice Kennedy: "persons [. . .] who are situated in relationships where consent might not easily be refused" (*Lawrence* 2003, 578). We can admit that for both the assistant professor and the stepdaughter, "consent might not easily be refused," but difficult refusals are differently difficult; the difference matters for sex ethics and sex law. If the professor is in a bind, the girl is in a vice. The professor can say *no* to the date and to the sex with the dean, risking her chances of promotion or tenure. She can report the dean's "throffer" (a threat masked as an offer; Wertheimer

2003, 179) to her chair and to Title IX campus coordinators. She can seek remedy. She can apply for appointments at other universities, even though she should not have to.

What if the stepdaughter does not desire the sex? To whom can she reasonably report? Her mother has a major conflict of interest (imagine if the Title IX coordinator were the spouse of the randy dean). She cannot apply for other positions in other families. There are no civil remedies available to her as there is no institution accountable for the injury (except the institution of the nuclear family).[28]

For what it is worth, and in light of #MeToo, Monica Lewinsky (2018, 177) is now far less sanguine about the validity of her consent to her former boss's sexual advances than she was just four years prior; she is "beginning to entertain the notion that in such a circumstance the idea of consent might well be rendered moot." Still, she recognizes the question as "very, very complicated" and is more willing to label Clinton's conduct as an "abuse of power" rather than sexual abuse.

The Race Problem

A conceit of this chapter is that if we care about targeting coercive or likely coercive sex, rather than incestuous or otherwise icky sex, then we ought to pay attention to postwar family formations. Not only are our country's current laws regulating sex and status too sanguineous and biological, but they typically presuppose a nuclear family of two married parents and their genetically related offspring. Our sex laws (and our sex thinking) should account for the growing number of single parent–led, stepparent-co-led, intimate-partner-of-parent-co-led, and other kinds of blended families. Persons superordinated in positions of familial authority are no longer biological fathers alone.

Here, though, is where we run into the race problem, which is more frankly a *black problem*. For while "today less than half (46%) [of children] are [. . .] living in a family with two married parents in their first marriage" (Pew Research Center 2015), and while "the number of U.S. adults cohabiting has continued to climb, reaching about 18 million in 2016 [a 29% increase since 2007]" (Stepler 2017), "the majority of white, Hispanic and Asian children are living in two-parent households, while *less than half of black children are living in this type of arrangement.* [. . .] The living arrangements of black children stand in stark contrast to the other major racial and ethnic groups. The majority—54%—are living with a single parent" (Pew Research Center 2015; emphasis added).

In other words, to the degree mothers' boyfriends are a feature of American family life, they are far more likely to be a feature of black American life than that of any other racial or ethnic group, in which case my proposal for extending the law's reach into sex across nonnuclear vertical status relations risks targeting a population—black men—already, disproportionately, and unjustly profiled and prosecuted under our criminal justice system.

This is the strongest objection to this chapter's proposals; the (racialized) costs might very well capsize the (gendered) benefits. Given the Trump administration's avowed commitment to "law and order" policing and the renewed drug war waged by Attorney General Jeff Sessions (M. Ford 2017; Nunberg 2016), any call for an expansion of criminal law, let alone an expansion that potentially screens in more black men, may simply be unpalatable and unsupportable. Yet I am inclined to agree with Stephen Schulhofer (2015) that "the danger of unequal enforcement [. . .] cannot be allowed to exert an all-purpose veto over efforts to fill gaps in the criminal law" (681).

Let me offer a few additional counterobjections that may ultimately be unconvincing (I am not sure they convince me).

First, the pool of newly criminalized conduct is shallow indeed. Most cases of sex between children and fathers, stepparents, and mothers' boyfriends are already proscribed by the jurisdiction's age of consent laws. So what is actually on the table is criminalizing sex between sixteen- and seventeen-year-old children and their mothers' boyfriends (or other intimate partners, or teachers, coaches, and counselors), conduct for which consent is often otherwise a legitimate defense. Yet once I concede that such revised vertical status laws would govern fairly little heretofore ungoverned conduct, I am conceding too that the laws have ultimately more symbolic than material function. That might be right, but the expressive power of law matters profoundly, reflecting and shaping the norms by which we abide and the values that we uphold (Sunstein 1996). "How we choose to label and classify offenses," Stuart Green (2017) observes, "sends important signals about why we are criminalizing the conduct, and the priority of wrongs and harms it entails" (13). Indeed, "incest," as I proposed above, should probably be stricken from criminal law and replaced with statutory language of gradated sexual assault and misconduct (13–14).

Second, while vertical status difference might potentially aggravate an existing crime—so that, say, a mothers' boyfriend who has sex with the fourteen-year-old daughter of his girlfriend has committed an offense more serious than would a stranger who had sex with the teenager—I have avoided any discussion of punishment. Perhaps this could be construed as naïve or irresponsible, but my suggestion that we pay more attention to coercive or likely coercive sex across vertical relations usually involving minors says nothing about the sentencing and punishment we should then dole out.

Third, the horrendously racialized history of rape law in the United States is not simply a history of overreach—in which black men are disproportionately charged, convicted, and more harshly sentenced for raping white women—but also a history of underenforcement—in which black women's claims of sexual assault are routinely ignored by police, dropped by prosecutors, and disbelieved by juries (Crenshaw 1991; Freedman 2013; Roberts 1993, 364–69; see also Chemaly 2016). The hundreds of thousands of rape kits that go untested in the basement shelves of police stations are not those of wealthy white college students.[29] While decades of anti-rape and anti-gendered-violence activism led by women of color have decidedly rejected policing and incarceration (INCITE! 2016), it is at least possible that restructuring sex law to be more attentive to heretofore neglected or discredited victim populations might be an ambivalently welcomed reform.

The Governance Feminism Problem

My response here is brief, not because I am unworried about the ways the state, corporations, and other institutions absorb and co-opt feminist projects of social and sexual justice, but because this chapter's proposals, given anything more than a superficial gloss, do not exacerbate the problem of governance feminism.

Janet Halley (2006) coined the term *governance feminism* in the early 2000s, using it to describe the ways feminist actors and organizations have both turned to the state to remedy injustice and installed themselves within state apparatuses. Developments in sexual harassment law (Halley 2002) and the regulation of sexual assault and misconduct (Halley 2008; 2015) are exemplary forms of governance feminism. The costs of aligning feminist projects with state power are myriad in Halley's view, not least of which is the cost to sex itself. Halley worries that once state policies and actors have been injected with strands of feminist thought, the state is more likely to criminalize sex and sexual expression that is nonnormative, kinky, and queer (Halley 2006; 2008). Halley likewise contends warns feminist-led efforts to revise sexual assault and sex discrimination laws, thereby expanding protections to women, may inadvertently solidify gender stereotypes of women as prudish and vulnerable and men as libidinal and aggressive (Halley 2015).

Several years after Halley put governance feminism to analytic work, Elizabeth Bernstein (2010) coined the related phrase *carceral feminism,* governance feminism's eviler twin. Here the issue is not simply turning to the state to redress sex-related injuries but turning to its criminal justice arm—putting allegedly bad men in prison to solve sex inequalities. Carceral feminism both individualizes problems that are more about neoliberal political economy than about predatory pimps (sex trafficking) and exacerbates an already-racist system (putting more black and brown men in prison—see "The Race Problem" above).

To possible charges of governance and carceral feminism, I reply with some tallies and political visions.

Tallies. I have argued here for the decriminalization of sex between adult family members; I have argued here and elsewhere (Fischel 2016) for the decriminalization of sex between same- or similar-age teenagers. In the following chapter, I argue that nearly all cases of sex involving "deception" or nondisclosure (for example, affirming to your girlfriend that you are a man even though you were not assigned male at birth by virtue of your external genitalia; or not disclosing your HIV status) should not be criminalized, either. And in chapter 4, I suggest that bestiality laws are overbroad.

I am, though, arguing that states which currently do not criminalize sex between stepparents and minor stepchildren, teachers and minor students, non-blood-related minor nieces or nephews and aunts or uncles, and finally between minors and the intimate partners of their parents should do so.

When all is tallied, then, the proposals probably amount to less overall governance, not more; or maybe net governance increase equals zero. And while these proposals tilt toward governance feminism rather than toward traditional morality or heteronormativity, surely they are an upgrade from existing law, whether from queer, anticarceral, or (probably even) libertarian perspectives.

As other feminist legal theorists have also argued, the question will never be between regulated and unregulated sex (see, for example, Nedelsky 2011, 342). Sex is *"always* shaped and regulated by social processes" (Appleton and Stiritz 2016). The question is: Which regulations are better than others? From the perspective of sexual autonomy— that is, from a pro-sex feminist perspective that takes as normatively central people's capabilities to co-determine their sexual relationships—along with a commitment to people's abilities to access intimacy and erotic experiences, I have suggested doubling down on sex in some vertical status relations and decriminalizing sex across horizontal relations.

Political visions. Nothing here or anywhere else in this book augurs for the winnowing of queer and feminist projects to legal fiat and state policy. To the contrary, sex-positive and anti–sexual violence activists and organizations do a great disservice to their missions by adopting the legal language of consent and by, at times, turning too hastily to punitive measures to redress bad, regretted, or otherwise unwanted but not assaultive sex. Suggesting that we repeal, reform, or revise sex laws says nothing about the kinds of nonlegal, cultural, creative, aesthetic, grassroots, intersectional, and global forms sexual justice politics can and should take.

But if we are going to have sex laws they might as well be the right ones.

CHAPTER 3

The Trouble with Transgender "Rapists"

The facts are undeniably unusual.
—*McNally v. R.* (2013)

Justine McNally, at the time a thirteen-year-old living in Scotland, and "M," a year younger than Justine and living in London, met through an online gaming site. For the next three and a half years, the two developed an intimate relationship over instant messaging, phone, and webcam. Across these technologies McNally presented herself as a boy named Scott.[1] Sometimes they had phone sex. "'Scott' would talk about what he wanted to do to [M] with 'it' and 'putting it in' which [M] took to mean 'his' penis" (*McNally v. R.* [2013]).

In 2011, after M turned sixteen, the two met in person in London. Beneath her pants, McNally was "wearing a strap-on dildo which resembled a penis." Over the course of four in-person visits that year, McNally performed oral sex on M and digitally penetrated her several times. "It was alleged [. . .] that M was penetrated with the dildo," though McNally later denied that charge. In their last visit together, M's mother "confronted" Justine/"Scott" "about really being a girl." McNally "came clean" to M and M's mother, though there is disagreement about whether M had earlier, in 2009, expressed doubts regarding McNally's birth sex.[2] In any event, M reportedly "felt physically sick" by the revelation, even as McNally "kept talking about wanting a sex change." Shortly thereafter police were notified, and M told officers that she "considered herself heterosexual and had consented to the sexual acts because she believed she was engaging in them with a boy called Scott" (*McNally* [2013]).

McNally would go on to plead guilty to six counts of sexual assault in 2012. A year later, she appealed her conviction and sentence to the England and Wales Court of Appeals, which dismissed the appeal on conviction but reduced her detention sentence. McNally was released from prison after eighty-two days. She must register as a sex offender for the remainder of her life (*McNally v. R.* [2013]; Rudd 2013).[3]

McNally is one of a handful of cases that have arisen in the past several decades in the United Kingdom, Israel, and the United States with similar fact patterns (A. Gross 2009, 168–73; 2015, 4–15). Defendants, typically in their late adolescence or early twenties, and assigned female sex at birth, are convicted of, or plea to, sexual assault against slightly younger women, typically in their mid-adolescence. In Israel in 2003, Hen Alkobi, sexed female at birth, was convicted on several criminal counts, some of them sexual offenses, relating to his intimate and sexual involvement with four teenage girls. Alkobi was in his early twenties at conviction, and "at least some of the time [. . .] live[d] as a male and present[ed] himself as such" (A. Gross 2009, 168). A few years after the Alkobi case (*Kashur v. State of Israel*), an Israeli court convicted "Jane Doe" for, inter alia, deceiving a fifteen-year-old female teenager into sexual contact. Jane Doe "was about twenty years old at the time of the described events [. . .] [but] presented herself as a sixteen-and-a-half-year-old boy and spoke in the Hebrew masculine form" (A. Gross 2015, 7–8). In the United Kingdom, Christopher Wilson, who identifies as a man but was sex-assigned female at birth, was convicted by the Edinburgh High Court of sexual offenses for kissing one teenage girl and for "penetrative sexual intercourse by means of a prosthetic device" with another (Sharpe 2014, 208). Wilson was also in his early twenties at the time of conviction. Prior cases in the United States from the late 1990s rehearse parallel narratives and comparable convictions, as does a case from the early 1990s in the United Kingdom (A. Gross 2009, 172–73).

In such cases, juries and judges have held that the young woman's consent to sexual contact (whether kissing or vaginal penetration) was vitiated by the defendant dissembling or misrepresenting their gender.[4]

Like other feminist scholars and activists, I find the conviction and categorization of this sexual conduct as a sexual offense troubling and wrong. These transgender "rapists" are not rapists,[5] the sex is not sexual violence, and consent—or so I will argue—is not necessarily polluted by the undisclosed absence of a penis, the fact upon which most such cases and convictions rely.

At the same time, these cases dramatize a central problem of consent's scope: What do we consent to when we consent to sex? What kind of background information, if undisclosed, embellished, misrepresented, or falsified, vitiates sexual consent, thereby converting sex into actionable sexual misconduct or assault? In this chapter, I propose that the deliberate contravention of an explicit conditional to sex should be a legal wrong, and that such a narrowly tailored solution to the problem of sex-by-deception best protects sexual- and gender-minority defendants from phobic juries and judges while also facilitating sexual autonomy.

The sexual assault cases involving gender nonconformity—and the limited scholarship about them—arise under (a) politically fraught circumstances for transgender people and (b) renewed legal theoretic attention to the problem that sexual deception poses for the consent standard of modern rape law. The chapter's first section overviews these two background conditions, and the following three sections correspond to these three arguments:

First, while the current transphobic political environment encourages us to understand these cases as pitting the sexual *autonomy* of young women against the *equality* and *privacy* of transgender men and butch women, I want to suggest that we should also be concerned about the sexual *autonomy* of transgender men and butch women.[6] In other words, our defense of transgender "deception" should be grounded not only in the fact of transgender oppression but also in the fact of transgender desire: transgender folks should not be legally forbidden from pursuing sex, searching for intimacy, or co-determining the conditions of their erotic relationships.

Second—and qualifying the first claim—because sexual deception truly problematizes the consent standard of modern rape law (to be explained below), a certain, highly particular form of sexual deception should in fact be considered a legal wrong. Namely, if sex is agreed to under an explicit condition and that condition is then willfully violated it should be a legal wrong, although not a crime.[7] "Explicitly conditioned sex" is perhaps a rather ridiculous notion (*I will have sex with you if and only if you voted for Bernie Sanders in the 2016 Democratic primary*); holding the violation of the conditional (lying to me that you voted for Bernie in order to bed me) as a legal wrong may seem even more absurd, but I believe it is the least-bad solution to resolving the deception-consent problem.

Third—and qualifying the second claim—some explicit conditionals are unanswerable by law, or at least should be, if we care at all about social constructions, historical contingencies, and cultural differences. For purposes of law, then, I do not think there is a "wrong" or "deceptive" answer to questions like *Are you a man?* or *Are you black?* for such questions may be unanswerable as truth claims. *Did you attend college?* and *Were you born with a penis and testicles?* are sensibly subject to a *yes* or *no* answer. *Are you a woman?* may not be.[8]

BACKGROUND CONDITIONS

Transgender Social Injustice

The second decade of the twenty-first century has been a rather tumultuous time for the lives and rights of transgender and gender-nonconforming people in the United States and across the globe.

Time magazine triumphantly heralded 2014 as the "transgender tipping point" for social equality and civil rights, putting the stunning and stunningly successful transgender actress Laverne Cox on its cover (Steinmetz 2014). Earlier that year transgender journalist Janet Mock published her autobiography, *Redefining Realness* (2014), which soon became an enormously popular and highly praised *New York Times* best seller. And of course, Caitlyn Jenner, formerly Olympic decathlon victor Bruce Jenner, became an international sensation when she came out as a woman in 2015. Jenner, featured on the cover of *Vanity Fair* about a year after Cox's debut on *Time,* has since been publicly advocating for queer and transgender lives and equality in many forums, including her own documentary series on the television network E! (Bissinger 2015).

Social equality should not be measured by celebrities, and "visibility is no silver bullet for transphobia" (Allen 2017). But it is not an exaggeration to say that Cox, Mock, and Jenner are but a few of "a great many transsexual celebrities, actors and activists [that] have exploded into the public sphere" in the past decade, and that this nationwide coming out signals a world-historical shift in the ways many of us understand, identify with, and respond to gender (Penny 2014). Correspondingly, in the past few years, many US states and cities have become increasingly accommodating to transgender needs and protective of transgender rights (Simon 2016; *New York Times* 2017). Some jurisdictions have relaxed requirements for transgender people to legally change their gender on official documents; some jurisdictions have amended their antidiscrimination statutes to include gender identity and expression. The US Justice Department and the Department of Education, under the Obama administration, issued directives interpreting existing federal civil rights legislation as protecting transgender students and transgender employees from discrimination, harassment, and assault. In 2016, the Departments of Justice and Education announced that Title IX of the Education Amendments of 1972 requires educational institutions to allow students to "access sex-segregated facilities consistent with their gender identity," including, now controversially, bathrooms (Department of Justice 2016; Peters, Becker, and Davis 2017).

Yet the conditions of transgender and gender-nonconforming lives are also deeply and persistently oppressive and unjust. Along every salient measure—experiences of violence (National Coalition of Anti-Violence Programs 2015), unemployment and underemployment (Movement Advancement Project et al. 2015), incarceration (Stryker 2017, 208–9; Zavidow 2016), homelessness (National Health Care for the Homeless Council 2014), suicide and attempted suicide (Haas, Rodgers, and Herman 2014), HIV/AIDS prevalence (Centers for Disease Control and Prevention 2017), and what Dean Spade more generally calls "distribution of life chances" (2011; 2013, 1042–43)—transgender people fair far worse than their nontransgender counterparts.

"Transgender men and women are harassed, assaulted, and killed at alarming rates" (Lee and Kwan 2014, 94). As of this writing, eleven transgender people were killed in the first half of 2017, all of whom were transgender women of color, a spike in what is an already–astronomically high annual homicide rate of transgender women in the United States (Marusic 2017; see also Bettcher 2007, 46; Lee and Kwan 2014, 95–96). We know too that ubiquitous stories of bullied "gay" schoolkids are, more often than not, stories of bullied kids not conforming to gender roles. It is typically the sissy boys and tomboys who get brutalized, regardless of their sexual orientation, not the gay high school quarterback (Higdon 2011, 836–43; Pascoe 2011).

Disappointingly if unsurprisingly, the Department of Justice and Department of Education under the Trump administration rejected the Obama-era transgender protective directives (Peters, Becker, and Davis 2017). In the past few years, several state legislatures, most notably North Carolina and Texas, have introduced "bathroom bills" that disallow transgender persons from using the public bathroom that corresponds to their gender identity (Fausset 2017).

All of this backsliding has led one commentator to wryly propose that 2017 might better be known as the "Transgender *Dipping* Point" (Allen 2017; see also Stryker 2017, 226–31).

These political and social circumstances are relevant for any consideration of the "transgender deception" cases because "deception" has been perhaps the most historically consistent and successful idiom through which transgender rights are abrogated and transgender lives are pathologized, demeaned, or cut short. The transgender woman with a "big secret" (her penis) was a staple, sensationalist formula of 1990s television talk shows (Gamson 1995). Audiences were expected not to sympathize with her but to scorn her for her betrayal (to her boyfriend, to gender binaries). Such genital-gender deception has been a central (but by no means exclusive or static) feature of configuring transgender bodies, characters, and "looks" in mainstream cinema (Halberstam 2005, 76–96). Likewise, the narrative mobilized to support bathroom bills is one of deception: men camouflaged as women will enter public bathrooms and molest children (Frank 2015). The narrative tropes on racist sexual anxieties of blacks entering whites-only bathrooms, but also on earlier feminist anxieties that transgender women would—stealthily, deceptively—infiltrate, commandeer, and "rape" women- and lesbian-only spaces (Frank 2015; Raymond 1979, 104).

In more than seven thousand news stories covering murders of transgender and gender-nonconforming people from 1990 to 2005, the dominant media frame "described the violence as a response to actual or perceived *deception* of the perpetrator by the transgender person" (Schilt and Westbrook 2009, 445–46; emphasis added). Nearly all these news reports are of cisgender men murdering transgender women (452);[9] men's violence is typically explained as a reaction to "feeling deceived" upon the discovery of the transgender woman's penis (453). The charge of deception serves as pretext for phobic and state violence against transgender people, especially but not only transgender women, and especially but not only racial minorities. "Trans/queer people," comments Eric Stanley, have "inherit[ed] a long history of being made suspect" (2011, 13).

Given these political circumstances and patterns, it is critical to consider the "transgender deception" cases in light of the stubbornly insidious stereotype (in law, literature, journalism, film, and elsewhere) of transgender people as duplicitous, as "counterfeit"—a stereotype that spurs and rationalizes discrimination, degradation, and brutality (Halberstam 2005, 48, 56, 71–72; Bettcher 2007, 47l).

The stereotype of transgender people as untrustworthy seems to hold greater salience among nontransgender people (cisgender men and women) in sexual and sexualized settings. While women may consider transgender men "men" in workplace environments, for example, "in sexualized situations [sex, discussion of sex], women frame transmen as *deceptive*—tricking women into seemingly heterosexual relationships without the necessary biological marker of manhood" (Schilt and Westbrook 2009, 450 [emphasis added]; see also Gross 2009, 190).

Sexual Deception and the Law, Redux

The first background condition, sociopolitical, scratches against the second background condition, legal theoretic. For if the first cautions us to be highly skeptical regarding claims of transgender and gender-nonconforming defendants "deceiving" women into sex, the second cautions us against our caution: we should take seriously sexual deception, and we should take seriously, too, the rather unexpected dilemma that sexual deception and misrepresentation pose for the consent standard of rape law.

The unexpected dilemma was brought into focus in 2013 by law professor Jed Rubenfeld's now-somewhat-infamous *Yale Law Journal* article, "The Riddle of Rape-by-Deception and the Myth of Sexual Autonomy" (2013a). The legal historical condition for the article's argument, and for Rubenfeld's riddle, is as follows. Over the past forty-five years, sexual autonomy has ascended as the governing principle of rape law in the United States and other postindustrial nations, as indexed by the substitution of nonconsent for force as the gravamen (key element) of rape and sexual assault (Rubenfeld 2013a, 1392–94). In the 1970s, liberal and feminist legal scholars and activists spearheaded this and other reforms of rape law (Caringella 2009, 13). The force requirement had been nearly impossible to prove and so only the narrowest subset of sexual misconduct was actionable (and even then, victim whiteness, chasteness, and marriage [not to the rapist] were all but prerequisites for conviction; Caringella 2009, 13–15; Freedman 2013). Presupposing that the problem of rape is the problem of the stranger with a knife, the force requirement was inhospitable to cases of acquaintance rape, coercive sex, and even sex that was resisted but not resisted "enough" (Estrich 1988). Nonconsent, it was hoped, would capture a wider range of sexual misconduct, emphasizing infringement of (women's) choice rather than violent violation.

It is against these progressive reforms, as well as a few outlier sexual assault convictions, that Rubenfeld's riddle surfaces (2013a, 1375–79). For according to Rubenfeld, if we take sexual autonomy seriously, by which Rubenfeld means people's sexual choices, then deceptions of any kind must be legally actionable, as they corrupt consent (1402–4, 1416). Under a principle of sexual autonomy so defined (nonmanipulated choice), "fraud is as great an evil as force" (1379). Any deception that induces sex—lying about your alma mater, your net worth, or your profession, or even the application of makeup—pollutes consent (2013a, 1416; 2013b, 391). Under a sexual autonomy regime, all such deceivers should be convicted of rape. Taken to its logical conclusion, sexual autonomy dictates that seventeen-year-olds who lie about their age in order to have sex with older partners would be perpetrators, not just victims, of sexual assault (2013b, 391–92, 402–3). For Rubenfeld, this outcome is both inevitable and ridiculous. Seeing no plausible limit to autonomy's reach and thereby to the scope of the consent standard, Rubenfeld proposes that we drop sexual autonomy—and therewith consent—from rape law. He advocates instead reinstalling the force requirement. Rape violates not a choice right, he reasons, but "the right to bodily self-possession," abrogated only by force (imprisonment, overpowering, physical restraint) or threat of such force (2013a, 390, 403). Consent re-enters sex law singularly as a defense against *forcible* sexual subjection, transforming rape into permissibly rough, kinky, or BDSM sex (1437–38; Dougherty 2013a, 326–27).

Heretofore, only two forms of deception have been recognized to vitiate sexual consent in Anglo-American law, thus criminalizing ensuing sex as assaultive. These deceptions are medical misrepresentation (e.g., a doctor claims to penetrate his patient's vagina with a medical instrument that is in fact the doctor's penis; the doctor has sexual intercourse with his patient by claiming such sex is medically necessary for the patient) and spousal (read: husband) impersonation. Yet as Rubenfeld rightly points out, the fact that these are the two and only two criminalized deceptions under rape law suggests that the rationale is patriarchy, not women's sexual autonomy (2013a, 1401–4). The legally cognizable deceptions protect a woman's virtue—she thought she was having marital sex (spousal impersonation), or she thought she was not having sex (medical misrepresentation). But in any other kind of deceptive sex, the woman has allegedly consented to the sex act, which means "she had willingly surrendered her virtue," whatever lies it took to get her to do so (1402). From traditional Anglo-American law's perspective, these deception exceptions maintain the property value of virtuous (chaste) women and wives; they are not premised upon respecting women's sexual choices.

So if we want to criminalize sexual deception to protect autonomy rather than promote patriarchy, we would need to radically expand the kinds of deception that vitiate sexual consent beyond the two historically recognized types. Yet once we go down that road, the road paved by consent-not-force, must we be committed to criminalizing all varieties of concealment, deception, and misrepresentation, such as a transgender man not divulging his assigned sex at birth?

Rubenfeld's essay revived earlier legal scholarly interest in the question of rape by fraud and deception, but to my knowledge he is the first to pose the dilemma of sexual deception as a fundamental challenge to modern rape law.[10] While scholars have sought to delineate permissible and impermissible forms of deception beyond spousal impersonation and medical misrepresentation—for example, by distinguishing fraud in the fact from fraud in the inducement, or deception over material information from deception over peripheral or immaterial information (e.g., Schulhofer 1998, 152, 155, 159; Larson 1993, 462–64)—Rubenfeld powerfully and provocatively argues that the dilemma of rape by deception may drive a stake through the very heart of modern rape law and its ascendant central principle, nonconsent.

Rubenfeld's dismissal of sexual autonomy alarms many scholars and activists, not least because "there is not much rape law left" if we take Rubenfeld's path (Falk 2013, 354). Consequently and more importantly, "the beneficiaries of Rubenfeld's proposal will be the perpetrators of all forms of nonviolent, nonforcible rape," which is to say most perpetrators of sexual assault (369). So, on the one hand, the evisceration of modern rape law advised by Rubenfeld in light of the contradiction he exposes risks further shielding sexual assault and its perpetrators from prosecution; on the other hand, if Rubenfeld is right about the consent contradiction—that a whole lot more sex should be criminalized, given the moral and legal value we liberals and progressives allegedly attribute to sexual choice—then what other options do we have but to either (a) rid rape law of "consent" and revert to a force requirement or (b) "jail all the beautiful people" for sexual deception (Rubenfeld 2013a, 1416)? Let's call this the Big Question.

TRANSGENDER EQUALITY, TRANSGENDER PRIVACY . . . TRANSGENDER AUTONOMY?

Before tackling the Big Question (*What do we consent to when we consent to sex?* or, *What (mis)information, nondisclosure, or concealment ought to legally vitiate consent?*), I want to point out a dominant discursive frame of the "transgender sexual deception" cases and of the scholarship surrounding them. The frame is misleading, I argue, yet my alternative frame only accentuates, rather than ameliorates, the Big Question.

Aeyal Gross (2009; 2015) and Alex Sharpe (2014; 2015) are the two legal scholars who have conducted the most thorough research and analysis on the "transgender deception" cases, and this chapter owes a great deal to their contributions. Sharpe's analyses accept the courts' central framing of the cases—that the defendants' "gender misrepresentation" does indeed undermine women's sexual choices. For both Sharpe and Gross, competing considerations outweigh the value of women's undiluted sexual *autonomy*, chief of which is transgender *equality*. Gross argues that the rulings of the Israeli, US, and UK courts "restor[e] the heteronormative regime against the complex queer reality" (2009, 207). By holding defendants guilty of sexual misconduct for "deceiving" as to their gender, courts reinstall binary gender and compulsory heterosexuality, marginalizing transgender people and queer sexualities outside the borders of normative social and legal relations (A. Gross 2015, 33).

Sharpe too argues that the UK cases are rooted in "unacknowledged cis-sexism" (2014, 218) and that, taken together, the rulings amount to "nothing less than the ontological degradation of transgender people" (2015, 385). In addition to valuing transgender equality (or rather, diagnosing the formalization of transgender inequality), Sharpe also contends that the "transgender deception" cases elevate the sexual autonomy rights of women against the *privacy* rights of transgender people (2014, 219–21; 2015, 388–89) and that there are medical, doctrinal, and public policy reasons to take privacy rights much more seriously. Too often, the forced exposure of gender history and genitals has dire, sometimes fatal consequences (2014, 220–21). We should therefore establish "privacy and/or human dignity as limits to sexual autonomy" (2015, 388).

Sharpe's critique largely keeps in place the terms of the debate, assuming that women's sexual autonomy rights must indeed be curtailed to respect the privacy rights of transgender people, and that transgender privacy is the central value competing with women's autonomy. I want to suggest, however, that we also take stock of the fact that criminalization impedes the sexual autonomy—not just privacy or equality—of transgender people too. This observation is intimated in Sharpe's first account of the "transgender deception" cases (2014, 217) and made more explicit in her second, if still unelaborated: "We should recognize that transgender people also value and have an interest in sexual autonomy" (2015, 388). Gross gestures in the direction of transgender autonomy, even as the bulk of his argument shores up how these cases police and promote gender and sexual-normative order: "Does imposing a duty to disclose on someone like the defendants in these trials not cause injury to him—to both his self-identity and *his ability to meet young women and have sexual intercourse with them?*" (A. Gross 2009, 201; emphasis added).

It rubs feminist readers the wrong way to imply a right "to meet young women and have sexual intercourse with them," yet must we not also accord moral and legal value to the kind of sex the transgender man or butch woman wishes to have? Gender-nonconforming folks are also entitled—or should be—to co-determine the conditions under which they experience intimacy and pleasure. The gender stylizations and sex preferences (e.g., using a dildo for penetrative sex) of transgender and butch defendants are exercises of the *defendants'* sexual autonomy. There is no reason, ipso facto, that gender stylization and sex preference must conform automatically and unalterably to the *complainants'* normative expectations.

It is, in part, an effect of the political conditions facing transgender lives enumerated in the section above (the first background condition) that we are encouraged to read these "transgender deception" cases as judicial imprimaturs of transphobia and transgender oppression and as violations of gender-minority privacy rights. They are, but we have a larger cultural repertoire of transgender people as victims to call upon than as erotic agents with desires, preferences, and sought-out pleasures. In a contiguous political context, Samantha Allen (2017) reminds us that while the marriage equality movement positioned gays and lesbians as subjects of *love*—and "almost everyone knows what it's like to love someone"—"transgender people, on the other hand, have to talk about going to the bathroom and getting fired and being physically abused." In other words, transgender folks, politically speaking, do not yet get to talk enough about love—whom they love, how they want to be loved, and how they wish to pursue sex and intimacy. What are transgender possibilities "to play," queries artist and activist Kai Lumumba Barrow? What are the opportunities for, as Hawaiian transgender activist and scholar Kalaniopua Young puts it, "decolonial lovemaking" (Spade 2017, 327, 330)?

To facilitate an incipient discussion of transgender sexual autonomy, consider the following scenario:

> Dude A goes to a kinky gay club to get fisted.
> Dude A accordingly positions himself in the sling, and dude B obliges.
> Dude B is a skilled practitioner, and so the two dudes meet up for several more fisting sessions at the club.
> One night the two dudes stay until the club closes. The lights come on and it is revealed that dude B has a prosthetic hand.
> "I'm a veteran," says dude B by way of explanation. "It feels even better than a 'real' hand, right?"

Has the fisting war veteran committed sexual assault by means of deception or misrepresentation, since the normative standard for fisting is one's biological hand? No. Moreover, ought we to deny dude B's pleasure and interest in fisting simply because he uses atypical equipment? What if dude B had been born with a vagina; would the sexual assault claim be any more legitimate (A. Gross 2009, 200)? And if dude B has a sexual autonomy right to fist a willing dude A, does not Justine McNally have a sexual autonomy right to penetrate a willing M? Does dude A really have an autonomy right to be fisted by a biological, not prosthetic, hand? Is dude A's sexual autonomy infringed simply because his normative expectation is not met? Sharpe (2015) nearly makes this point regarding the "transgender deception" cases. If nondisclosure of gender history to one's sexual partner is not deceptive, and if gender history is irrelevant to the validity of the sexual partner's consent (218–19), then is the sexual autonomy of the partner actually infringed by nondisclosure?

Under present social and political conditions, we are inclined to make sense of these "deception" cases as pitting women's sexual autonomy against transgender social equality. I am suggesting we have it backward. It may be more apt to understand these cases as placing transgender sexual autonomy alongside women's equality.

This is something of a legal analogic stretch, but consider that "courts are generally quite permissive of sex discrimination in privacy cases," and that the "ideal underlying and driving courts' permissiveness toward discrimination in such cases," posits law professor Kimberly Yuracko (2016), "is focused on the value and importance of *protecting personal and sexual autonomy*, particularly from forced exposure in the market"

(115–16; emphasis added). Courts tend to uphold sex-based hiring policies, for example, if the employment pertains to intimate modes of caretaking or guardianship, on the premise that recipients of such care possess the right to decide under what conditions and under whose supervision to expose their bodies. Yuracko argues that courts are more forgiving of sex discrimination in these cases than in other kinds of discrimination cases because there is a legitimately competing normative value (as opposed to, say, the value the boss places on his assistant wearing revealing attire) to balance against the value of formal sex equality: care recipients' intimate autonomy.

I reach for the analogy in sex discrimination law because this body of law, like rape law, is not simply about the fair application of neutral principles. Both bodies of law are also substantively rooted in (or in rape law's case, repurposed for) women's equality. Rape and sex discrimination not only prohibit women from doing and being in the world but are also instantiations of women's subordinate status. As Jonathan Herring (2005) observes, "the protection of these rights [of sexual autonomy and sexual integrity] is also essential as part of the wider programme of the law to promote equality between men and women" (516; see also Cahill 2001, 32–33; Ramachandran 2013, 375). In other words, the difference that most matters between *McNally* and my fisting dudes scenario, yet the difference typically left unarticulated, is that dude A is a man and M is a young woman. This is not a double standard; sex inequality exists. Indeed, we should be especially concerned about the ways sex practices perpetuate sex inequality. So the central normative issue in the "transgender deception cases"—nearly all of which feature young female defendants—should not be women's autonomy (for the same reason dude A's sexual autonomy is not infringed by dude's B prosthetic hand), but women's equality. Does this sex subordinate women? The answer is still ultimately no: women are not categorically made less equal by sex with transgender men and butch women; in fact, women's alleged inequality may function as pretext for transphobic policing and prosecution. But it is an important question to ask, and to press against the particulars of each case.

My brief for transgender sexual autonomy, though, only dramatizes Rubenfeld's riddle, the Big Question. Perhaps McNally and other gender-nonconforming subjects should retain rights to sexual interactions that contravene normative expectations (e.g., presenting oneself with a chosen masculine name rather than disclosing one's more feminine birth name; using a dildo for penetrative sex; calling oneself a "man" when one is assigned female sex at birth), but as one version of the liberal legal adage goes, the right to swing my arm stops at your face. Surely transgender folks, just like nontransgender folks, do not have unfettered sexual autonomy rights. I do not enjoy a "right" to sex with Zac Efron simply because I wish to have sex with Zac Efron (Rubenfeld 2013a, 1418). Moreover, even if the feeling were mutual, might not certain misrepresentation, concealment, or nondisclosure on my part vitiate Efron's consent to any ensuing sex between us? So if, as I have argued, McNally's genital configuration and gender stylization ought not to vitiate M's sexual consent, what sort of (mis)information should, if any? Where does one's sexual autonomy right to stylize and present oneself in one's own image (e.g., "I'm Scott"; "I'm a millionaire"; "I'm your husband"; "I'm Jewish"; "I'm HIV-negative") give way to another's autonomy right to know with whom (and with what) he or she is having sex?

EXPLICITLY CONDITIONED SEX

The first background condition, sociopolitical, directs us toward transgender inequality and transphobia as explanatory variables for the conviction of transgender men and butch women in sexual deception cases. I have proposed, however, that we not lose sight of transgender autonomy: that not only should this sort of sexual contact not be criminalized (or even be considered tortious) but this sort of sexual contact (procured under whatever stylization of gender identity and expression) may reasonably fall within the autonomy rights of transgender and gender-nonconforming people.

The second background condition, legal theoretic, pushes against that proposal, and quite profoundly. If the wrong of rape is the wrong of nonconsent, asks Rubenfeld, should not an enormous range of sex procured under deceptive or misinformed conditions (e.g., Jill assumes John was sexed male at birth but he was not; Jill tells John she is thirty years old when she is in fact older) be reclassified as rape? And to check state overreach, must we not replace the ascendant consent standard of rape law with what we thought was the waning force requirement? In which case, argues Rubenfeld, the wrong of rape is not a violation of sexual autonomy, an absurd abstraction, but a violation of bodily self-possession, as with the wrong of torture and slavery (2013a, 1426–27).

Several legal scholars have had a go at Rubenfeld's riddle, some of which were published together in a special forum of the *Yale Law Journal Online*. Professors Patricia Falk (2013) and Gowri Ramachandran

(2013) both balk at the consequences of Rubenfeld's pared-down rape law for prosecuting sexual assault and protecting women. Ramachandran contends that Rubenfeld's norm of "bodily self-possession" is no less riddled with contradictions than is sexual autonomy (2013, 378–79), and both Ramachandran and Falk argue that a better way to resolve Rubenfeld's riddle is by "developing a more robust understanding of which types of fraudulent (or deceptive) representations violate our right to sexual autonomy and which do not. How do we draw the line?" (Falk 2013, 365). Professor Deborah Tuerkheimer (2013) suggests that "sexual agency" is a preferable alternative to "sexual autonomy" as the primary value for rape law to uphold, since the former admits that we all make sexual decisions under constraints and imperfect conditions whereas the latter presupposes the fiction of the sovereign subject (338; see also Abrams 1999). Tuerkheimer would therefore allow for the validity of sexual consent under most imperfectly informed conditions, though she draws her line at impersonation: "When a person has been deceived as to *which* human being she is choosing sex with, what would be sex becomes rape" (2013, 346).

In a critique published outside the special forum, Corey Rayburn Yung (2016) takes Rubenfeld to task for wrongly presupposing that sexual autonomy is the single underlying fundamental value of rape law when instead, argues Yung, criminal rape law is or should be premised on several core values, among them that rape terrorizes its victims, subordinates women, and causes grave harms (20–27). For Yung, whatever "inconsistencies in doctrine" Rubenfeld has revealed are far outweighed by the prevalence of sexual violence and the underenforcement of rape law (45).

All of these criticisms—Falk's, Ramachandran's, Tuerkheimer's, and Yung's—raise important theoretical and political concerns about both rape law and Rubenfeld's account of rape law, but ultimately all fail to resolve the troublesome riddle. Falk and Ramachandran want us to draw better lines regarding which sexual deceptions are legally actionable and which not, but what can be the objective basis for that line drawing if we take as morally paramount (a particular woman's) choice? Tuerkheimer draws the line at impersonation, but why is impersonation so much morally or legally worse than other forms of deception? And if transgender men or butch women adopt traits, even names, of actually existing men in the world to stylize their identity and expression, should this be considered impersonation?[11] Yung's conceptual reconstruction of rape law is compelling (it is not all about autonomy, nor should it be), but it provides no cabining of consent's scope. While he too supposes that material deception can be confined to impersonation and fraud in the fact cases, it remains unconvincing that these kinds of cases necessarily disrespect people's choices any more or less than, say, a wife who continues to have sex with her husband despite her extramarital affairs, knowing the husband would end the marriage (and the sex) if he knew of her infidelities (Rubenfeld 2013b, 401).

Indeed, it is the intractability of the riddle that leads political philosopher Tom Dougherty, in his response to Rubenfeld, to concede that "we must bite this bullet: when the deception is material to someone's sexual consent, then sex-by-deception is a serious wrong" (2013a, 331). Dougherty's resolution to Rubenfeld's riddle is to expand the scope of rape law (and thereby, the meaning of nonconsent) in exactly the ways that alarm Rubenfeld. Dougherty concludes, to Rubenfeld's shock (2013b, 391), that "we should reluctantly accept that someone can be guilty of rape-by-deception by falsely saying he went to Yale" (Dougherty 2013a, 333). Dougherty refines his argument elsewhere (2013b) but maintains that if forms of sexual deception are "deal breakers" for a partner then the subsequent sex is nonconsensual and "seriously wrong" (2013b, 719–20). Yet I want to suggest that, for M, Justine McNally's not having a penis was just such a deal breaker and that there is nothing "seriously wrong" about their ensuing sexual contact, penetrative or not. If Rubenfeld's proposal renders too little unwanted sex "rape," and Dougherty's counterproposal renders too much wanted sex "rape," what, finally, might be a middle path?

Making actionable the contravention of *explicitly conditioned* sex, or such is my argument. This sort of deception should classify as tortious, probably not criminal, sexual misconduct. Normatively, the deliberate contravention of an explicit condition to sex is a violation of sexual autonomy in a way that other forms of concealment, deception, and misrepresentation are not. As far as I know, nobody has offered the "explicit conditional" solution to Rubenfeld's riddle, but I think it succeeds. For it both concedes and accommodates the scope problem of consent Rubenfeld rightly identifies, but without jettisoning consent altogether from sexual assault law and thereby excluding from its reach most unwanted sex.

Alexandra Brodsky's excellent analysis of "stealthing"(2017), the rather nasty phenomenon whereby a man removes the condom from his penis unbeknownst to the sexual partner he is penetrating, arrives at the same conclusion as I do about penalizing violations of explicitly conditioned sex, albeit in a different vernacular and for different reasons.

Still, Brodsky's argument for rendering nonconsensual condom removal a legal wrong illuminates a better path for thinking and regulating sexual deception.

Brodsky explains that there are two theories by which we might pinpoint what exactly is nonconsensual about nonconsensual condom removal during penetrative sex. The first theory, which she calls the "literal theory" of consent is that the receptive partner consented to genital contact with a condom-covered penis, not a bare penis. The second theory, which she calls the "risk-enhancement theory" of consent, is that the receptive partner consented to sex assuming x degree of risk but not y, regarding, mainly, pregnancy or sexually transmitted infections (2017, 190–96).

Brodsky opts for the first theory, for she notices several drawbacks to the second. Among them, we risk "overly punitive responses to STI non-disclosure," to nondisclosure or misrepresentation of reproductive (in)capacities, and, indeed, to rape by deception. "Too often," Brodsky points out, "courts use rape by deception to validate and operationalize bigotry, like a Jewish Israeli woman's horror to learn she had slept with an Arab man or a partner's horror to learn a man with whom she had been sexually intimate is transgender" (2017, 193–95; internal citations omitted).[12] Holding nonconsensual condom removal nonconsensual on "literal grounds," or what I am calling a violation of an explicit conditional, better contains state interference in sexual and intimate decision making.

Brodsky's literalism is the condition of the explicit conditional. She prefers the thin theory of consent on mainly consequentialist grounds (we risk criminalizing nondisclosures of sexually transmitted infections and misrepresentation of reproductive capacity), while I prefer it on both consequentialist and absurdist grounds. Otherwise, we risk criminalizing too many deceptive practices, like embellished or inaccurate Grindr profiles. "HungTwink" states he is twenty-one and has a ten-inch penis but is actually twenty-eight and has an eight-inch penis; we probably do not want to throw our still-young but not that young, and still-hung but not that hung Grindr user into prison (or hold him accountable for damages, for that matter).

Yet we must acknowledge that the "literal theory" of consent, or the explicit conditional, at least potentially invites broader criminalization or legal liability (were such a wrong a tort). Imagine the following scenario, given that Brodsky's "literal approach focus[es] on different physical touches" (196):

Dude C will bottom for dude D if and only if dude D does not wear a condom. Dude C may or may not have articulable reasons for preferring "raw" anal sex, but suffice it to say that sex without condoms turns dude C on and sex with condoms turns him off; more than that, the very notion of sex with condoms is an affront to dude C.[13]

Dude D agrees to penetrate dude C without a condom.

When dude C is not looking, dude D slips a condom on his penis and penetrates dude D.

Has dude D committed a legal wrong against dude C? In most if not all courts of law (where "dude sex" is legal to begin with), no. But should dude D's conduct be considered a legal wrong? I hesitantly think so, and so, I think, does Brodksy. Tom Dougherty (2013b) agrees too, supposing that if "Victoria makes it clear that she wants to have sex only with someone who shares her love of nature and peace," and that someone, "Chloe," fabricates a love of nature and peace to sleep with Victoria, Chloe's lie vitiates the moral validity of Victoria's consent, and the subsequent sex by deception is "seriously wrong" (728, 733, 743–44).[14]

While the literalist or explicit conditional theory of legitimate sexual consent (or more precisely, the literalist or explicit conditional theory of what counts as nonconsensual, wrongful sexual deception) may seem to indulge people's trivial or bigoted or otherwise "bad" sexual preferences, it bypasses the deeper trouble that recourse to a content-based or risk-based theory would enmesh us in. We might find this latter alternative attractive at first: deception or nondisclosure regarding a fact like marital or HIV status may appear "objectively" important, or material to any reasonable sexual partner, whereas deception as to goldfish caretaking may appear trivial and unworthy of state redress. However, this approach imposes a universal standard for legitimate criteria in sexual decision making, when the very moral crux of consent is that people make different choices from one another and for different reasons. "As such, it is up to each individual to determine which features of a sexual encounter are particularly important to her" (Dougherty 2013b, 730; see also Herring 2005). Dude C's preference for condomless sex may be just as passionately held as Jane's preference for sex with condoms, each breach experienced equally as violation.

Let us remember that "much deception in romance is not material to someone's decision to consent to sex" (Dougherty 2013a, 333). That Jane says she graduated from Yale may make her more attractive in the eyes of Jill; this is a far cry from Jill agreeing to have sex with Jane if and only if Jane went to Yale (326, 333). Let us remember, too, how infrequently this sort of explicit conditional is asserted; such infrequency minimizes the risk of overcriminalization. Explicit conditionals are rare because "sexual consent is, typically [. . .] not directed at types of agents [*I have sex only with Yale graduates*]; it is directed at a unique particular agent [*I want to have sex with Jane, who says she went to Yale*]" (Manson 2017, 426).

This does not mean we should dismiss, however uncommon, type-particular, explicitly asserted sexual preferences. If Jane sleeps only with surgeons, and says so to Ben, then Ben's lying about being a surgeon vitiates, to my mind, Jane's sexual consent. (On the other hand, if Jane sleeps only with "men," and says so to Ben, Ben's genitals are or should be legally irrelevant; I reluctantly propose in the following section that there is no consent-vitiating way to answer the question *Are you a man?*). These sorts of explicit conditionals are perhaps most common, and not ridiculous-sounding, in regard to condom use and in regard to commercial sex—sex for and only for money. The contravention of explicit conditionals ought to be considered legal wrongs in the case of sex work and condoms; but contraventions of other explicit conditionals to sex should be taken no less seriously just for being unusual.

As a final hedge against state overreach, note that being deliberately deceived about an explicit conditional is distinct, and actionably so, from consenting to sex that you would not have consented to had you known this or that fact. Had I known the man I went home with from the bar had voted for Trump, I would not have slept with him. But I did not ask for his voting record. Nor should I expect—*unless I explicitly ask*—him to confess his voting history, even (especially!) if he knows it will ruin his chances to bed me. Carol might not sleep with Ken again, knowing now that Ken used a dildo to penetrate her, as Ken has a vagina, not a penis. As Neil Manson points out (2017, 427–28), if you give clothes to a man whom you assume to be homeless based on his appearance, and he turns out not be homeless, your consent is not vitiated. But your consent is vitiated if your charitable giving was unequivocally conditioned on the recipient being homeless and the recipient lied (427–28). Sexual regret, though, is not nonconsent; and the past perfect tense (*had I known then . . .*) is the realm of unhelpful counterfactual (Manson 2017, 415; but see Herring 2005).

The explicit conditional exemption has the added advantage of heeding Tuerkheimer's intuition about sexual agency. Since so many decisions about sex are made under conditions of constraint and imperfect information, we cannot criminalize all that sex, nor should we. We should, for the most part, respect people's sexual choices, even if adulterated. The explicit conditional makes unequivocally manifest a sexual agent's choice—in effect she says, *There is a whole lot I do not know about you, some of which might make you even more appealing or much less, but it is only on this condition that I will have sex with you* (e.g., if you were born with a penis; if your dildo is made from silicone; if you wear a condom; if you do not wear a condom). Unlike law professor Jonathan Herring, I am unwilling to retrospectively classify as "rape" sex between a client and a sex worker for which the client refuses to pay the previously agreed-to fee (Herring 2005, 523–24). But the legal wrong against the sex worker does amount to more than the unpaid fee (512–13, 523); it is a wrong against the sex worker's sexual autonomy. The explicit condition of the sex was contravened by the client.

The language of *explicitness* is used by two of Brodsky's interviewees, women whose male sex partners removed condoms without consent: "I set a boundary. I was very *explicit*"; "I agreed to fuck him with a condom, not without it" (2017, 187; emphasis added). Partners explicitly agreed to a certain kind of sex, sex with condoms, that one partner unilaterally disregarded. So regardless of whether unanticipated (risks of) pregnancy and sexually transmitted infections are or should be legal wrongs, and what kinds of legal wrongs they would be, it is the violation of the explicit conditional that is the sexual autonomy wrong and a violation of consent. By equating a violation of an explicit conditional to sex as a violation of consent to sex, we are able to retain consent as the preferred standard for rape law without either (a) reverting to a force requirement (Rubenfeld's solution) or (b) criminalizing or otherwise penalizing all sex under conditions of imperfect information, which is most if not all sex (Rubenfeld's reductio ad absurdum).

UNANSWERABLE CONDITIONS

Based on the elaboration of explicit conditions, we could reconstruct the facts of the *McNally* case in the following way:

> *M:* I am heterosexual and engage in sexual conduct only with men. Are you a man?
>
> *McNally:* Yes.

There are three ways we might interpret McNally's (reconstructed) *yes,* with two different legal results.

The first interpretation, which was the court's: McNally lied and the ensuing sexual conduct occurred nonconsensually. This interpretation seems genitally fixated, transphobic, facile, and wrong.

The second interpretation: McNally was telling the truth. Alex Sharpe (2015) adopts this interpretation: "McNally appears to have genuinely identified as male at the time of the offences. *Therefore* criminal liability ought not to have been founded on 'gender fraud'" (387; emphasis added). As Sharpe writes of transgender men more generally: "There is nothing fabricated about their feelings or performance of masculinity" (2014, 215). So McNally has answered M's (reconstructed) explicit conditional, the answer is truthful, and the ensuing sexual conduct occurs consensually.

The third interpretation: *Are you a man?* is a bullshit question. Rather, and put with slightly more sophistication, the coordinates, constructions, experiences, identifications, histories, physiologies, and stylizations of gender—manhood, womanhood, and everything in between and beyond—are so multiple, so variable, so contradictory, so personal and so impersonal, that *Are you a man?* cannot be answered incorrectly, at least for the purposes of making deceptive sex actionable. This last interpretation is the one Aeyal Gross seems to favor (2009, 215–17), as do I.

Why? For what does it mean to "be a man"? Or to "be a woman"? The "queer reality" of social life—the interplay of permanence and plasticity that animates sex, gender, desire, and identification—undercuts the immutability of legal classification (A. Gross 2009, 167, 207). What makes a "man" or a "woman"—genitals, gonads, chromosomes, or hormones (Fausto-Sterling 1993; A. Gross 2009, 183–84)? Or is it subjective feeling, social recognition, legal classification, or heterosexuality? Or the doctor's famously performative speech act, *It's a girl* (Butler 1997, 49)? (Hint: it's a trick question.)

Are you a man? or *Are you a woman?* cannot be comprehensively answered by recourse to genitals, genital history, gonads, chromosomes, "brain" sex, hormones, legal records, or any particular permutation of factors (Fausto-Sterling 1993). Nor, however, contra Sharpe as I read her, can we rely fully upon subjective feeling and identification for gender determination. Perhaps McNally felt unequivocally "like a man" when she engaged in sexual conduct and online conversation with M, but McNally alone can verify that feeling. More important, McNally's culpability should not hinge on the purity of feeling. Gender identification is often ambivalent, uncertain, locally conditioned and constrained, and in a word, queer (Halberstam 2005, 34, 41–45). Moreover, gender and sexuality are not only identifications but also ascriptions, however much we prefer our preferred gender pronouns.

For our last scenario, consider:

> By way of genitals, gonads, hormones, chromosomes, and secondary sex characteristics, E is "male."
> E identifies as a woman; her preferred gender pronouns are "she" and "her."
> E has sex with dude F.

If E believes herself a woman, phenomenologically feels and proprioceptively senses herself a woman (Salamon 2010), and dude F believes himself to have had gay sex with E, are not they both right? We would be hard-pressed to say dude F had heterosexual sex; it would stretch linguistic credulity to say he had gay sex with a woman; and yet it would be wrong to claim E a "man" too. And it seems resolutely absurd to charge E with sexual assault for not disclosing her gender identification, her "subjective sense of fit," to dude F before having sex with him (Stryker 2017, 21). So if a transgender man defendant alleges heterosexual sex with his girlfriend, but the girlfriend sees the sex as lesbian, whose account should be given credence (A. Gross 2009, 214–15)? Subjective feeling is no more but no less exhaustive of gender than any other criterion, not least because gender, like sex, like sexuality, is made and remade relationally, not individually.

Furthermore it is not or should not be just dude F's sexual autonomy rights that we take into moral or legal consideration, but E's too. E's gender identification, and her decision whether and when to disclose that identification, are (or might be) elemental to E's sexual autonomy: her ability and choice to have sex *as a woman*.

It should not go unnoticed, finally, that these legal and cultural discourses—transgender women with penises "deceiving" men; transgender men or butch women without penises "deceiving" women—revolve around penises, start to finish (see also Halberstam 2005, 53–54; as the following chapter shows, it is likewise phallocentrism that converts placing a penis into a corpse as "sex" when such conduct is no more "sex" than placing a penis into a tube sock). In addition to reasonably asking why the presence or absence of a penis dictates sex or gender, we might also ask, embracing the phallocentrism, why the presence or absence of a penis is any more important than characteristics of the penis itself. Does a sexual partner have a reasonable expectation of a standard-sized penis? What if the man has a micropenis, an enormous penis, or genitals that do not bear significant resemblance to a penis, on account of birth figuration, surgery, accident, or the like (A. Gross 2009, 200–1; Lee and Kwan 2014, 118n230)? If this all seems ridiculous, it is because the phallocentrism of the whole debate is ridiculous. The expectation that genitals correspond to gender identification is a normative one, a resolutely heteronormative one (A. Gross 2009, 192–93). That an expectation is socially normative need not entail that the failure of the expectation be legally actionable. By rendering the question *Are you a man?* legally unanswerable for purposes of criminalizing sexual conduct, we help undermine the "systematic representational alignment between gender presentation and sexed body" that indicts transgender people as always already deceivers and that shackles all of our gender identities to our genitals (Bettcher 2007, 55; Halberstam 2005, 57–58). Under these lights, the real deception is the lie by which most of us still operate, even as the compulsoriness of compulsory heterosexuality has been relaxed: that there are two and only two genital forms, which constitute two and only two sexes, which correspond perfectly to two and only two genders (Rich 1980; Butler 1990).

CHAPTER 4

Horses and Corpses

*Notes on the Wrongness of Sex with
Children, the Inappositeness of Consent,
and the Weirdness of Heterosomething
Masculinity*

I could never believe that an animal would do this on their
own. We don't allow adults to abuse children sexually.
Children cannot consent. Children are innocent, and so are
animals. They cannot consent and they are innocent.

—Washington state senator Pam Roach

How do they know the horse didn't consent? [. . .] If
the horse didn't consent then none of this would have
happened!

—Rush Limbaugh

The horse was fucking the guy. It's honestly not that bad. It's
not as if a human was fucking the animal.

—Ilana Wexler, "Game Over," *Broad City*

HORSES

In 2005 a man known as Mr. Hands died from peritonitis after his
colon was perforated by a stallion's erection. The death of the Boeing
engineer, whose given name was Kenneth Pinyan, revealed that a group
of men regularly convened at a farm near Enumclaw, Washington, to
venture into the stables together to bottom for the well-endowed horses.
A grainy, graphic video of Mr. Hands getting plowed by the stallion was
leaked online and went viral. The scandal catalyzed Washington State
to promptly enact an antibestiality law, sponsored principally by state
senator Pam Roach and voted for unanimously by her colleagues. The

incident and its surrounding circumstances—men meeting up for horse sex—were the sympathetically, nonsensationally portrayed phenomena of Robinson Devor's documentary *Zoo* (2007). Slowly sequenced against soft, sad instrumentals, the recurring images are of lush green landscapes; the recurring motif of light surrounded by darkness (figs. 4, 5, and 6). Paced glacially, almost boringly, *Zoo* asks its viewers to resist the breakneck pace of the viral video, its aversion-attraction stimuli, long enough to have a thought. What does the unlikely case of a human-horse sex exposé help us see more clearly, if we suspend our (performance of) disgust? What is revealed by the distant light, surrounded by the darkness of our cultural conventions?

Rush Limbaugh knows, maybe. As he half-jokingly asks his listeners (and as replayed in *Zoo*), how might a horse penetrate a man without the horse's "consent"? The joke, or the argument, is this: animal erection = consent. The stallion erection betokens consent to sex with humans (Devor 2007). This is a tempting supposition, and one with which *Zoo* flirts. The documentary offers up images of frozen meat and discussions of meat-eating, along with a stirring sequence of animal welfare officials anesthetizing and then gelding the stallion that had topped Mr. Hands (figs. 7 and 8). Senator Pam Roach is incorrect about animals' capacity to consent, Limbaugh says (and *Zoo* implies). If animals' refusal to consent were ethically relevant, we should be far less concerned with interspecies sex than with, say, mass meat consumption, factory farming, and the fishing industry (Singer 2001; 2009, 95–157; see also Foer 2009). And if "interspecies sexual assault" has any meaningful referent, it would not be a horse topping a man but men and women anesthetizing a horse and removing its testicles (Beirne 1997).[1] Perhaps the equation of an animal's erection with consent explains why *Broad City*'s Ilana Wexler, in the epigraph, defends the horse sex incident (and the video recording of it, and her tweeting the clip to unsuspecting followers) to her best friend Abbi as "not that bad." Were the man topping, or "fucking the animal," we might not as reliably infer the animal's consent from the encounter (Aniello 2016).

Yet despite the "moral magic" consent promises in proximity to sex, any sex, it is an altogether inapposite, unproductive ethical analytic for thinking about our relations with animals, sexual or otherwise (Hurd 1996). Consent is undeniably a human construct in relation to human transactions under conditions of human cognition. Asking if your dog "consents" to sit when you yell "Sit," or if a horse "consents" to be washed or trained, is nonsensical (Case 2005, 1148–49). We initially

FIGURE 4 (Top). Film still (00:00:30) from Robinson Devor (dir.), *Zoo* (New York City: THINKFilm, 2007), DVD.

FIGURE 5 (Middle). Film still (00:04:21) from *Zoo*.

FIGURE 6 (Bottom). Film still (00:39:18) from *Zoo*.

What does bestiality illuminate about our (sexual) ethics?

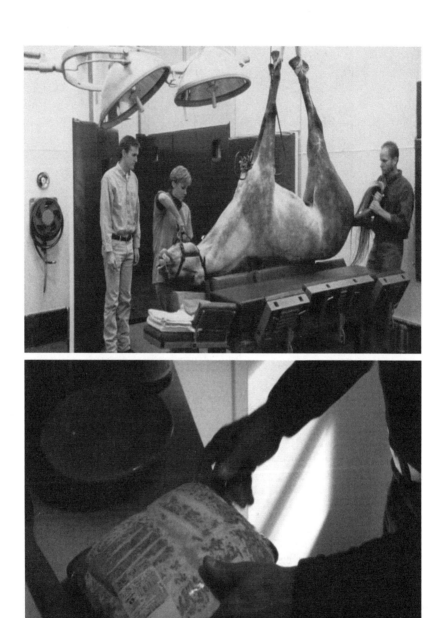

FIGURE 7 (Top). Is gelding sexual assault? Film still (01:07:47) from *Zoo*.

FIGURE 8 (Bottom). Is bestial sex as morally objectionable as dinner? Film still (00:19:07) from *Zoo*.

consider such an inquiry sensible only because when liberals think sex we think consent. This is not to deny profound intelligence and cognitive capacities within and across nonhuman animal species (de Waal 2016). However, even without a clear-cut definition of what consent means or should mean among humans, it suffices that consent, conceptually, presupposes a combination of expression, information, reason, and reflection that is unavailable to nonhuman animals (Westen 2004, 1–10). It is this combination that differentiates consent from simple expressions of want or manifestations of an urge, like a dog pawing its owner to be taken out or fed.[2]

So state senator Roach is wrong to frame the problem of human-horse sex as the problem of nonconsent. But Rush Limbaugh is wrong too, and so is *Zoo* and Ilana Wexler, insofar as their provocations presume that the "consent" of the horse ethically matters, since consent is inapposite as applied to interspecies relations, whether sexual or scientific, companionate or veterinary, commercial (zoos and circuses) or consumptive (farming). Requiring, as a matter of justice, a stallion to consent to sex with a human is like requiring, as a matter of justice, a rabbit have the right to vote (Nussbaum 2007, 360).

Perhaps Ilana Wexler's moral theory, like Peter Singer's (2009), is utilitarian and pivots on suffering and nonsuffering: we assume the stallion does not suffer as a top, but might suffer as the bottom. Utilitarian emphasis on sentience and nonsuffering has had significant influence on our treatment—philosophically and practically—of nonhuman animals, but it is not the only moral orientation available. Our approach might instead be rights-based, demanding duties to animals as "moral patients" (Regan 2004, xxv). We might focus on our love (Rudy 2011), care (Adams 1996; Luke 1996) or sympathy (Donovan 2007) for companionate animals, and that love, care, or sympathy might generate or heighten our concern for the well-being of other animals. We might find moral import not only in nonsuffering but also in "animal pleasure" and animals' capacity for pleasure across an array of life activities (Balcombe 2009). Finally, we might repurpose the capabilities approach to clarify what is either morally acceptable or morally required in our animal relations, insofar as animals ought to be able to realize a minimum-capabilities threshold in accordance with their "species-specific norm" (Nussbaum 2007, 325–407, 365). These approaches (rights-based, utilitarian, capabilities, love and care, imaginative substitution) unanimously agree that many farming, research, and commercial practices involving animals are wrong. However, not all of these philosophies reach the same verdict on the painless killing of nonhuman animals. More to the point, but more speculatively, none of them would likely outright proscribe interspecies sex, though the capabilities approach might find such sex prima facie morally questionable[3] (Nussbaum 2007, 377–78), and a feminist analysis might find such sex prima facie dominative (Adams 2015, xviii, 34–37; Beirne 1997, 332; MacKinnon 2007a, 320–22).[4] In any case, these approaches focus less on human intent than on consequences to the animal as a result of conduct by "moral agents" (Regan 2004, 151–52). Indeed, these approaches shore up the idea that our aversion to human-animal sex is ultimately about human intent—a presumptively peculiar desire—not animal welfare (Case 2005, 1144). We are disgusted by a man having sex with a dead chicken (Haidt, Koller, and Dias 1993, 617–18, 624–25); should not more of us be morally outraged that we killed the chicken? Disgusting humans, apparently, are more outrageous than suffering animals.

The bestiality law enacted by Washington State exempts human-animal genital contact or penetration if performed as part of "accepted animal husbandry practices or accepted veterinary medical practices."[5] What is being policed and criminalized is not sex with animals but human desire. To exempt certain animal husbandry practices from the bestiality law while criminalizing all other animal genital contact under the aegis of cruelty is cruel indeed. Surely, many animal husbandry practices are nonbeneficial to the animals, cause pain and suffering (often to the animals' genitals; Rosenberg 2017), and are exploitive (extracting human benefits from the vulnerable position of animals), while some sex practices are beneficial and pleasurable, or at least not painful.

CORPSES

When it comes to sex and consent, corpses are simpler than horses.

In 2002, a few years before the horse sex–death incident in Washington, twin brothers and their friend, all twenty years old, attempted to dig up the corpse of an attractive woman, also twenty, so one of the brothers could have sex with it. Since "having sex" with a corpse is the very semantic-cum-ethical presumption I am disputing, it is more accurate to write: *Twin brothers and their friend . . . attempted to dig up the corpse . . . so one of the brothers could place his penis in the human remains of a vagina.*[6]

Spurred and evidently seduced by a newspaper obituary and picture of the deceased young woman, Nicholas Grunke hatched his plan and convinced his twin brother Alex and friend Dustin Radke to help with the disinterment. On a September evening the three drove a van into the cemetery and to the woman's gravesite, "with shovels, a crowbar, a tarpaulin, and a box of condoms" (*State v. Grunke* [2008], 771). Despite effortful digging they were unable to open the concrete vault housing the corpse. A police officer, responding to a phone call regarding a "suspicious vehicle" in the cemetery, soon thereafter located the twenty-year-olds, the van, the condoms, and the disinterment tools (771).

In addition to charging Nicholas, Alex, and Dustin with attempted theft and damage to property, Wisconsin also charged the three for attempted third-degree sexual assault. Lower state courts held that the state's sexual assault statute "did not apply to circumstances in which the victim is deceased due to no act of the accused," and that the statute is ambiguous as applied to victims that are corpses (*Grunke* 2008, 772). The Supreme Court of Wisconsin reversed the earlier decision by a court of appeals, and held that Radke and the Grunkes could indeed be charged by the state with attempted third-degree sexual assault against the young woman's corpse.

The sexual assault statute at issue in *Grunke* criminalizes "sexual intercourse with a person without the consent of that person." Consent is defined as "words or overt actions [. . .] indicating a freely given agreement to have sexual intercourse or sexual contact." And the statute "applies whether a victim is dead or alive at the time of the sexual contact or sexual intercourse" (*Grunke* 2008, 775). The defendants, the Grunke brothers and Radke, "contend that, because a corpse cannot provide or withhold consent," they cannot be charged with sexual assault (775; the distinction between *withholding consent* versus *cannot withhold consent* is clarified below). The court found the defendants' argument unpersuasive. First, the meaning of the statutory clause "applies whether a victim is dead or alive" is plain on its face. Second, that a corpse cannot offer consent does not render the statute contradictory; it just makes the state's case easy. In the court's reading, the state's task to prove sex without consent is a simple one "when the victim is a corpse," because, well, the victim is a corpse, and could not possibly consent (776).

At first blush, *Grunke* looks like a terrific if terrifically bizarre case to demonstrate all the liberal and feminist benefits that come from the codification of an affirmative consent standard in sexual assault law. Wisconsin is one of few states whose laws contain such a definition ("words or overt actions [. . .] indicating a freely given agreement"); accordingly, in *Grunke,* the burden of the state was to show not that the corpse refused sex but that the corpse did not positively agree to it (776). It did not. The corpse is a corpse. This makes one wonder: In states *without* an affirmative consent standard, might sex with corpses—in the absence of a freestanding necrophilia statute—be legally permissible? And this leads one to wonder, more alarmingly still, whether, if a corpse satisfies a nonresistance requirement, live women do also (MacKinnon 1991, 1300). All that sex that is unwanted but not resisted; all that sex in which women freeze, remain silent, or acquiesce; indeed all those scenarios in which sex with a woman looks more like sex with a corpse—all is consensual and thus permissible. If what we (say we) dislike about sex with corpses is that corpses cannot consent, and if nonconsent is defined as silence, acquiescence, or frozenness, then perhaps our sympathy for penetrated corpses might be converted into sympathy for assaulted live women.

Whether such a rhetorical maneuver appeals politically, the argument is illogical. Judge Ann Walsh Bradley, in her dissent in *Grunke,* exposes the fallacy and shreds the majority opinion—or rather, the dissent would have shredded the majority opinion had its criticisms been clearer. Despite its imprecisions, Judge Bradley's dissent accentuates the critique of sexual consent (inappositeness) that I begin above with horses and that I extend below with children.

Judge Bradley's opening swing nearly knocks out the ruling: "The majority reaches a desired result through an undesirable analysis" (*Grunke* 2008, 780). That "desired result" is criminalizing necrophilic sex. The "undesirable analysis" is getting to criminalization by way of consent. Italicizing her point, Judge Bradley restates the state's sexual assault law: "whoever has sexual intercourse with a *person* without the *consent* of that person is guilty." She concludes, "I don't think a corpse can give consent" (781).

To put her reply this way, though, is a mistake on Judge Bradley's part, as she intends an altogether different sort of criticism than the phrasing intimates. "I don't think a corpse can give consent" sounds as if sex with corpses is impermissible because corpses are unconsenting, when what she means is that subjecting a corpse to a consent inquiry is nonsensical because corpses are not persons, in any ordinary sense of the word *person*. While corpses may look like human beings, as Aristotle (2017, 21–22) tells us and Thomas Aquinas (for example, 1999, 164, 573) reminds us, they are not.[7] Although Judge Bradley later asserts that Wisconsin's affirmative consent standard "cannot apply to a corpse," she never says why, perhaps because it is obvious to her (*Grunke* 2008, 781). But that obviousness is obfuscated by the powerful pull of consent for those judging all matters sexual. Bradley should have made explicit the implicit: affirmative consent cannot apply to a corpse because corpses are insentient things like socks or inflatable dolls. We might disapprove of sex with corpses for proprietary or dignitarian reasons, or because we think it repulsive or pathological, or a public health concern, but surely not because the corpse, like a sock or a doll, did not "consent."

Judge Bradley explains that the clause of the sexual assault law specifying that it "applies whether a victim is dead or alive at the time" was codified to target rape-homicide, in situations where it is unclear whether the victim was alive during the sexual assault (782). Here again, Bradley's argument is easily misconstrued. It seems as though she is suggesting that the clause should govern only the sort of conduct that led to its codification, a point to which the majority and concurring opinions reasonably respond that nothing prohibits the "dead or alive" clause from governing cases in which the victim is already deceased at the time of the sexual assault (777–80). But this back-and-forth again misses the point. The "dead or alive" clause allows jurors *to assume the victim was alive at the time, and did not consent to sex before she was murdered by the same assailant.* If the victim is unquestionably dead, then she—*it, really*—cannot be sexually assaulted, because sexual assault happens to persons (and maybe other sentient beings). Read otherwise, the sexual assault law is not just vague but absurd.

The most affirming affirmative consent standard cannot solve this problem; it would only dramatize it. The issue is not, as the majority opinion would have it, that the Grunkes and Radke would not have been convicted for attempted sexual assault had they committed this conduct in a state where silence counts for consent, but unluckily found themselves in a state with a codified affirmative standard. Posing the problem this way betrays the performative contradiction at the heart of the majority opinion. Corpses are not persons. They cannot affirmatively consent any more than they can dissent. They also cannot "be" silent as if there were other alternatives for the corpses to choose from. When the majority writes that "Nicholas planned to have sexual intercourse with it," the analysis should have ended there (771). We cannot subject an "it" to a consent inquiry, and not because the inquiry will always fail, but because the inquiry is an impossible one to perform. Did this keyboard consent to my typing on it? But did it affirmatively consent?

Even more than horses, then, corpses reveal the stranglehold of consent on our thinking about sex: *sex with corpses is wrong because corpses cannot consent,* we might initially suppose. And even more than horses, which can, minimally, manifest "behavioral analogue[s]" to consent like willingness, interest, or arousal (Levy 2003, 446),[8] corpses evidence just how inapposite consent may be under certain sexual circumstances: is intercourse with a corpse even "sex"? And if it is, is sex thereby defined as a man placing his penis into anything, and is this not a bit, in fact literally, phallocentric (see also Gavey 2005, 124–26)? Phallocentrism aside, is not consent, as Judge Bradley and I have supposed, a preposterous analytic for our treatment of corpses? Should I be convicted for digitally assaulting my laptop? Should Jim Levenstein be convicted for sexually assaulting his mother's apple pie (Weitz 1999)?

Consent is inapposite for our ethical assessment of (sexual) conduct with corpses and horses. Unlike corpses, however, horses are sentient, and that sentience grounds a strong presumption that what likely distinguishes our ethical assessment of (sexual) conduct with horses from that with corpses is that the former assessment will incorporate the well-being, flourishing, or suffering of the horse.[9] Corpses neither feel nor flourish, so if anything is wrong about placing a penis in human remains, it is not that the corpse suffers.

But what about the ethics of sex with other "moral patients," such as children?[10]

WHAT IS WRONG WITH ADULT-CHILD SEX?

Sentience and the preceding analyses bring us to the uncomfortable question of sex and the child. It is not simply that adult-child sex is patently more ethically complex than sex with corpses or horses. More challenging, it is that the very upshot of the considerations so far—centrally, the depreciation of consent and the appreciation of other moral metrics—make the following considerations more fraught.

Throughout the 1970s, feminist activists garnered major national attention for child sexual abuse. At the end of the decade, David Finkelhor, now a renowned expert in child victimization, published his article

"What's Wrong with Sex between Adults and Children?" (1979). His answer: nonconsent.

That such an article, with such a title, needed to be published and propounded strikes many of us today as incomprehensible. The heinousness of child sexual abuse seems so obvious, the harms so undeniable, that the very performance of proving its wrongness appears morally questionable, like an essay explaining the wrongness of rape or murder (or bestiality? or sex with corpses?).

And yet the motivations for and shortcomings of Finkelhor's argument—grounded in nonconsent—anticipate a recurring definitional crisis of "child sexual abuse" and point to the uncomfortable fact that there is no reliable answer to the wrongness of adult-child sex (which does not mean such conduct is permissible). For if consent is immaterial when it comes to animals and corpses—that is, if consent is a product of sloppy thinking as we inventory our ethical encounter with animals and corpses—why would it be any more relevant for young children?[11] I will arrive at this point more gradually by way of examples and through rehearsing Finkelhor's claims from 1979.

Finkelhor's moral and political commitment is liberal. The wrongness of adult-child sex, he writes, cannot be (tautologically) rooted in unnaturalness, as traditional morality prohibits all kinds of sex, including gay sex, that liberals accept.[12] Nor can the wrongness of adult-child sex be located on the supposed premature sexualization of otherwise innocent children. Contra Pam Roach, kids are sexually curious, innocence is a social construct, and protecting children from sex tout court (even from sexual information and education) only exacerbates their vulnerability (Finkelhor 1979, 693).

But, and this is Finkelhor's most provocative intervention, the wrongness of adult-child sex cannot be premised on findings of injury, as such findings have an empirical, not moral, grounding (1979, 693–95). This worries Finkelhor since it leaves us with the unsavory conclusion that in cases where adult-child sex does not result in harmful consequences such cases would not be wrongful. The problem cuts the other way too. "Compulsory education, divorce, even going to the doctor cause harm and trauma to an important number of children" (694).

Finkelhor thus searches for a moral basis for the wrongness of adult-child sex, and the basis he locates is consent. "The key argument here is that children, by their nature, are incapable of truly consenting to sex with adults. Because they are children, they cannot consent; they can never consent" (1979, 694).[13]

Finkelhor's argument regarding sex and children is the opposite of mine regarding sex and animals. "Suffering" is subject to empirical validation and invalidation; nonconsent is not, if nonconsent is both a moral and a legal construct. By avoiding that hard place of "harm," though, Finkelhor runs into the rock of "nonconsent," and his argument suffers similar, though not identical, shortcomings as applied to animals. If we assume, as Finkelhor does, that children are incapable of consent, if they are not the kinds of beings to whom a consent inquiry is a meaningful exercise, then the fact of their incapacity to consent to any activity whatsoever should have only so much moral force. Asking whether young children consent to be bathed, be spanked, be fed, be fed vegetables they do not like, go or not go on a playdate, be or not be on timeout, get vaccinated or not get vaccinated, get circumcised or not get circumcised would be beside the point.

While Finkelhor's argument intervenes against traditional sexual cultural attitudes already waning in the 1970s, it is seduced by the rising cultural tide of consent. Consider his conclusion: proscribing adult-child sex on the basis of consent aligns with the "progressive attitude [. . .] that consent be the sole standard by which the legitimacy of sexual acts be evaluated" (1979, 697). Whether or not consent ought to be the "sole standard" for measuring the moral permissibility of sex, it is at least defensible regarding adults (and teenagers). Consent is indefensible as a sole criterion—or really a criterion at all—for sex involving children, whose lives are so thoroughly cared for, superintended, and intervened upon, precisely because they are unable to consent. We refuse children's expressions of willingness and unwillingness as indices of meaningful consent.

This is the dilemma, put sharply: Finkelhor proposes that we understand the wrongness of adult-child sex to be located in the child's inability to consent since young children's cognitive capacities are not fully developed. Because children, like animals, are not considered beings able or unable to consent, we need other moral terms to evaluate the permissibility of sexual conduct. One such term is suffering, but whereas I make the almost palatable point that not all sex with animals may entail suffering, Finkelhor makes the nearly unpalatable point that not all sex with children may entail suffering. Yet while many (or a few) readers might concede my point that some sex with animals may be permissible, likely no readers would concede that adult sexual activity with children is permissible even if that activity proves to be not directly harmful to the child; for example, rubbing the child's genitals for too long while bathing her (Haugaard, 2000, 1037)[14] or uploading a picture of a naked child onto a website, even if the posting is forever unknown to the child (Ost 2009, 143–44). This is why Finkelhor turns to consent, but consent in no way clarifies the ethical dilemma just as consent in no way clarifies the problem or nonproblem of interspecies or necrophilic sex.

So if children do not always suffer as a result of adult sexual activity, and if consent is moot or minimally useful for our assessment of children's activity, sexual or otherwise, what is wrong with adult-child sex?

THE INAPPOSITENESS OF CONSENT

I sketch two answers that are question-begging on their face but that I hope point to more careful deliberation, un- or less sutured to the flag of consent.

The first answer: rather than focusing on incapacity to consent or bad consequences, we might classify the wrong of adult-child sex as *exploitation*. Exploitation sounds with the way 1970s feminists framed adult-child sex: as reflective and reiterative of patriarchal *domination*. Whereas *domination* focuses on setbacks of the victim's interests, however, *exploitation* concentrates on the illegitimate satisfaction of the perpetrator's interests (Pettit 2013; Wertheimer 1996). Framing the harm of adult-child sex as exploitation thus avoids the difficulty of determining whether children have identifiable interests, and whether or under what conditions their subjective interests outweigh their objective ones. (What if the thirteen-year-old believes having sex with a twenty-one-year-old is in her interests? See Levine 2002, 68–89).

Exploitation is the moral harm that Suzanne Ost (2009) identifies as the wrong of child pornography and sexual grooming. For her, exploitation "revolves around one person's wrongful misuse of another, a situation or context in which an individual takes unfair advantage of someone else for his own ends" (139). She proposes that it is better to understand the harm of these practices as exploitation rather than child sexual abuse because viewing or possessing child pornography, or grooming a child, does not necessarily entail actual sexual abuse. But since, as I have been intimating, "child sexual abuse" may not entail actual child sexual abuse, it may be helpful to turn to exploitation. For if abuse is abuse because children are incapable of consent, nearly every activity undertaken with young children is abuse; this is why Ost herself avoids consent as a legal determinant, since it could criminalize a "holiday snapshot" of a child (2009, 143). If *abuse* refers to trauma or other negative consequences, we face uncomfortable empirical variability; we want to classify an uncle's sexual activity with his underage niece as wrong and unlawful regardless of whether the sex is sweet, violent, wanted, or nontraumatizing (see chapter 2). And if sex with children just is abuse, we need to know why; exploitation may provide the reason. Adults who engage in sexual activity with a child, as well as "pornographer[s] and groomer[s,] exploit the child's body for their benefit [. . .] they make use of the child's vulnerability and taking advantage of this vulnerability enables them to benefit-exploit the child's body" (Ost 2009, 140–41).

Except now we face what we might call the *Toddlers & Tiaras* problem. Doesn't this TLC show and the child beauty pageant industry, not to mention child acting generally, unfairly benefit—financially, psychically, socially—parents, guardians, and filmmakers by exploiting the child's (often primped, exposed, and sexualized) body? What about all those kids who hate team sports but their participation makes their parents feel good, important, parental, or young again? Might framing the harm of adult-child sex as exploitation indict an assortment of activities involving children?

This suggests a second speculative answer to the wrongness of adult-child sex: there is no one answer. That consent, exploitation, and harm all fall short of identifying *the* wrong of adult-child sex indicates that we may never find a singular, summary wrong. Perhaps what is wrong with sex between adults and children is composite: the likelihood of negative consequences of many sex practices, joined with the cultural or phenomenological specialness of sex, joined with unequal relations between adults and children, joined with the probability of exploitation, joined with gendered dominance instantiated so often through adult-child sex, means adult-child sex is a particularly bad idea and a particularly impermissible form of conduct.

In zones of erotic life where consent is *inapposite*, there might not be as clean an alternative "solution" to consent as there is in zones of erotic life where consent is *insufficient* (kink; mothers' boyfriends) or where the *scope* parameters of consent are contested (transgender "deception"; the deliberate contravention of an explicit conditional).

In any case, these speculative conclusions have no bearing on the difficult task of determining who is a child, what counts as sexual, and what qualifies as abuse (Haugaard 2000; see also Rubin 2011, 37–38). But at the very least I have hoped to trouble—by way of horses and corpses—the ethical efficacy of consent in resolving the question of sex and the child (and animals and human remains).

CODA: WEIRDLY STRAIGHT MEN

Taking a break from consent allows us to see ethical dimensions of the horse and corpse sex cases we might otherwise miss, but at the same time these unusual cases expose how easily but misguidedly we are drawn to consent as our summary sexual-ethical metric. I have asserted—perhaps provocatively—that the inappositeness of sexual consent in matters of horses and corpses carries over, if not comprehensively, to the problem of adult-child sex. Feminists' earlier framing of child sexual abuse—as cause, effect, and instantiation of gendered dominance (refined as exploitation)—may better track its moral wrongness. Child sexual abuse is then perceived in "terms of power and gender, rather than pathology or consent" (Whittier 2009, 24). In this way, nonconsent—or rather unwillingness or resistance, as young children are assumed incapable—might be a strong indicator of, but not tantamount to, exploitation (Ost 2009, 143). But I want to conclude by cautioning against adopting (only) a feminist dominance frame to make ethical sense of the Washington and Wisconsin cases. For taking a break from feminism (Halley 2006) yields notable returns for getting at the weirdness of heterosomething masculinity in the early twenty-first century.

If we relax our reliance on consent without relaxing our allegiance to dominance feminism, here is what we might say about the Washington horse sex case: sure, we would do better to consider the suffering, well-being, or even pleasure of nonhuman animals (and children?) rather than their incapacity to consent, but ultimately men's use of animals for sexual gratification is part and parcel of their use of women and children for the same purposes. On this reading, the men who gathered to have sex with horses are no worse but no better than men who objectify women as "bitches," "sluts," or "pieces of meat"; than men who film themselves penetrating nonhuman animals or employ or coerce women to be penetrated by them; than men (and corporations) who demean by feminizing vegetarianism and nonmeat products; than men (and corporations) who eroticize meat-eating by advertising meat as women or as parts of women: "Are you a breast man or a leg man?" (Adams 2015, 39).[15]

I am unconvinced, however, that gendered domination—specifically, a horse as a stand-in for a woman and, more generally, the superordination of men through the subordination of something figured as nonman—has much to do with the Washington horse case or even the Wisconsin corpse case, cases that nonetheless have everything to do with masculinity and its recuperation. A bunch of straight- or straightish-identified, mostly white men convene at a farm in rural America to go out in the stables and help one another get fucked by horses, by enormously large horse penises.[16] The men are bottoming, willingly (this is not a hazing ritual). Unlike your run-of-the-mill homosociality, there is no woman, feminized man, or subjugated other around whom their worth as men is valued against (Sedgwick 1985). As for the young Wisconsin men, Nicholas Grunke, his twin brother, and their friend, all white twenty-year-olds, join their exhuming forces so Nicholas can penetrate a corpse. It's strangely sweet, a little gay, and vaguely incestuous. This is not, though, a story of young men cavorting around town to sexually assault a (live) woman; nor is it the story, as it was in Wyoming years earlier, of men beating up and killing a young gay man, Matthew Shepard. The Washington and Wisconsin cases are stories of men helping one another—with great intimacy and shared vulnerability—to have wildly strange but noninjurious, nondominative, not particularly heterosexual sex. These nonnormative sex practices seem to be less about "proving masculinity" than recuperating it (Dean 2009, 52).

I am unsure there is any analytic in theoryland to comprehensively take stock of what is happening to and for these men and their masculinity, although (not getting beyond) the pleasure principle comes to mind: as in the minimization of "unpleasurable tension" through an "avoidance of unpleasure or a production of pleasure" (Freud 1990 [1920], 7). Consider some of the reflections of the "zoos" themselves, the men who seek out the horses: "It was pretty much a classless society of our own little small world." "I could just let my hair down." Animals do not hierarchize humans, they only care that "you're either a good person or a bad person." While one cannot discuss "Madonna and Tolstoy" with the horses, they promise a "simpler, very plain world." One zoo ventriloquizes Mr. Hands's motivations: "I don't have to impress anybody. I don't really have to deal with relationships" (Devor 2007).[17]

These men express longings to withdraw from homosocial competition, for pleasures unadulterated by pressures of adulthood or normative manhood. The longing for simplicity undoubtedly syncopates with their desire for the capsizing sensation of "massive cocks" in their anuses (Charles Mudede, quoted in Sokol 2015), which presumably delivers the same degenitalized sensorial overloading, the same self-dis-solving ecstasy, of being fisted (Halperin 1995, 90–91; Rubin 1991, 126–28). As *Zoo* reenacts Mr. Hands's fatal encounter with the horse, we hear an agitated voiceover speeding through mathematical equations, as if to say the obliterating pleasure on the farm stills the everyday stresses wrought on the Boeing engineer.

As for the Grunkes and Radke, who all resemble overgrown Harry Potters, one could speculate that a pretty corpse seduces because it requires no other skills but shoveling. Nor can a corpse reject Nicholas. Maybe what these men want is a time-out from the grind of hetero manhood, the pressure to impress, to appear renaissance, to compete with one another, get hard, stay hard. And they are seeking that time-out not through channels like rape (dominative), pornography (still spurring a sense of inadequacy; likely dominative), sports (still competing with other men), or sex with one another (Ward 2015),[18] but through sex that is actually, not allegedly, relationally uncomplicated (albeit logistically complicated, certainly), through sex that requires other men's noncom-petitive collaboration. This is all too speculative. I have interviewed nei-ther the horse-men of Washington nor the corpse-men of Wisconsin, but then again, I have interest neither in their intentions nor their uncon-scious. Rather, I am proposing that these outlier cases might dramatize something important about the state of (white, American) masculinity in the early decades of the twenty-first century. Consent as an ethical frame-work takes us nowhere in parsing that masculinity; dominance feminism takes us somewhere, but it's the wrong location.

Let's take a final loop back. If the will to simplicity of some millen-nial masculinity covers explanatory ground regarding men's sex with horses and corpses, what about men's sex with minors? Is it all about domination or pathology? Might masculinist domination commingle with millennial masculinity's will to simplicity? Two years after his corpse conviction, Dustin Radke was once again charged with sexual assault, this time for having sex with a (live) fourteen-year-old girl when he was twenty-four. "The girl told detectives that she had sex with Radke twice in late September, once in a parked car [. . .] and the [*sic*] again in the back seat of a car as it was driven around [. . .] by a friend of Radke's" (Treleven 2011).

I wonder if what Dustin wants from a teenage girl and what Nicholas wanted from a corpse and what Mr. Hands wanted from a horse amount to the same thing: ungay pleasuring simplicity sheltered from homosocial competition and live women. Again, I do not actually wonder if these men want this—but what might these failed men and their unlikely objects of desire tell us about strictures of millennial, neoliberal, postindustrial masculinity, strictures undetectable from the paradigms of consent or dominance? What social and sexual worlds do these men wish to access?

CHAPTER 5

Cripping Consent

Autonomy and Access

WITH HILARY O'CONNELL

In 2012 the Connecticut Supreme Court affirmed that Richard Fourtin was not guilty of sexually assaulting a significantly disabled woman. Referred to as "L.K." in court hearings, the alleged victim had been diagnosed with hydrocephalus and cerebral palsy and used a wheelchair. L.K. was nonverbal and communicated through a messaging board. She was also the daughter of Fourtin's then-girlfriend (*State v. Fourtin* [2012]; Tepfer 2012).

The trial jury's conviction of Fourtin hinged on whether L.K. was "physically helpless" and thus unable to consent to sexual relations. In the crude vernacular of the previous chapter, the question before the jurors was *Is L.K. more like a corpse, a nonhuman animal, or a child than an adult woman?* Is consent simply *inapposite* in regard to someone with disabilities as significant as L.K.'s? The juries answered *yes*—L.K. is not the type of being who can or cannot consent to sex, so Fourtin's sexual encounter with L.K. was assaultive (*Fourtin* [2012], 674). The legal question was not *Did L.K. refuse or give consent to the sexual encounter?* but rather *Is she able to give consent?* Thus, by determining L.K. to be more like a child or nonhuman animal than an adult woman, the trial court could convict Fourtin of sexual assault.

The Appellate Court of Connecticut reversed the trial jury's conviction, holding that because L.K. had a demonstrable history of registering displeasure or discomfort through "biting, kicking and scratching," she could not be deemed physically helpless, as unable to consent (*State v. Fourtin* [2009]). The Connecticut Supreme Court affirmed the appellate court decision and Fourtin's conviction was overturned. Thus, while the higher courts treated L.K. more like an adult woman than a horse, corpse, or child, her elevated moral status came with a pernicious consequence: letting Richard Fourtin go.

The *Fourtin* case and its aftermath capture some of the most salient consent contradictions elaborated in the preceding pages regarding *inappositeness, insufficiency,* and *scope.* The case also intimates other concepts, beyond consent, that might help us better think about and regulate sex for people across the spectrum of ability.

The first part of this chapter describes *Fourtin* in more detail, as it is easy to misunderstand the case's facts and findings, as many critics did. This first part also warns of the inappositeness of *inappositeness* for regulating some forms of sexual conduct. When it comes to sex with horses and corpses, we gravitate toward consent when we probably ought not to, and when it comes to sex and cognitive disability, we gravitate toward competence and capacity when we probably ought not to so readily jettison consent. Again, let's not screw consent altogether.

And yet, for all the reasons outlined in the previous chapters, and for many reasons spelled out by others (MacKinnon 1983; Pateman 1980; West 2000), consent will never be a guarantor of erotic flourishing. The second part of this chapter makes the case for *sexual autonomy* and *sexual access* as more promising, less damaging concepts for facilitating the promotion and protection of intimacies and erotic flourishing.

There is something of a paradox in reclaiming these concepts, autonomy and access, for a broad-based, coalitional sexual justice politics. While *autonomy,* particularly sexual autonomy, has been revalued by liberal and even many feminist theorists, disability scholars and activists have long been wary of the notions of self-sufficiency, mastery, and control lurking behind the term's typical usage (Garland-Thompson 2002; Shuttleworth 2007a). If autonomy excludes the dependent or denigrates dependency, is it a worthy aspiration? And while *access,* even lately sexual access (Mingus 2011; 2017; Shuttleworth 2007b), has been a staple organizational point for disability studies and politics, it conjures something sinister in nondisabled feminist and liberal imaginations: the sexual access that institutions like churches, school athletics programs, and fraternities provide for men to assault women and children.

The paradox makes the case for reconstruction stronger. It is precisely the historically exclusionary, even degrading implications of autonomy and access that drive the imperative to resignify them to enable democratic sexual culture. The reforms heralded by the reconstruction of sexual autonomy are legal; the reforms heralded by the reconstruction of sexual access are institutional and social.

But let us first make sense of *Fourtin* and the negative externalities of consent politics, even feminist consent politics, for disabled populations.

THE INAPPOSITENESS OF INAPPOSITENESS, OR HELPLESS TO HELPLESSNESS

We delineate the facts and case history of *State v. Fourtin* before outlining the legislative response to the decision. We then offer a critique: by proposing to safeguard disabled victims of sexual assault like L.K. under the shelter of the "physically helpless" and "mentally defective" statutory subsections of criminal sex offenses, advocates and legislators prematurely disqualify the sexual autonomy of all significantly disabled adults.

At trial, the state alleged that the defendant, Richard Fourtin, sexually assaulted L.K. in February 2006 at the victim's home. L.K. was unable to verbally communicate or walk without assistance, yet conversed with others by "gesturing and vocalizing and through the use of a communication board" (*Fourtin* [2012], 677, 691). Appearing "'aggravated' and 'scared,'" L.K. relayed to a staff member of her adult day care program that Fourtin had sexually assaulted her. "A subsequent medical examination disclosed physical symptoms consistent with the complainant's report" (*Fourtin* [2009], 264).

The state charged Fourtin with sexual assault in the second degree and sexual assault in the fourth degree. The applicable subsections of both statutes extend protections to victims who are "physically helpless," defined as "unconscious or for any other reason [. . .] physically unable to communicate unwillingness to an act."[1] State prosecutors argued that L.K. was "physically helpless" due to her inability to verbally communicate, her dependence on others, and her "limited cognitive abilities" (*Fourtin* [2012], 688–89).

Fourtin appealed his conviction, asserting that "the complainant could communicate [displeasure] using various nonverbal methods, including screeching, biting, kicking and scratching," thereby proving her physical abilities (her nonhelplessness, as it were; *Fourtin* [2009], 266). In 2009, the Connecticut appellate court overturned Fourtin's conviction: L.K.'s nonverbal communication in commonplace, nonsexual circumstances contravened a jury finding of physical helplessness (266).

The intermediary court was "not persuaded that the state produced any credible evidence that the complainant was either unconscious or so uncommunicative that she was physically incapable of manifesting to the defendant her lack of consent to sexual intercourse at the time of the alleged sexual assault" (267).

In 2012 the Connecticut Supreme Court upheld the state appellate court's ruling, affirming that the statutory definition of "physically helpless" excludes L.K. (*Fourtin* [2012], 689–90). As in the appellate ruling, the state supreme court majority cited as precedent *State v. Hufford* (1987), which acquitted an emergency medical technician of sexual assault. Although Hufford's alleged victim was "restrained on a stretcher" while being "transported to the hospital," Hufford's conviction was nevertheless overturned because the victim was able to verbally "communicate unwillingness to an act" and was therefore not "physically helpless." Despite the *Fourtin* majority's concession that "no one would dispute that [L.K.] is physically helpless in the ordinary sense of that term," the court was bound by *Hufford:* "Even total physical incapacity does not, by itself, render an individual physically helpless" (*Fourtin* [2012], 682).

The point of unanimous agreement across media and stakeholder responses to *Fourtin* is what seems at first blush to be dispositive: Fourtin sexually assaulted L.K. Yet what is so distressing about *Fourtin* may not be the ruling itself, which neither denied nor questioned the occurrence of the assault. Rather, the ruling reveals the tragic bind of Connecticut sexual assault law (and those in many other states) for significantly disabled victims: they are disabled enough that assailants need not use requisite force for their conduct to qualify as criminal, but abled enough to class out of physical helplessness. L.K., then, is not victimized under the general sexual assault statute, because her disability makes force moot; but she is not victimized under the "physically helpless" subsections either, because she can resist just enough not to be helpless. Caught between force requirements and blanket exclusions from sexual contact, there is nowhere for L.K. to turn to seek redress.[2]

Fourtin's failure to protect disabled subjects propelled a pursuit for remedy: how might the law better protect L.K. and people similarly situated from sexual assault? In the months and years following the 2009 appellate ruling, Connecticut state representative Gerald Fox III, the *Fourtin* prosecutors, and the Connecticut General Assembly's Permanent Commission on the Status of Women (PCSW) led a team of policy makers and advocates to amend state sexual assault law in order to extend protections for disabled persons like L.K. (Younger 2012).

Legislative bills proposed in 2010 and 2011 would have eliminated the phrases "physically helpless" and "mentally defective" from the sexual assault laws altogether. Instead, perpetrators would be found guilty of sexual assault in the second degree if "the victim's ability to communicate lack of consent was *substantially impaired because of a mental or physical condition*" (Younger 2012; emphasis added). The language revisions suggest a lowered threshold of impairment to reach a successful conviction, and a departure from the limited capture of "physical helplessness" set in existing state law. Neither bill passed the Connecticut House of Representatives, and legislators revised their amendments in 2012. The proposed changes, more limited than in previous years, altered only the statutes' "mentally defective" clause. Perpetrators would be found guilty of sexual assault if "the ability of [the victim] to consent or to communicate lack of consent to such sexual intercourse is substantially impaired because of mental disability." The final bill, passed in the Connecticut General Assembly's 2013 legislative session, signaled a win for anti–sexual assault and disability advocates.[3]

This victory, though, seems superficial at best. Although catalyzed by Richard Fourtin's acquittal, the statutory revisions would likely not have changed the *Fourtin* ruling. The same language and standard of "physical helplessness" remain in Connecticut sexual assault law. Legislators changed the language only of Connecticut General Statutes §53a-71(a)(2), replacing "mentally defective" with "mental disability."

We worry that the facial change to the statute reflects a discomfort among policy makers with the ableist and archaic language of "mentally defective," rather than a more substantial investment in the flourishing (sexual and otherwise) of intellectually and physically disabled people. If the amended statute does more to assuage policy makers' distress over unseemly language than it does to protect victims of sexual assault, the statute has not meaningfully changed at all.

Yet there is another, larger problem with the political effort to stretch the "helplessness" cover over vulnerable populations and to legally render a greater number people unable to consent to sex. Connecticut state representative Gerald Fox III noted that drafters had worked diligently to tailor the language so as not to be "overly broad" and thus "[ban] handicapped people from consenting to sexual activity" (Golladay 2013). We share this concern. Like feminist, anti-violence, and disability activists, we are troubled by the verdict issued in *State v. Fourtin* and troubled also that the threshold requirements for "physically helpless" and "mentally incapacitated" do not protect persons with disabilities from sexual assault. But we are also troubled that the expansion of blanket protections for disabled victims of sexual assault may render mentally or physically disabled adults legally unable to consent to any *wanted* sexual contact (see, for example, Appel 2010; Denno 1997; Finger 1992; Hahn 1994; O'Brien 1990; Siebers 2012). While *Fourtin* commentators objected that L.K. did not qualify as "physically helpless," a crip theoretic perspective alerts us to the potential consequences of expanding the coverage of "physically helpless" to include all adults whose intellectual or physical disabilities present similarly to L.K.'s.[4] If we stretch the parameters of "physically helpless" such that any disabled adult with restrictions similar to L.K.'s so qualifies, we may derealize L.K.'s and others' sexual (and nonsexual) agency, the possibility of their sexual flourishing, whatever form that might take. We risk codifying the stifling norms of ableism that deny access to sex, intimacy, and sexual culture.[5]

In the following sections, which build on law professor Deborah Denno's earlier proposals (1997), we suggest reforms to sexual assault law that might better protect vulnerable and disabled persons while still promoting sexual autonomy across the spectrum of ability. Our reforms, as with Denno's, excise disability as a special category of sexual assault law, stressing instead relational conditions and constraints. Yet—and perhaps because our reforms are principled not on the notion of universal human dignity but rather on relational *autonomy* and on *access* to a more democratically hedonic sexual culture[6]—we especially canvass ways the state might facilitate the sexuality and intimacy opportunities for persons with significant disabilities in particular.[7]

AUTONOMY AND ACCESS

Throughout this book, sexual autonomy is referred to as the *capability to co-determine sexual relations,* as if that is both an accepted and a well-understood definition of the concept. It is neither.

We offer here a feminist reconstruction of sexual autonomy before elaborating the legal reforms that such a reconstructed principle might portend. We begin with a summary and critique of Stephen Schulhofer's version of sexual autonomy (1992; 1998; 2015). What Schulhofer intends by "sexual autonomy"—something like sexual self-determination, indexed by affirmative consent—is widely accepted and supported by anti–sexual violence activists and scholars. The section then marshals political and legal theorist Jennifer Nedelsky's persuasive account of relational autonomy (2011) in order to distinguish our notion of sexual autonomy from Schulhofer's: we disrupt the equivalence between sexual autonomy and sexual consent. Nevertheless, and despite the rupture, in the following subsection we propose that our feminist reconstruction of sexual autonomy portends an affirmative consent standard for sexual assault law (a standard that resonates with the arguments in the introduction and chapter 3). We also argue that sexual autonomy portends restrictions on sex in certain vertical status relations (an argument that resonates with the data and arguments in chapter 2).

We then explore the notion of access as reconstructed and politicized by disability scholars and rights activists, before sketching some policy implications and institutional reforms that a commitment to a more democratically hedonic conception of access might entail.

The proposed reforms, in law and life, promote the sexual autonomy of people across the range of physical and cognitive abilities. They are applicable to you, to us, to L.K., and to diverse sexual cultures, even as we primarily focus on populations recognized as cognitively disabled.

SEXUAL AUTONOMY, RECONSTRUCTED

In the 1990s, law professor Stephen Schulhofer helped steer legislative, scholarly, and cultural debates about rape away from questions of requisite force, resistance, and violence and instead toward the question of sexual autonomy (1992; 1998; and he continues to do so—2015). For Schulhofer, core wrongs of sexual assault are or should be contraventions of a victims' sexual decisions and impermissible constraints on a victim's set of sexual choices. The pertinent issue should be not only *whether the sex was forced* but also *whether the victim's sexual decision making was unduly constrained.* Schulhofer's normative reconstruction is thus far removed from Kant's influential elaborations on autonomy, which emphasize temperance, rationality, self-legislated morality, and behavior in accordance with universalized norms (and Kantian autonomy is famously incompatible with sex, or so Kant thought).[8] Indeed, in *Unwanted Sex* (1998), Schulhofer explicitly sidesteps these hefty matters in his advocacy for sexual autonomy as the governing principle for rape law. Instead of getting entangled with temperance and rationality, Schulhofer hones in on individual choice and choice structure (112). He seemingly—but only seemingly—lowers or all but eliminates Kant's self-definition side of autonomy (who, or what kind of subject, is eligible for sex), while valuing up the self-determination side (who or what a subject can choose; 108–9).

Schulhofer proffers three reasons for his normative shift from self-definition to self-determination in his defense of sexual autonomy. First, his is an intervention in a particular vector of criminal law, and he contends persuasively that "legal and philosophical conceptions of autonomy are not identical" (1998, 105). In other words, autonomy as a protected legal right may and should mean something other than autonomy as a moral human attribute. Second, in what is a direct counterclaim against the Kantian conception of autonomy, Schulhofer rejects the notion that the choices of the autonomous subject must be self-generating or uninfluenced by others (106). Our choices are all a bit heteronomous—autonomy is exercised in the act of choosing, uncoerced. By "deciding for herself what goals [are] valuable," the subject performs autonomy, even if those goals entail nonmarital sex, earning money for sex, rough sex, and so forth (86). Third, Schulhofer wants self-determination as a core normative value to withstand strands of second-wave feminist thought that, as he perceives them, implicate heterosexual sex as coercive tout court (109). Schulhofer's move from self-definition to self-determination portends, therefore, permitting commercial, consensual sex between adults while proscribing a high school principal's conditioning a student's graduation on their having sex (87, 196). For Schulhofer, the sex worker's choice is not forced by social and economic inequality in the same way that the student's choice is forced by the principal's conditional.

Schulhofer's moral premiums on choice and the choosing person generate overlapping definitions of sexual autonomy throughout *Unwanted Sex*. Sexual autonomy is, variously, the "right to self-determination in matters of sexual life" (11); "every person's right to control the boundaries of his or her own sexual experience" (15); the "right to determine the boundaries of our own sexual lives" (16); "a woman's right to control her own sexual choices" (69); and "the freedom of every person to decide whether and when to engage in sexual relations" (99). In Schulhofer's reconstruction, any expressed preference (of adult able-minded persons—see below) is autonomous because sexual autonomy is simply expressed preference about sex.

Among other reforms, Schulhofer's thinned notion of sexual autonomy as sexual self-determination requires a more robust standard of consent as voluntary, freely given, and affirmative, rather than silent, acquiescent, or coerced (267–73). An affirmative consent standard better tracks persons' expressed wants over their reluctant concessions; expressed wants reflect voluntary choices that in turn reflect, without remainder, sexual autonomy (273, 283).

Adult women are the primary beneficiaries of Schulhofer's sexual autonomy: the purpose of the proposed reforms in *Unwanted Sex* is to better protect women and women's sexual choices.

Minors and—more apropos of our analysis—persons with intellectual disabilities are not main characters in *Unwanted Sex*. Peppered through *Unwanted Sex* are figurations of minors and persons with intellectual disabilities as, perhaps unwittingly, the constitutive outer limits for sexual autonomy. Schulhofer asserts without argument that "teenaged prostitutes" lack the "capacity to make competent decisions" (1998, 87). He states, as if forming a predicative and not a postulate of sexual autonomy, that "if a fifteen-year-old girl initiates a sexual encounter with a twenty-year-old man, he violates her autonomy by having sex with her" because of "her incapacity" (111). And Schulhofer equates minority status with disability only to eject both from autonomy: "Intercourse with an apparently willing fifteen-year-old or with a mentally incompetent woman is not prohibited because the [assailant] is a potential killer; it is prohibited because the preconditions for meaningful choice are absent" (102). Tellingly, Schulhofer's Model Criminal Statute for Sexual Offenses adopts the retired language of the Connecticut Penal Code: "Consent is not freely given [. . .] whenever: (1) the victim is physically helpless, mentally defective, or mentally incapacitated" (283).

So sexual relations with teens and the intellectually disabled are categorically banned. These subjects are rendered incapable of meaningful choice and self-determination, and one gets the sense that they must be for Schulhofer's post-Kantian, revisionist sexual autonomy to be cogent (101). By focusing exclusively on individual choice as the nexus for sexual autonomy—even while thinning the self-definition prerequisites left over from Kant—Schulhofer rhetorically and normatively relies upon a clean distinction between competence and incompetence, minors and adults, abled and disabled, meaningful and illegitimate choice.

We are not counterproposing that all minors and all persons with intellectual disabilities should have an unfettered right to wanted sex. But it seems as though in order to make consent carry all the normative and morally transformative weight Schulhofer wants it to, these other characters are rendered immediately, unquestionably, and without any distinctions, ineligible for autonomy. Anything other than able-minded adult choice is unduly heteronomous choice and can therefore be supervened by law. Schulhofer's downplaying of background conditions, cultural context, and social structure ultimately dehistoricizes and atomizes his subjects (108–9). Autonomy is thing-like, there or not on arrival: either you have it or should (adult women), or you do not have it and cannot (minors and persons with intellectual disabilities). Indeed, it is this ascendancy of individual choice and its attendant binaries (rationality-irrationality, capacity-incapacity, adult-minor, abled-disabled) that may underlie well-intentioned but potentially regressive political campaigns to shield the cognitively disabled from sex. Can we instead retrieve or reconstruct a version of sexual autonomy that does not box out groups of people to purchase its moral and legal force?

Sexual Autonomy (Re)Thickened

Jennifer Nedelsky's notion of autonomy, elaborated in her *Law's Relations* (2011), is more promising than Schulhofer's from the vantages of vulnerability and disability.

Contra Kant, Nedelsky's autonomy does not depend on sacralizing "independence" and "control" (2011, 118–19, 163, 285). Because Nedelsky understands the self as multidimensional, relational, and (variably) dependent on others, independence and control are neither possible nor desirable. Independence, were it achievable, would lead to an impoverished and isolated existence (145). And total control ultimately necessitates domination (279). Attempting to master intimate relations, social scenes, and political bodies implicates a refusal of receptivity to others' creativity, spontaneity, and input; control requires the refusal of others' autonomy (297–98). And because we are relational beings, because we become autonomous through "constructive relations," dependency may be *exemplary* of autonomy. Those relationships that are explicitly or particularly dependent—say, between a teacher and a student—reflect acutely how intersubjectivity amplifies autonomous action (151, 305).

Contra Schulhofer, Nedelsky points to broader social restructuring for the realization of autonomy. Autonomy is realized through relations, textured through emotion and care (118–19; see also M. Friedman 2003, 95). State-sanctioned relationships like marriage, for example, that might otherwise be understood as a threat to autonomy (by mandating commitments and obligations) can be reconceived as a condition of possibility for autonomy (Ball 2009, 302–3). Relationally reconceived, autonomy is not merely a right to be let alone (Ball 2009, 311; Nedelsky 2011, 97, 105). "I see autonomy," Nedelsky writes, "as the core of a capacity to engage in the ongoing, interactive creation of our selves—our relational selves" (2011, 45). Nedelsky qualifies that she takes this "capacity for creative interaction" as "just one component" of autonomy, but it is nonetheless a "key" component (166). The *creative* of "creative interaction" refers to human thought and action that generate something new, unpredicted, and not routinized (48). The *interaction* of "creative interaction" nods to Nedelsky's notion of the self as relational. Autonomy materializes with and because of others. Even famed inventors and entrepreneurs of American lore are supported by a set of "nested relations" (45). Autonomy, therefore, as entailing the "capacity for creative interaction" with others, requires positive provisions and state support, not merely noninterference (3, 46, 74–5).

It is at this juncture that the feminist theoretic reconstruction of *autonomy* and the crip theoretic reconstruction of *access* imbricate. Reconstructed as a *capability* for self-determination and not merely self-determination as such, an individual's sexual autonomy necessitates broader access to a democratically hedonic sexual culture.

As cause and consequence of such broader access, Nedelsky's autonomy pivots on "self-creation" (2011, 167) and not, like Schulhofer's, on "self-determination." The latter, suggests Nedelsky, obscures the many ways we are "determined" by forces outside ourselves, and clings to the fiction of the rational agent whose choices summarily govern her or his life course (162–67).[9] The former, self-creation, values up human inventiveness and imagination but without disavowing our social enmeshment. As opposed to the rational agent presupposed by Anglo-American law (whose rational agency is the guarantor of her equality), Nedelsky's subject is affective, embodied, and relational. Self-creation is not the exclusive jurisdiction of the intellect, but registers through all sorts of human activity (158, 162).

Evidently, Nedelsky's reconstruction of autonomy bodes better than Schulhofer's (or Kant's) for persons with intellectual disabilities.[10] This is because "those who value autonomy [e.g., Kant, Schulhofer] must not simply posit it as a human characteristic [e.g., Schulhofer] but also inquire into the conditions for its flourishing" (2011, 167). So, unlike Schulhofer (but like Kant), Nedelsky is attentive to autonomy as a human achievement that must be nourished through social relations. Autonomy requires investment, care, and "constructive relations," which translates into a set of reforms that broadens and democratizes access. Thus, Nedelsky's examples of statutory reforms that "foster autonomy" include a guaranteed annual income neither means-tested nor conditioned by unannounced state surveillance (154–55); legislation that facilitates parents' greater involvement in educational policies affecting their disabled children's lives (141–43); and revisions to Canadian sexual assault law that relaxed mens rea as an element of the crime (consent or nonconsent are now determined under a "standard of reasonableness"; 218–21). These sorts of reforms, argues Nedelsky, structure social relations in a way that permits and promotes a greater degree of autonomy across a larger, more diverse population (315–17).

Dependents—children, the elderly, and persons with intellectual disabilities—therefore can, or could with the help of others, be autonomous to some degree, if autonomy is linked to embodied creativity and delinked from disembodied rationality (2011, 162–73). Persons with intellectual disabilities may be capable of achieving some degree of autonomy, but that achievement is guaranteed through social, not just individual or legal, transformation. Nedelsky recalls a colleague's story of a quadriplegic Swedish law student who "was entitled to four attendants who, on a rotational basis, cared for her twenty-four hours a day so that she was able to attend law school and did not have to rely on her family for care" (192–93). For Nedelsky, this scenario illustrates relational autonomy, as well as state action that structures relations so that all persons—the student, the student's family members, and the student's attendants—are institutionally buoyed to act autonomously. The story references a physical, not intellectual, disability, but it is not difficult to imagine analogous restructuring of relations that enhances the autonomy of persons with intellectual disabilities. Whereas Anna Yeatman calls for restructuring relations for persons with intellectual disabilities to enhance their autonomy in *social* life (2000), and Martha Nussbaum (2010, 86–94) calls for restructuring relations for persons with intellectual disabilities to enhance their autonomy in *political* life, we call for restructuring relations for persons with disabilities (and for temporarily abled persons) to enhance their autonomy in *erotic* life.[11]

Sexual Autonomy as the Capability to Co-determine Sexual Relations

Triangulating from Schulhofer's sexual autonomy and Nedelsky's relational autonomy, we reconstruct sexual autonomy as the *capability to co-determine sexual relations,* the operative yet unelaborated definition of the preceding pages. Each of the key terms requires brief clarification before we posit the kind of legal policies, institutional reforms, and broad-based access such a reconstructed principle of sexual autonomy entails for people across the spectrum of ability.

· Capability

Unlike other autonomy theorists, we emphasize "capability" over "capacity." In common parlance this might be a distinction without a difference, but in theoretical expositions of autonomy *capacity* veers us toward determinations of individual competencies and toward categorical qualifications and disqualifications; *capability* steers us toward institutional reforms, statutory provisions, and alternative divisions of labor and play that cultivate human (sexual) flourishing. While Nedelsky's conception of autonomy includes a "capacity for creative interaction" that can and ought to be enhanced through legal and institutional restructuring, capacity is more often associated with the subject's supposed internal constitution. And despite Nedelsky's measured reservations concerning the individualistic aspects of Martha Nussbaum's capabilities approach (CA) to social justice, it strikes us that *capability* more adequately directs us to the kinds of reforms Nedelsky's ecological accounting of autonomy requires (Nedelsky 2011, 30, 433n23; Nussbaum 2001; 2007). Indeed, for Nussbaum, the state and its actors are responsible for providing meaningful opportunities across a range of social, educational, political, and economic dimensions in order for persons to reach a minimum threshold of predetermined central human capabilities. Resonant with our reconstructed model of sexual autonomy, Nussbaum's model of social justice commands political institutions to guarantee a set of enumerated capabilities that realize our common human dignity (2007, 160).

Sexual autonomy is not a central human capability for Nussbaum.[12] But there is no prima facie reason that sex, sexuality, and intimacy should be any less important, or any less possible, for persons with intellectual disabilities than, say, attending school or voting. Insofar as Nussbaum's central human capabilities include "being able to have good health, including reproductive health"; "[being] secure against violent assault, including sexual assault[;] *having opportunities for sexual satisfaction* and for choice in matters of reproduction"; "being able to use the senses, to imagine, think, and reason[;] *being able to have pleasurable experiences* and to avoid nonbeneficial pain"; being able "to love those who love and care for us"; being able "to engage in various forms of social interaction"; and "being able to laugh, to play, to enjoy recreational activities," there seems to be more than enough material for a composite capability in sexual autonomy (Nussbaum 2007,

76–77 [emphases added]; see also Kulick and Rydström 2015, 286; Riddle 2014, 280). Enshrining sexual autonomy as a nonfungible central human capability also means that the sexuality and erotic flourishing of persons with (and without) disabilities cannot be so readily trivialized in relation to other human needs, rights, and aspirations (Kulick and Rydström 2015, 285, 292).[13]

· Co-determination

Co-determination is not synonymous with equality or reciprocity. Co-determination need not require equal abilities, education, experience, income, strength, or the like between or among sexual agents.[14] "The relational approach does not require a utopia of (impossible) relations of perfect equality," Nedelsky argues (2011, 303). Co-determination instead anticipates that all parties can plan the existence, directions, and trajectories of their sexual relations. Ann Cahill (2016) similarly describes sexual agency as the *"ability* to contribute meaningfully to the quality of the sexual interaction in question" (754; emphasis added). It is not that the person must co-determine his or her ensuing sexual activity. Sometimes one wishes to let one's partner call the shots. As a "capability," co-determination need not be actualized, its function not required for sexual justice or sexual autonomy (Nussbaum 2007, 79–80). But co-determination must at least be possible. Choosing to let one's partner make the choices is itself an exercise in co-determination, as long as that choice can be revoked or revised.

Co-determination, like "capacity for creative interaction," avows the relationality at the heart of autonomy. Not incidentally, codetermination sounds with Kantian respect for others' aims and goals.

· The "Sexual" in Sexual Autonomy

We are disinclined to restrictively define the sexual. As feminist, queer, and disability studies have made clear, the borders of the sexual are porous, variable, historically and culturally contingent, not always genitalized but too often masculinist, and eroticized if not necessarily saturated by social inequality. For our purposes, it is sufficient to underdefine sexual conduct as conduct that generates or is intended to generate erotic pleasure. To avoid tautology, erotic pleasure can be understood as pleasure phenomenologically distinct from other sorts of embodied pleasures (Alcoff 1996, 127–28). And (sometimes) excepting masturbation, what is sexual is relationally determined between or among parties. Thus, whipping someone might be (a) a homosocial prank, (b) assault, or (c) sexual, depending on the relations and the relational determination.

Schulhofer's autonomy is "sexual"; Nedelsky's is "relational." Ours is a relational approach to sexual autonomy. We place a premium on sexual decision making, but step back from the immediacy of the sexual (or sexually assaultive) encounter to inquire about the laws, institutions, and social and educative practices that cultivate or diminish sexual autonomy.

With sexual autonomy so reconstructed, we endeavor to better protect and promote the intimacies and erotic lives of people across the spectrum of ability by reconceiving two legal reforms discussed earlier: affirmative consent and restrictions on sex in vertical status relationships.

PROMOTING SEXUAL AUTONOMY: AFFIRMATIVE CONSENT

The controversy surrounding *Fourtin* and the defanged legislative reform that followed revealed that the "physical helplessness" and "mentally defective" subsections of the sexual assault statutes potentially leave persons with disabilities unprotected by law.[15]

Left unexamined were the general sexual assault statutes historically reserved for able-minded adult victims. These statutes—in Connecticut and in many other states—retain a force requirement.[16] If the touchstone of sexual assault were consent, not force, might Fourtin have been successfully convicted under the general statute? What if the law recognized unwanted sex, not just forced sex, as an actionable wrong? And might such a shift recognize as normatively valuable and desirable people's ability to determine their sexual and intimate relationships?[17]

Consent is all but nonexistent in the sections of the Connecticut Penal Code that address sexual offenses.[18] First-, second-, and third-degree sexual assault criminalize sexual conduct that involves the use or threat of force (including force involving weapons), the infliction of bodily injury, and victims deemed *unable* to consent (as the state unsuccessfully argued with L.K.).[19]

Over the past couple of decades, as discussed in the introduction, liberal and feminist legal scholars and advocates have proposed an affirmative consent standard for sexual assault law and for university sexual misconduct codes (see, for example, Schulhofer 2015; Friedman and Valenti

2008). An affirmative consent standard rejects force, resistance, and non-consent thresholds, and instead requires evidence—a verbal or nonverbal, noncoerced indication of agreement—in order for sexual activity to be rendered noncriminal or not in violation of university policy.[20] By requiring minimal evidence of positive agreement one degree above acquiescence, an affirmative consent standard may better track a subject's participation in co-determining her or his sexual relations. To reiterate an earlier argument, the shift is not to a standard that requires enthusiasm, full sobriety, creativity, mutuality, or multiple orgasms for sex not to be assaultive. The shift, instead, is away from force or silence to some minimal but additional form of verbal or bodily indication of agreement to sex.

How might the introduction of an affirmative consent standard impact the outcome of cases like *Fourtin*? If the touchstone of sexual assault were the absence of affirmative consent rather than the victim's incapacity to communicate nonconsent, Fourtin's misconduct might have been more readily recognizable. No party ever claimed the sex was consensual.[21] In sexual scenarios involving persons with intellectual disabilities, affirmative consent may register even more precisely under law than in sexual encounters involving persons without such disabilities. L.K., after all, has a message board with the words *Yes* and *No* imprinted on it (*Fourtin* 2012, 691n77; see also Boni-Saenz 2015, 1234). In their monograph on disability and sexual assistance, Don Kulick and Jens Rydström (2015, 105–8) document "plan of action" contracts that caretakers draft to help their disabled clients masturbate (the placing of sex aids, the positioning of pillows, duration of time to leave the client alone, and so forth). These contracts specify in advance the sexual activities disabled clients wish to pursue and set parameters for caretaker assistance (107). Such plans of actions are adaptable to sexual contact between disabled persons and between disabled and nondisabled persons, and could be indicative, if not dispositive, of affirmative consent.

What counts as affirmative consent will depend on particularities. A *yes* procured through threats is not affirmative consent (Schulhofer 1998, 114–36). If a person with intellectual disabilities smiles in response to all social interactions, however injurious, affirmative consent will require more than a smile (Denno 1997, 387–89). "All smiles, of course, do not betoken consent," reasonably remarks psychiatry professor Jacob Appel (2010), "yet rather than enforcing a restriction that is over-inclusive [. . .] caregivers of institutionalised individuals should evaluate smiles and other forms of non-verbal and indirect assent in the context of the patient's life" (153). Because the "affirmative" component of affirmative consent can and should be tailored, the standard reaches persons with intellectual disabilities who thus no longer need be cast out into "statutory isolation" (Denno 1997, 343). Dedifferentiating disability in sexual assault law minimizes the potential for underprotection (not helpless enough) and overprotection (always helpless, always incapable of consent), while remedying the codified entrenchment of social stigma and marginality (both literal and figural) against persons with disabilities (Mairs 1997, 59).

Whereas in the introduction I offer affirmative consent as the least-crappy standard to adjudicate sexual assault as compared to force or desire, in this chapter we have been arguing that an affirmative consent standard best indexes, from the available alternatives, sexual autonomy, once it is reconstructed as the capability to co-determine one's sexual relations. Requiring some minimal, not necessarily verbal,[22] indication of positive agreement to the sex one is having—even if that sex is not desired—demonstrates respect for a person's sexual decision making better than the metrics of silence or resistance. Sex in the absence of affirmative consent, like the deliberate contravention of an explicit condition for sex (see chapter 3), at best disregards and at worse extinguishes another person's capability for determining her sexual choices.

A final note on the peculiarity of advocating for an affirmative consent standard in a book titled Screw Consent. By speculating on the adoption of an affirmative consent standard into the Connecticut Sex Offenses (and other states' sexual assault laws), we do not equate sexual autonomy with sexual consent. Sexual autonomy, relationally reconceived, is attentive to broader social and material opportunities for the realization of intimate and sexual choices, and is thus irreducible to individual consent. Furbishing consent in sexual assault law is but one possible reform for better protecting and encouraging the sexual autonomy of persons across the spectrum of ability. Below is another, a reform that cuts more protective of than promotional for one's capability to co-determine one's sexual and intimate relationships.

PROTECTING SEXUAL AUTONOMY: STATUS RESTRICTIONS

Another compensatory reform to close or narrow the gap in sexual assault protections for people with significant disabilities is the expansion of laws to regulate or criminalize sexual conduct within relationships of dependence unaddressed by extant status restrictions.

As chapter 2 shows, status restrictions on sexual relations are neither unprecedented nor uncommon. Sexual assault laws frequently contain provisions restricting or prohibiting sexual contact within particular relationships. These status provisions include restricting sexual conduct between parents and their children, teachers and their students, employers and their employees, and doctors and their patients. Laws regulating sex within family relationships (often codified as "incest") commonly target consanguinity or biological relation over power inequality. Age of consent statutes, perhaps the most widespread example of status restriction codifications, are generally understood to address both the uneven social power dynamics between adults and minors as well as the presumptively limited developmental capacity of young people.

At their best, restrictions track manipulations of relational dependence; they reflect that there are certain professional, familial, and other social relationships in which a person's ability to negotiate sex and intimacy—his or her sexual autonomy—is unduly curtailed on account of dependence or inequality or both.

Like other states, Connecticut criminalizes sex not only between adults and minors (and between older and younger adolescents), but also within specified relations of dependence.[23] Connecticut proscribes sexual relationships between parents or guardians and their children, custodial supervisors (in the justice system, hospitals, and other institutions) and their charges, psychotherapists and their patients, school employees and students, coaches and players at the secondary school level, and employers and employees—if the employer is twenty years or older and the employee is under eighteen. Sexual contact is also limited among familial relatives.[24]

But are these restrictions sufficient? Or, how often do perpetrators of sexual assault "look" like Richard Fourtin—the mother's boyfriend, an informal caretaker, a person of trust? As chapter 2 demonstrates, quite often.

Although fathers—the most common perpetrators in our data from Connecticut—are prohibited by status restriction from engaging in sexual contact with their children, mothers' boyfriends, and unmarried partners of parents generally, are not. The statutory focus on fathers rather than unmarried parents' partners as potential perpetrators seems, superficially, commonsensical: the relationship involves neither consanguinity nor a formal, legal relationship of dependence. But mothers' boyfriends, like Fourtin, may perpetrate sexual assault at close to the same rate as fathers: they are the second-most common perpetrators in our case review (see appendix A).

If we shift from a model of status restrictions based largely on age and consanguinity to a model based on significant dependence and inequality, other relationships are regulable. Sexual autonomy provides normative grounds to restrict, for example, sexual contact between a young woman and her mother's boyfriend (chapter 2): the young woman may be unduly impeded from co-determining (or, as in the *Fourtin* scenario, exiting) the relation despite the absence of a formal (legal or consanguine) relationship. Sexual autonomy may also warrant extending proscription on sex between certain caretakers and dependents with intellectual disabilities. Yet proscribing sex across certain vertical status relations, as opposed to legislatively broadening the definition of "physical helplessness" or "mental incapacity," renders sex in relationships like the one between Richard Fourtin and L.K. impermissible without the risk of criminalizing all sex involving persons with disabilities.

Viewed alongside our data from appellate sexual assault cases in Connecticut, Michigan, and Wisconsin (appendix A), *Fourtin* appears both exceptional and typical. Exceptional because the statutes under which Fourtin was charged are so infrequently exercised by the state, and because reported assault cases rarely involve victims with identified disabilities.[25] Typical, though, because the relationship between Richard Fourtin and L.K. was one of significant dependence and power imbalance due to Fourtin's dual roles as L.K.'s mother's boyfriend and one of L.K.'s informal caretakers.

Research suggests that women with disabilities are approximately four times more likely than women without disabilities to experience sexual assault (S. Martin et al. 2006, 834; see also Casteel et al. 2008; Plummer and Findley 2012). For persons with intellectual disabilities, risk of victimization may be as much as ten times higher than for persons without intellectual disabilities (C. Wilson and Brewer 1992, 115). Comparative rates of lifetime risk of sexual assault do not capture the heightened risk of repeated victimization: in one study of persons with diverse disabilities who had experienced sexual assault, nearly half (49.6%) had experienced ten or more sexually abusive incidents in their lifetimes (Sobsey and Doe 1991, 247). Especially instructive are the rates at which disabled people are sexually assaulted within the context of relationships of intimacy and dependence. The same study found that 37.5 percent of perpetrators held supervisory positions over their victims, contracted on the basis of the victims' disability (248).[26] Another

28.8 percent of perpetrators had other kinds of supervisory positions over the victims.[27] Factors associated with increased dependence, including decreased mobility and increased social isolation, are strongly predictive of experiencing sexual violence as a disabled person (Nosek et al. 2006, 846; see also Gill 2015, 33–34).

We recognize that the trope of sexual victimization itself can be oppressive, if that trope is leveraged to categorically ban sex with, or withhold sexual information from, persons with disabilities (Finger 1992). Far from pointing toward a *general* prohibition, however, these data support expanding status restrictions to restrict or prohibit sexual conduct across *specific* relationships of dependence.

We find a host of compelling reasons for expanding status restrictions in Connecticut (and beyond) to capture certain relationships of dependence for both disabled and nondisabled persons alike (mothers' boyfriends, caretakers). However, we concede that categorical restrictions on sex between disabled persons and their caretakers could, like overextending the "physically helpless" or "mentally defective" subsections of Connecticut sexual assault law, impede the sexual autonomy of persons like L.K. Caretakers may be the ones best equipped to act as sexual assistants or sexual partners for their significantly disabled clients. Those best able to sexually gratify persons with significant disabilities are often those best positioned to abuse them. One possible way to circumvent this conundrum is to render affirmative consent an affirmative defense within certain status relations. In this way, sex in certain relationships of dependence may be proscribed unless the defendant can prove affirmative consent on the victim's part. This defense should probably not be available to mothers' boyfriends when the complainant is the minor child of the mother; the defense probably should be available to a caretaker of someone who is intellectually disabled, especially if the people were in an intimate relationship prior to the onset of the disability.[28]

A refurbished consent standard and revised restrictions on sex in vertical status relations are two legal reforms that follow from a feminist theoretic reconstruction of sexual autonomy. What social practices and institutional reforms follow from a crip theoretic reconstruction of sexual access?

SEXUAL ACCESS, RECONSTRUCTED

No concept has been more critical to modern disability rights activism and to disability studies scholarship than *access*, except perhaps for the concept of the *social model of disability,* which itself politicized access as a legal right and normative aspiration.[29] For readers unfamiliar with the social model, we offer an overview below to demonstrate how the model and its proponents forefront access for persons with disability, even if sexual access, or access to sex, sexuality, and intimacy, have not always been a political priority. We then return to Gigi Engle's *Teen Vogue* anal sex guide (2017) for teenagers (recall the discussion of Engle's gloss on consent in the introduction) to clarify how access syncopates with our brief for a democratically hedonic sexual culture (punchline: access is not license, nor does it license the gratification of any sexual predilection or pursuit whatsoever). We next rehearse a powerful criticism of the social model of disability.[30] By demonstrating how our advocacy for access survives this criticism, we are better positioned to delineate and defend what sorts of institutional reforms and cultural transformations a commitment to sexual access recommends for people across the spectrum of ability.

Access and the Social Model of Disability

The social model of disability emerged out of disability rights activism in the United Kingdom in the 1970s, although the term was coined in 1983 by Mike Oliver (Oliver, Sapey, and Thomas 2012 [1983]; Oliver 2013, 1024). A major premise of the social model is the distinction between impairment and disability. The former connotes a bodily limitation, atypicality, or, in less sensitive language, defect or deficiency, whether congenital or acquired. The latter describes how institutional and physical arrangements convert or compound the impairment into a hindrance for sociality and everyday living (Shakespeare 2006, 198).[31] Blindness, for example, is an impairment; blindness is disabling in a world without Braille signage, audio or Braille alternatives to written texts, readily available guide dogs, and accessible pedestrian signals at crosswalks.[32] Whereas the focus of the "medical model" is on the individual and her or his supposed deficiency, the social model presumes the problem is with the disabling world, not the impaired person. "Social model thinking mandates barrier removal, anti-discrimination legislation, independent living and other responses to social oppression. From a disability rights perspective, social model approaches are progressive, medical model approaches are reactionary" (Shakespeare 2006, 199; see also Oliver 2013). The pulse of the social model is participatory rather than protective or paternalistic. Whereas the medical model was put to the service of institutionalization and diagnosing pathology, the social model developed from the wide-scale deinstitutionalization of disabled people and has been put to the service of integration.[33]

In the social model frame, the core problem requiring redress—philosophically, politically, and physically—consists of barriers, the minimization or elimination of which demands *access*. Rather than isolate students in special education classrooms or accommodate one disabled person's office space, schools and workplaces ought to be transformed to foster the equal participation and to equally value the contributions of disabled people. The social model of disability intends a politics of access—that is, redesigning work, school, cultural institutions, transportation, and so on to foster the broadest involvement across ability (see, for example, Satz 2008).

What about redesigning sex? Or redesigning sexual culture (Siebers 2012)? In light of the political victories of the disability rights movement alongside the retrenchment of the welfare state and engorgement of the militarized state, both of which make more and more of the population increasingly susceptible to disability (Puar 2017), why not advocate for democratized access to sex, sexuality, and intimacy? Over a decade ago, Russell Shuttleworth (2007b) called for disability politics and disability studies to include sex on their agendas, postulating that a "narrow technical understanding of access," localized mostly to transportation, work, and school, keeps us from imagining and lobbying for more-accessible sexual culture (179).[34] Likewise, politicizing sex in this way cuts against a dominant trope of disabled people as asexual. Cognizant that "sexual access" conjures figures of sexual predation, Shuttleworth nonetheless maintains that "this masculinist and heterosexist understanding of access does not render the concept itself flawed but only the interpretational framework on which it is based" (178). Likewise, disability rights activist Mia Mingus (2011; 2017) argues for extending access demands into realms of sex and intimacy. For Mingus, foregrounding democratized intimacy access transforms the political meaning of access itself:

> Access for the sake of access is not necessarily liberatory, but access for the sake of connection, justice, community, love and liberation is. We can use access as a tool to transform the broader conditions we live in, to transform the conditions that created that inaccessibility in the first place. Access can be a tool to challenge ableism, ablebodied supremacy, independence and exclusion. I believe we can do access in liberatory ways that aren't just about inclusion, diversity and equality; but are rather, in service of justice, liberation and interdependence. (2017; see also McRuer and Wilkerson 2003, 7)

We think Shuttleworth and Mingus are right. What might a feminist politics of sexual access, beyond a feminist politics of sexual consent, augur for disabled (and, speculatively, temporarily abled) people? But first: How exactly ought we to distinguish, in our "interpretational framework," access for a democratically hedonic sexual culture from access in its "masculinist and heterosexist understanding"? And second: How might the integrationist impulse—the social model's will to participation—of "sexual access" be potentially limiting or even counterproductive for intellectually disabled populations?

Access for a Democratically Hedonic Sexual Culture

The introduction looks at *Teen Vogue*'s "A Guide to Anal Sex" (Engle 2017) to caution against the conflation of consent, pleasure, and desire, as well as the narrow sexual politics the conflation invites. Here we want to reexamine Engle's imperatives about what makes for good and bad sex, and good and bad sexuality, in order to refine what we mean by "democratized sexual access." The point is not to pick on Engle—quite the contrary. The analysis is offered as a way to begin imagining a more expansive sexual justice politics that facilitates exactly the kinds of intimacy, candid communication, and honesty Engle advocates.

In her anal sex guide, Engle writes, "There is no wrong way to experience sexuality, and no way is better than any other."

We get what Engle means. Preempting the admonishment *That's gross!* from unforgiving peers, Engle reminds her young audience that sexual variation is benign: not all sexual preferences are the ones held by you (Rubin 1993 [1984]). Yet there are wrong ways to experience sexuality. Some ways are better than others. Coercing people into sexual submission, sneaking off a condom when one's partner is not looking, or demanding to be dismembered or killed during sex are insidious, unfortunate ways to experience sexuality. Experiencing sexuality with multiple orgasms tends to be better than experiencing it with dread. Engle might likely reply: duh. But in the same way that encomia for consent obfuscate our sexual values, recourse to *You do you* shortchanges a more thorough engagement with sexual ethics. We specify that the kind of sexual access we are advocating is *democratically hedonic* in order to make manifest, in a Millian vein, that fostering some kinds of sex practices inhibits access to sex for many others. Democratic hedonism need not mean we provide fraternity brothers with more beer because some of them like to experience their sexuality with intoxicated girls. And while we should encourage parents, siblings, and teachers to support the typically neglected sexuality of a cognitively disabled individual, we also want to take care that such sexual expression is not coercive or unwantedly dominative over others. Does permitting a teenage boy with intellectual disabilities to masturbate publicly in school, for example, help realize his otherwise denigrated sexuality? Or does such allowance make his classmates, particularly girls, feel sexually objectified? Or is our hang-up with public masturbation moralistic? Or might sexual educators sensitively redirect the boy to masturbate elsewhere, so he remains unashamed while other students get to go about their learning (see Goodley and Lawthom 2011, 93–94)? These are thorny questions for which we do not have certain answers, but they are questions we ought to address in the ongoing project of fostering feminist sexual culture and eliminating sexual violence.

Achieving democratically hedonic sexual culture must also be done collaboratively and collectively, such that it is not simply the university bureaucrat—or armchair feminist theorists, for that matter—directing the masses to have better sex. In that regard, the following assertion from Engle may be well intentioned but cuts against coparticipation: "Condoms are also nonnegotiable. There is no risk of pregnancy during anal sex, but STIs are widespread and abundant. Protect yourself and practice safe sex every single time."

We appreciate Engle's unembarrassed account of anal sex and her plea to young people that they inform themselves about all kinds of sex and safer sex practices. Worrisome, though, is the "nonnegotiable" injunction and the injunction's moralistic tenor ("every single time"). Admittedly, Engle is a sex educator for young people and we are not. But this sort of top-down directive inhibits necessary conversations about sexual health information and resources. For example, should we talk to teenagers about pre-exposure prophylaxis (PrEP), a pill taken daily to prevent contracting HIV (Burda 2015)? Might we discuss that the follow-up protocol for PrEP itself functions as a safer-sex practice (for example, by requiring screening for sexually transmitted infections [STIs] every three months; Summers 2017)? Or that the Centers for Disease Control finally announced that if a person's HIV viral load is undetectable on account of antiretroviral therapy, the person cannot transmit HIV (Z. Ford 2017)? Could we be honest and also tell young people that condoms can be uncomfortable and desensitizing? Should we mention the joys of ultrathin condoms? Or larger condoms for bigger toys and penises? Must a young monogamous couple, dating throughout high school, be as insistent with condom use as their peers? Should not high schools have on-site facilities for STI screening? Young people, like people with disabilities, and all people for that matter, should have input in their own sexual education curricula, and should be encouraged to have forthright conversations rather than to simply absorb what we tell them (Kendall 2013). After all, the mantra "Always wear condoms" has had mixed success (Sifris and Myhre 2017).

A Cognitive Disability Caution of the Social Model (and Why Access Survives the Caution)

The social model of disability arose specifically from oppressive experiences of living with physical impairments; correspondingly, the model may be most limited in regard to cognitive impairments. "Physical and sensory impairments are in many senses the easiest to accommodate," Tom Shakespeare explains, but "what would it mean to create a barrier free utopia for people with learning difficulties?" (2006, 201). It is not clear that this is even an advisable political imperative. Not only might people with intellectual impairments not be capable of performing some of the same tasks as, or working and learning alongside, their nondisabled peers, but they might also find such tasks and integration unpleasant or unsafe. Michael Bérubé (2010), in an otherwise sympathetic reply to Martha Nussbaum's argument (2010) that we ought to facilitate the political participation of the intellectually disabled, cautions against the integrative impulse of the social model. He argues, contra Nussbaum, that it is ill-advised for his son Jaime—who has Down syndrome and about whom Bérubé has written two beautiful books (1996; 2016)—to serve on jury duty. Jaime might do so successfully, but jury duty would be exceptionally taxing, try Jaime's attention span, and likely frustrate him. Coordinating his jury service would be fatiguing for Jaime, Jaime's parents, other jurors, and court officers (2010, 104–5). Bérubé writes that he and his wife prioritize meaningful employment and adequate health care for Jaime over jury duty. Bérubé reports, sensibly, that he must often make decisions for Jaime "without taking his wishes into consideration" and likewise calls for disability scholars to "think more seriously about the role of guardians" (103–4).

Is jury duty like sex? That is, is it too risky and too complicated for someone like Jaime? This is the wrong question. A more defensible version of the social model is not that integration and participation are required for each and every person across the spectrum of ability, but that integration and participation are attempted in good faith. Indeed, Bérubé's *Life As Jaime Knows It* (2016) catalogs his son's stunning athletic, artistic, and educational achievements. Bérubé insists that those achievements were made possible, even probable, by the assumption that Jaimie is capable of many things, that his life is richer and more joyful if he is given opportunities to creatively participate in social life (even if participation sometimes fails). Institutions and social services calibrated to a presumption of participation and integration, rather than a presumption of protection and isolation, cultivate capabilities (Nussbaum 2011).[35]

Out of respect for Jaime's wishes, Bérubé omits from his book discussion of his son's intimate life, except for the following: "Jamie would like a life partner, a companion, who loves him and wants to spend her life with him" (2016, 18). If we are committed to building worlds that are wheelchair accessible, should we not also build worlds that foster more-accessible opportunities for love and intimacy? Bérubé's recommendation that Jaimie not serve jury duty is not made willy-nilly and uninformedly; it is instead based on more than a decade of experiences encouraging his son to be and do in the world, and on the assumption that he can and should be and do in the world.

The father of one of this chapter's authors, Fischel, suffers frontotemporal dementia and occasionally wishes to drive his old car. His driving would undoubtedly endanger himself and others; if the social model demands accommodating his preference to drive, the model is wrong. While Fischel's father cannot operate a car, his family and friends drive him to his guitar lessons, to the movies, to the frozen yogurt store, to musical concerts, and to the public library. The unspoken assumption is that the imperative toward integration and participation is ethically right, even as integration and participation recede from possibility. Should this not be true for sex, intimacy, and love?

PROMOTING SEXUAL ACCESS: RESOURCED SEX

Sexual access portends the following recommendations, but so does ableism, and the ugly history of the wide-scale denigration or outright denial of the sexuality of persons with disabilities, particularly intellectual disabilities (Appel 2010; Block 2000; Denno 1997).[36] Persons with disabilities have been figured—by medical experts, scientists, journalists, and cultural commentators—as sexually predatory or, more often, as childlike and innocent (Mollow 2012, 286). Both constructs, predator and child, have authorized the refusal of sexual information to, and impeded the sexual opportunities for, persons with disabilities, especially women (Denno 1997, 333–34; Finger 1992).[37]

While the silence around sexuality and disability has broken in the past several decades, journalistic, documentarian, pornographic, scholarly, and autobiographic accounts of sex and disability generally feature persons with physical disabilities (for example, Dean 2014; Mairs 1997; O'Brien 1990; H. Rubin and Shapiro 2005), thereby sidestepping challenging moral and philosophical questions regarding sexual flourishing for L.K. and others with cognitive disabilities.[38]

Let us consider in more particular ways how to facilitate sexual access for persons with recognized cognitive disabilities before speculating, in broad strokes, how such initiatives might translate for, or provide models to people of all abilities.

One way to promote the sexual culture of persons with disabilities is to provide publicly funded sexual assistance. Compensated sexual assistants for persons with disabilities operate legally in Germany, Switzerland, and Denmark (all countries where prostitution is legal and regulated) and operate illegally in Sweden and the United States (where purchasing sex is criminalized; de la Baume 2014).[39]

To elaborate sexual assistance, we turn to Don Kulick and Jens Rydström's *Loneliness and Its Opposite: Sex, Disability, and the Ethics of Engagement* (2015). The authors offer a stunning ethical defense for publicly funded assistance for the erotic flourishing of persons with significant disabilities. Kulick and Rydström compare policies, practices, and public opinion regarding the sexuality of persons with disabilities in Sweden and Denmark, documenting that Sweden is resolutely hostile toward the sexuality of persons with disabilities while Denmark is consistently if not always facilitative (17–18). Explanations for the differences between these two countries are multiple, but particularly important is the fact that Danish social workers and caretakers may train to become "sexual advisers" who "assist people with disabilities perform activities like masturbate, have sex with a partner, or purchase sexual services from a sex worker" (18). These advisers undergo specialized training to assist not only persons with disabilities but also caretakers and group home administrators (101–5). These modes of assistance undoubtedly enhance sexual access (and autonomy) of persons with significant disabilities. The practices Kulick and Rydström observe could and should be integrated into US state and group home policies regarding the sexuality of persons with disabilities.

Facilitating Masturbation

We cite the following anecdote from Kulick and Rydström, as it aptly captures how assistance with masturbation may facilitate sexual autonomy for persons with significant intellectual disabilities:

> One particularly inventive solution to a seemingly unmanageable problem involved a young man with intellectual impairments in Denmark who insisted on masturbating at the edge of a highway. Every day this young man managed to elude staff members at his group home, turning up by the side of the highway and prompting near accidents and outraged calls to the local police. Desperate, the staff called in a sexual advisor for advice. The woman who came to help managed to figure out that what the young man found exciting was the sound of traffic. At her suggestion, the staff recorded a video of the highway at the site where the young man liked to stand, and they gave that video to him, telling him that whenever he felt like looking at cars and touching himself, he could do so—in his room, with the sound up and the door closed. Problem solved. (2015, 26–27)

What is ethically noteworthy about this incident is not that the young man can now masturbate free from the danger of oncoming traffic. Rather, it is that the solution to this problem was promotional, not punitive, of the man's sexual autonomy. By recording the sounds of traffic instead of, say, attempting to recircuit the man's desires toward more hetero-palatable materials, the group home staff permitted and encouraged the man to co-determine the contours of his sexuality.

Kulick and Rydström also recount the case of Helle, a young woman in a group home who was nonverbal, was diagnosed with cerebral palsy, and used a mechanism akin to a message board to communicate. Helle shared some classificatory similarities with L.K. (2015, 106, 116). A sexual advisor drafted a plan of action for Helle's assistants to help Helle masturbate. The plan of action detailed how Helle should be laid on the bed and where mirrors and pillows should be placed. The document directed assistants (though assistants are not mandated to facilitate sex for clients) to "place the sex aid on [Helle's] privates," and to ask Helle how long she would like to "lie alone." When Helle finished masturbating, the assistant was to wash the sex aid and make sure Helle was content (104–6).

In Helle's case, as in the case with the young man masturbating to traffic, sexual advisers and clients' assistants collaborated with one another and with their patients to enable access and autonomy. The plan of action for Helle was co-determined by Helle, and practices of sexual co-determination themselves recursively strengthened the capa-

bility of (sexual) co-determination: the sexual advisor "had long conversations with Helle to determine what kind of sex aid she wanted, and
she helped Helle try out several before they settled on the ones Helle
liked best" (116; see also Dukes and McGuire 2009, 732).[40]

Facilitating Sex

Kulick and Rydström tell the story of Marianne and Steen. Residing in
separate group homes, they became a romantic couple after meeting in
an activity center. Steen is nonverbal, "spastic," autistic, and paralyzed
from the neck down. Like Helle and L.K., Steen uses a form of message
board to communicate to his assistants. Marianne is intellectually disabled, deaf, and "nearly blind" (2015, 97–112).

Enabling Marianne and Steen to share intimacy and sex required great
effort on the part of their assistants and the group home social workers.
Social workers collaborated to rearrange schedules, coordinate transportation, and delegate supervisory responsibilities. They also prepared rooms,
beds, pillows—as well as Steen's body—in such a way that the couple could
have and enjoy sex. Assistants continually consulted Marianne and Steen
to make sure everything was all right (2015, 98–101, 111).[41]

Evidently, facilitating sex for persons with significant disabilities
requires more than assisting the sex act itself. Preparations must be
made beforehand, and evaluations of wantedness must be recurring. In
Danish group homes visited by Professor Kulick, staff organized role-
playing activities and discussion groups for persons with disabilities in
order to familiarize them with modes of intimate communication and
negotiation, to explain boundaries of permissible social-sexual behavior, and to help them cope with the rejection of a love interest (108–9).[42]
These sessions are exemplary in their promotion of sexual autonomy,
designed to enhance disabled persons' capability to co-determine their
sexual relations.

Facilitating the Purchase of Sexual Services

The sexual facilitation described above is publicly funded. But sexual
services can be and are purchased privately as well, directly by persons
with disabilities (Kulick and Rydström 2015, 174–216).[43]

The "private purchase of sexual services" is not simply a euphemism
for hiring a sex worker; it encompasses a wide variety of activities. If
they wish to pay for sex directly, persons with disabilities may also need

help finding sex workers willing to meet persons with disabilities (207); combing through websites and newspaper advertisements for such escorts; locating brothels that are accessible (195); and navigating what can often be complicated and detailed menus of services and prices (203). Particularly for persons who are nonverbal or are intellectually disabled, or both, caretakers are often needed as "translators" for hired sex workers, since caretakers are more familiar with their patients' communication patterns and better suited to interpret the meanings of patients' gestures and sounds (203). In addition, persons with significant intellectual disabilities or mobility limitations may need to be bathed in advance of a sexual encounter, and their rooms properly prepared (198–99).

The private purchase of sexual services, including the purchase of sex, provides some persons with disabilities access to sexual pleasure that might otherwise not exist or be unduly difficult to obtain. Just as important, these sorts of paid-for sexual experiences can help boost the confidence of persons with disabilities; persons with disabilities recognize themselves not only as sexual beings but also as capable of successfully "having sex," whether or not such sex is penetrative (209). The purchase of sexual services allowed one paraplegic man, as Kulick and Rydström put it, "the opportunity to engage with others in ways that extend his capacities" (211). Mark O'Brien, famed poet and journalist paralyzed from polio, wrote of seeing a sex surrogate: "I knew I could change my perception of myself as a bumbling, indecisive clod, not just by having sex with someone, but by taking charge of my life and trusting myself enough to make decisions" (1990; see also Wilkerson 2002). These kinds of experiences expand disabled persons' erotic repertoire and, more generally, invite them to participate in navigating their life trajectories.

What would it look like to translate these forms of sexual assistance—enabling access—for persons across the spectrum of ability, including temporarily abled people?

There are sound moral and strategic reasons for democratic states—and liberal arts universities—to choose neither to subsidize sex workers for their citizens and students nor to directly facilitate, mechanically, sex and masturbation for folks without significant impairments. One reason is limited resources. Another is conservative blowback. Another is erotic totalitarianism.

But two wonderfully simple moral assumptions underlie the facilitation of sexual access for persons with disabilities that ought to carry across the spectrum of ability: first, sex is or can be a source of joy in people's lives, and second, sex is socially coordinated and mediated.

Danish sexual advisors would not do what they do if sex and intimacy did not make their clients' lives better. And they would be unemployed if masturbation and sex were just one- and two-person acts that require no learning, training, or experience. But given how insufficient and inaccurate so much sexual education is in the United States, and given how stubbornly sexist, heteronormative, and uninformed our dominant sexual culture is, temporarily abled folks will likewise benefit from resources and assistance so that their erotic lives and relationships are not only free from coercion and violence but are also joyful.

In the 1970s, sexologists Lorna and Phillip Sarrel led sexual health initiatives on university campuses, first at Yale, and then, through their publications, they "advised more than thirty universities about developing sex education and counseling programs" (Appleton and Stiritz 2016, 57). Programming included courses on human sexuality and sexual communication and on medical and gynecological care. "The sexologists recognized that post-secondary institutions should provide supportive environments for students' sexual development to fulfill the mission of educating the whole person" (56). That is to say, the Sarrels understood resourcing and advising—and thereby improving—sex and sexual health as contributing to a liberal arts education, just like resourcing and advising—and thereby improving—athletics and arts. One does not, or should not, just say *no* to sex any more than one should just say *yes*. Sex, good sex, is an acquired skill, one that entails candid communication, openness to intimacy, and an ability to recognize and express sexual preferences (56–57). The view of sex as a skill rather than something hardwired is captured in the sexologists' concept of "sexual unfolding," a set of processes, realized educationally and collectively, by which young people become confident and healthy sexual agents (Sarrel and Sarrel 1981; Appleton and Stiritz 2016, 57n60).

Following Sarrel and Sarrel, and Appleton and Stiritz, a politics of democratic hedonism, at the most general level, might entail providing girls and women, queers, and everyone else with information about sexual health and pleasure; readily available, publicly funded access to birth control, other reproductive services, and pre-exposure prophylaxis (Burda 2015; Caron 2017); workshops on improved sexual communication, better sex, safer sex, better masturbation, and so forth; good lube; and a variety of contraceptive options. Many universities currently offer these sorts of programs and resources.[44] Nevertheless, such programs are too easily perceived as gratuitous in comparison to the "real issue" of sexual violence. Rather, these programs should be understood as essential to transforming immiserating sexual culture that leads to so much unpleasant and unwanted sex.

If we are going to train young people to labor in markets and participate in what is left of our democracy, perhaps we should make sure too that they are skilled at sex and sexual decision making. This does not mean we must train boys and young men to be exceptional cunnilingus (or fellatio) performers. But such an imperative might augur, for example, more candid, comprehensive discussions about oral sex, about its pleasures and risks, and about ways to minimize those risks and even maximize the pleasures. We might also want to facilitate conversations that examine the misogyny and male privilege that attend to too much oral sex discourse, in which fellatio is casualized as entitlement and cunnilingus is too often considered "gross." Why do boys and men pressure their partners into giving them oral sex? Why do partners accede to performing oral sex when they do not want to? What resources, material and discursive, allow people access to sex and a sexual culture that revolves not around pressure but around redistributed pleasure? We use oral sex as an example in part because as a practice of nonprocreative sex it has no alibis for itself but pleasure, experimentation, and curiosity.[45]

Promoting democratically hedonic access necessitates interrogation of institutions and cultural dictates that continue to make pleasurable sex and egalitarian sexual culture inaccessible. Namely, consider the more rigid and unforgiving aesthetic, comportment, and behavioral norms of femininity and masculinity that stifle most people's sexuality, especially the sexuality of people with disabilities. In his interviews of men with mobility impairments, Russell Shuttleworth found that the men's perceived failure to meet "hegemonic expectations of masculinity such as competitiveness, strength, control, endurance, and independence" impeded them from exploring sex and sexual intimacy (2007b, 189). On the other hand, and promisingly, Shuttleworth also reports that "those men [. . .] who did not view hegemonic masculinity as a total index of their desirability and who could draw on alternative gender dispositions and embodied practices [. . .] could better stand rejection and remain open to [. . .] interpersonal connection and sexual intimacy, and, in fact, were able to cultivate significantly more successful sexual relationships than those who could not" (190–91).

What institutions and spaces cultivate "hegemonic expectations" of masculinity and femininity, and how might those expectations quash sexual autonomy or, worse, encourage sexual coercion and misconduct (Grigoriadis 2017, 229–48, 291–93)? "Having institutions with cemented gender norms controlling social life on campus seems like a really bad idea," writes Vanessa Grigoriadis (229). So is having "boys in charge of social life" (57). Might we consider rerouting resources from fraternities, binary-gendered bathrooms, and other sex-segregated spaces, and toward facilities that desegregate sex, thereby encouraging a wider latitude of gender expressions and stylizations? Might we understand sex desegregation campaigns as rooted not only in equality but also in a commitment to democratizing sexual access? Reactionaries worry that facilities like all-gender bathrooms provide "sexual access" for sex offenders and mythic transgender sex predators. But in a way, all-gender bathrooms and the gender desegregation of privileged social spaces like fraternities *do* promise greater sexual access, if by that we mean that queers, people with disabilities, transgender people, and women are enabled to fully participate in the curricular and extracurricular life of the university, to pursue friendships, partnerships, and sex, without being harassed, beaten, or made to feel inferior (Herman 2013; see also Kafer 2013, 154–57).

PROMOTING SEXUAL ACCESS: EDUCATED SEX

A commitment to sexual autonomy—as a capability that needs to be cultivated—also requires access to a minimal level of publicly funded comprehensive sexuality education (CSE).

Comprehensive sexuality education programs were all but rubbed out in the United States between 1981 and 2009. Until recently, "abstinence only until marriage" (AOUM) programs dominated public schools, especially those in poorer communities. AOUM programs were first federally funded under the Reagan administration, and "funding for these unproven programs grew exponentially from 1996 until 2006, particularly during the years of the George W. Bush Administration. [. . .] Congress has funneled over $2.1 billion tax-payer dollars into abstinence-only-until-marriage programs" (SIECUS 2018). AOUM programs are both scientifically inaccurate and ineffective against their own success measures. They elide or demean queer sexualities and reproduce presumptions of male aggression and female vulnerability or unruliness. Such programs promote not sexual autonomy but sexual incompetence and ignorance (Grose, Grabe, and Kohfeldt 2014; Fine and McClelland 2006; Kendall 2013, 151–223; Lamb, Graling, and Lusting 2011; Malone and Rodriguez 2011).

While the Obama administration relaxed the funding stranglehold of AOUM, most publicly funded sexuality education programs remain abstinence-only or "abstinence-plus,"[46] and the great majority of US teen-agers either do not learn anything at all (in school) about sex or learn only that sex should be deferred (SIECUS 2018; Sifferlin 2014). Compre-hensive sexuality education, while certainly a major improvement from AOUM, does not extend broadly or deeply enough to foster the capabil-ity to codetermine sexual relations. Some CSE programs avow and respect minority sexual orientations and provide accurate information about contraceptives, sex, reproduction, and disease (Kendall 2013, 225–31; Lamb 2011).[47] Yet CSE programs generally run on the "disaster preven-tion model," emphasizing how to delay sex and avoid pregnancy and STIs (Vernacchio 2014, x; see also Fields 2008; Kendall 2013).

From the perspective of facilitating sexual autonomy and democra-tizing sexual access, federal initiatives under the Obama administration at least signaled a turn for the better, away from ideological, irresponsi-ble, and endangering abstinence "education" and toward evidence-based programming targeted at teen pregnancy, sexual violence, and sexually transmitted infections (R. Stein 2010; B. Wilson 2010). As of this writing, the Trump administration is rolling back even these limited gains. In the summer of 2017, without warning or justification, the Department of Health and Human Services announced that it would be terminating the Teen Pregnancy Prevention Program two years early, a program inaugurated during the Obama era that granted $213 million to more than eighty organizations across the country. Left scrambling, many of these organizations have shuttered their comprehensive sex education projects (Cha 2017; Ingold 2017). The funding cuts, in com-bination with the Department of Education's advisory that Title IX does not protect transgender students, along with its guideline that educa-tional institutions are no longer bound by the proof standards regarding sexual misconduct hearings set under the Obama administration, spell out a grim future for sex (Kreighbaum 2017; Saul and Taylor 2017). That the Trump administration has relaxed the Affordable Care Act's requirements for employers to cover their employees' birth control costs adds fuel to the fire (Levintova 2017): sexual autonomy for women and sexual minorities is being aggressively curtailed, and sexual access regressively narrowed. Perhaps more than ever in recent history, sexual progressives ought to be keenly invested, financially and politically, in feminist, sex-positive sexuality education.

Virtually non-existent—either now or in the past four decades—are publicly funded sexuality education programs in which sexual desire is celebrated as a "force for good" (Vernacchio 2014, 10; see also Gill 2015,

81). Rarely are sex acts—what they include, why they (should) feel good, how to refuse or initiate them, how to perform them well and safely—discussed plainly and positively. Infrequently too are "plumbing" lessons of sexuality education taught alongside critical interrogations of gender normativity, heteronormativity, and cultural valorizations of able-bodiedness and able-mindedness. Nor does comprehensive sexuality education typically entail less lofty but no less important lessons regarding how to start and end relationships, how to respectfully argue with intimate partners, and how to determine and revise one's sexual and relational values (Fine and McClelland 2006, 325–28; Haberland 2015; Lamb 2011; Lamb and Peterson 2012; McRuer 2011; Owens-Reid and Russo 2014; Vernacchio 2014).

Comprehensive sexuality education programs that extolled sexual pleasure and sexual safety, emphasized sexual and intimate decision making, and assessed the force and ethicality of cultural norms would democratize sexual access and better foster sexual autonomy as a capability for all people (Gill 2015, 80–81).

Evidently, there is nothing about such programs that is disability specific. But we might think of comprehensive sexuality education (what it could be, not just what it is) as a policy reform with universal objectives (e.g., sexual literacy; cognizance of physiological development; familiarity with contraceptives, their use, and effectiveness; critical apprehension of cultural, media, and pornographic stereotypes around gender and sexuality; see M. Jones 2018) that should be differentially tailored to persons across the spectrum of intellectual and physical abilities (Dukes and McGuire 2009; Swango-Wilson 2011). While we may expect all students to reach some specified threshold of sexual literacy— a threshold that should be co-determined by persons with disabilities— reaching such objectives may require customized teaching lessons and many more resources for persons with disabilities (Swango-Wilson 2008, 168–69; 2011, 117–18; Whitehouse and McCabe 1997; see also Nussbaum 2007, 190–91).

Although sexuality education programs over the past two decades have been created for and targeted to disabled audiences, they tend, as with sexuality education programs for nondisabled adolescents, to emphasize ways to minimize risk of abuse, STIs, and pregnancy, rather than ways to enhance decision-making skills, to interrogate gender and ableist norms, or to experience pleasure (Gill 2015, 69–79; Rohleder and Swartz 2009). And sex education, particularly for persons with intellectual disabilities, cannot be administered solely through decontextualized knowledge banking. Because a person's intellectual disabilities wax and wane across different social settings (depending on comfort, anxiety, newness, and so forth), those with such disabilities need practice and experience communicating about sex and intimacy in different contexts. For example, a study in Japan that administered specially tailored, social-situational sexual education to persons with intellectual disabilities found that the intervention improved the subject population's skills in "communication," "management," and "problem-solving" (Hayashi, Arakida, and Ohashi 2011, 14–15). And a small study in Ireland found that one-on-one sexual education interventions for persons with moderate intellectual disabilities not only improved the subjects' knowledge of sex, sexuality, and sexual safety, but also "improve[d] capacity to make sexuality-related decisions" (Dukes and McGuire 2009, 727–32). Both the Ireland and Japan studies demonstrate how sexuality education can better not simply sex but sexual autonomy as a decision-making capability.

Many researchers have argued too that the dearth of sexuality information and education available to the disabled makes the population more susceptible to sexual exploitation and abuse. Some persons with disabilities neither know they can say *no* nor recognize themselves as decision makers in matters of intimacy and sex. Sexuality education can destigmatize conversations about sex, sexual health, and sexual abuse (Cuskelly and Bryde 2004; Swango-Wilson 2011; but see Whitehouse and McCabe 1997).

L.K., the alleged victim in *Fourtin*, had had no sex education whatsoever (2012, 695). While expert testimony regarding L.K.'s cognitive abilities is conflicting (691, 695), we wonder if she had no sex education because nobody ever thought to offer it, and that nobody ever thought to offer it because of the presumptive asexuality or sexual disorderliness of disabled people (Cuskelly and Bryde 2004, 256; Swango-Wilson 2008, 167–68).

Our proposal for more robust, feminist sexuality education for persons with (or without) disabilities is not naïve regarding the disciplinary power of schooling and the unsavory side of sexuality education for the disabled. Patrick White (2003), for example, describes how 1970s sex education for the blind was organized around biological sex difference, dominant gender roles, and gendered traits of desirability. While earlier superintendence of the blind denied their sexuality altogether, the seemingly liberal reforms and reformers of the 1970s reinstalled compulsory heterosexuality, ignoring the ways intimacy and sexuality might otherwise, alternatively be expressed by blind persons. "Ultimately," summarizes White, "sex education is about the assimilation of the blind into the heterosexual matrix" (2003, 139).[48]

But if no social practice is free or purified of power, some practices are better than others; sexual autonomy is or ought to be our ethical barometer. Sexuality education should be geared toward facilitating people's ability to co-determine their intimate and erotic relations, and to democratizing access to sexual culture.

Better-resourced and better-educated sex redistributes sexual access and cultivates sexual autonomy. In seeking to build a democratically hedonic sexual culture, then, these are the questions we might ask about consent, instead of the usual ones: why do we consent to so much sex that is miserable or unwanted (West 2000)? How might enthusiastic, affirmative consent belie the fact that the consented-to sex is nevertheless mediocre, rote, and hedonically "one-sided" (Oberman 2000, 714)? Under what circumstances is consent insufficient or inapposite as a guarantor of sex that is either good or ethical? Are there any sexual circumstances in which consent *is* a sufficient ethical guarantor?

If consent is a subpar standard for the ethicality or goodness of sex, let alone the ethicality or goodness of sexual culture, then is sex special or ordinary?

Or to put this differently: if kinky sex is different from the gendered violence of football, if eating nonhuman animals is different from fucking them, if lying to get laid is different from lying to get out of class early, if agreeing to sex with an uncle is different from agreeing to babysit his kids, and if sexual pressure is different from other peer pressures, consent is of little to no help in marking these differences. Consent mystifies those differences and the values that underlie them.

Screw consent . . . mostly. Sexual justice politics deserve and demand more.

Conclusion

#MeFirst: Undemocratic Hedonism

#MeToo arrived, you may have noticed. Fomented directly by reports of sexual assaults perpetrated by film producer Harvey Weinstein and perhaps indirectly by a nation reeling under President Trump, "Sexual Harasser in Chief," #MeToo has launched a cascade of courageous coming-out stories from (mostly) women detailing the sexually violent, harassing, or otherwise unbecoming conduct of powerful men (Chozick 2018; K. Locke 2017). #MeToo has instigated a cultural, international reckoning, not only a reassessment of men's untoward or criminal conduct but also, more broadly, a reassessment of gendered and (hetero) sexual norms of the workplace and beyond. Inevitably, with movement comes pushback as journalists, pundits, and self-identified feminist leaders question whether #MeToo has overreached and is catastrophizing some instances of bad or regretted sex as harassing or assaultive.

I am uninterested in relitigating the facts of the #MeToo cases in order to reinterpret the conduct of particular men as either assaultive, harassing, nasty, or assertive, or to readjudicate which incidents "properly" fall under the hashtag. Nearly all of us were not there. What we have available for public record are women's (and some men's) testimonies of unwanted sexual advances and trespasses alongside news and magazine narratives of those narratives. These accounts sometimes ignite our inner *Law & Order: SVU* detective, prompting us to search for inculpatory or exculpatory evidence even as the scene of the crime, or the scene of bad sex, or the scene of *really* bad sex, is so remote and remediated (even while sexual assault is too proximate for too many). It is hard not to draw the conclusion that much of that investigatory impulse—as a default readerly analytic—finds its source in the stubbornly persistent refusal to believe women.

Instead of asking what part of which story is accurate and what part of which story rightfully classifies as wrongful sex, I want to query, albeit gesturally, how the #MeToo movement and all of the sexual harassment, bad sex, and assaultive sex it has cataloged attunes or might attune feminist activism to undemocratic hedonism, sexual access asymmetrically privileged for a few men at the expense of everyone else. While critics of #MeToo have criticized the movement for "lumping"—lumping regretted or unpleasant sex or a grope with rape, for example (Peyser 2017; Roiphe 2018; Young 2017)—I want to applaud the movement's will to lump. Feminist consciousness raising is, after all, a relumping project; and identifying a continuum of bad behaviors is not equivalent to "collapsing" them as one and the same (Roiphe 2018). But it may be conceptually and politically helpful to clarify more precisely the lumping rubric. In other words, what are all these #MeToo stories stories *of*? Or if the Harvey Weinstein stories are nonidentical with the Glenn Thrush stories, what is their connective tissue? Is there connective tissue?

These last pages retrieve concepts and arguments from earlier in the book to suggest that #MeToo and its leading voices avow what is already the target of much of its campaign: men's leveraging of power and celebrity to extract and territorialize pleasure from women and sometimes other men—in a clunky phrase, undemocratic hedonism.

I argue first that *nonconsent* is neither the core nor the common wrong of #MeToo's wrongful sex, despite some advocates contending otherwise. Furthermore, positing #MeToo's wrongful sex as ubiquitously *nonconsensual* leads to bad, as in antifeminist, political outcomes: the sentimentalizing of (white) children and the pathologizing of men; a myopia regarding sexual culture and gender hierarchy; and conservative backlash. And while *discrimination* and *harassment* hold better explanatory purchase over #MeToo's wrongful sex than nonconsent, these terms too do not quite capture some of the central and centrally unethical aspects of these sexual or sexually assaultive encounters.

Triangulating between criticisms of #MeToo sexual encounters as nonconsensual and #MeToo sexual encounters as harassing or discriminatory, I propose instead that what might hold all this bad and really bad and assaultive sex together is undemocratic hedonism, a problem of asymmetric sexual access. Reframing #MeToo as exposing both violations of sexual autonomy and impediments to sexual access helps accentuate the movement's aspirations while buttressing it against familiar conservative criticisms.

On my read, it is more useful from the perspective of sexual justice politics to think of powerful men like Harvey Weinstein and Aziz Ansari less as sexual predators (although perhaps the appellation is not so wrong for Weinstein) than as the men who bottomed for horses in Washington or hoped to penetrate a corpse in Wisconsin. Except that the horse men are ethically exemplary by contrast, attentive as they are to equine pleasure. The celebrity men, on the other hand, leverage their superordination to exploit women's subordination: men barricading against the risk of live women's judgment and rejection in order to unduly limit women's sexual choices and to diminish access to the sex they want.

SCREW CONSENT, REDUX

A first problem with lumping all #MeToo sex as nonconsensual sex is that it potentially mystifies men's usurpations, their sense of sexual entitlement, behind the twinned specters of ruined innocent children and pathological predators (Kincaid 1998; for my gloss on intergenerationality, consent, and sex offense, see Fischel 2016).

Take as a primary example the hashtag campaign #MeAt14, which arose in response to allegations leveled against then–US Senate candidate Roy Moore from Alabama that he pursued, kissed, and molested teenage girls when he was in his thirties. The youngest of the girls was fourteen. In the weeks leading up to Moore's election day defeat hundreds of women, Alabamans and non-Alabamans, celebrities and ordinary folk, posted pictures of their fourteen-year-old selves online, with the hashtag #MeAt14 with comments like "Can't Consent at 14. Not in Alabama. Not anywhere" and "When I was 14, I got braces . . ." (Contrera 2017). The images feature dorky kids doing dorky stuff like homework; they are not dressed up for the school dance. The images and captions bespeak the supposed naïveté and incompetence of any and every teenage girl. National Public Radio summarized the campaign succinctly: "#MeAt14 Reminds Internet 14-Year-Olds Are Innocent, Immature, Unable to Consent" (Benderev 2017).

Feminists should be skeptical if not outright dismissive of such a campaign. #MeAt14 converts the phenomenon of an older man leveraging age and power to sexually assault or advance upon girls (for example, by driving a victim to a remote spot in his car to grope her) into a phenomenon of a pedophilic man who spoils purity, the frivolous joys of child-hood. What about all of Moore's alleged victims who were older teenag-ers (Cleves and Syrett 2017; see also MacKinnon 2007b, 245–56)? Are they undeserving of sympathy or support because they are not minors and so are above the age of consent? If Moore sequestered girls and young women from their communities to force himself upon them, what difference does age difference make? On the other hand, what about fourteen-year-olds who willfully and joyfully engage in sexual activity? Refiguring ruined preadolescent and adolescent innocence as the social problem, rather than male sexual entitlement buttressed by privilege and power, substitutes pervasive sex inequality for Sick Men and Cute Kids. #MeToo, unlike #MeAt14, recalls that sexual manipulation, coercion, assault, and misconduct are practiced by superordinated men against subordinated girls and women (and boys and men) of all ages. Young age aggravates women's vulnerability but young age is not ipso facto vulnerability.

The sentimentalization of childhood and the pathologizing of sexual misconduct also orbited the Kevin Spacey scandal. The actor was accused of making drunken, aggressive sexual passes at the actor Anthony Rapp in 1986, when Rapp was fourteen. In his public apology, Spacey came out as gay, which immediately triggered outrage from gay leaders and pundits distancing gayness from pedophilia (Victor 2017). But lost in the back-and-forth over whether or not to classify Spacey as a pedophile, or whether Spacey used his gayness to distract us from his misconduct, was a deeper consideration of what this story has in common with so many other stories: the normalization of men's coercive behavior to extract, and sometimes exploit, sex from others.

In late November 2017, when the Spacey scandal was cooling down and the Moore one was heating up, I received an email from an editor at *Fortune* Magazine who requested that I write an op-ed for the maga-zine answering the question: "Is it time for Congress to step in and establish a national age of consent? What age should it be? Should our laws be changed in any other way to prevent such behavior?"[1]

I replied that I would rather write about the persistent norms of mas-culinity and femininity that lubricate unwanted sex for too many women and young people, and about men's leveraging of authority, power, and prestige to extract sex from others. I pointed out that age of consent laws in New York and Alabama stopped neither Spacey nor Moore, and that age of consent laws would not help older victims in any way. The editor withdrew the offer.

To be clear, Kevin Spacey and Roy Moore allegedly attempted or had sex with young teenagers and those teenagers refused their advances. So my point is decidedly not that the problem of rendering these #MeToo incidents as nonconsensual is that these teens in fact consented; to the contrary. But perhaps we need not imagine that these fourteen-year-olds, like horses, corpses, or, according to a trial court in Connecticut, a severely disabled woman, are "unable to consent." Rather, these young people's sexual autonomy was run roughshod by older men with status. Then-twenty-six-year-old Kevin Spacey might still be culpable had then-fourteen-year-old Anthony Rapp engaged enthusiastically in sexual conduct with him, but that is not what happened, according to Rapp.[2] Rapp dodged Spacey and maneuvered himself out of the room. The consent paradigm, which so quickly collapses into the age of consent paradigm, risks reframing men's abuses of power as individual, pedophilic perversions, thereby distancing the teenagers' experiences from those of adult women (and some men) and potentially discrediting adult victims (*But why didn't you leave?*).

A second problem with lumping all #MeToo sex as nonconsensual is that some of the sex was or might have been consensual, nonetheless deeply unwanted, but still rightfully a target of feminist movement.

In her discussion with Rebecca Traister and Terry Gross on National Public Radio's *Fresh Air,* famed political journalist Jane Mayer commented, "What matters to me most is that kind of the fundamental building block is consent, that women give sexual consent to whoever they're involved with. [. . .] And a lot of women do meet people and men meet each other through work; it's where we spend most of our time. And again, this gets back to the subject of consent. [. . .] It's a little complicated maybe, but it's not necessarily a situation that is harassment" (T. Gross 2017).

Recall Gigi Engle's guide to anal sex for teenagers (2017). Mayer, like Engle, is magnetized by consent because that is what liberals and progressives do when moralizing good and bad and wrongful sex. But is (non)consent really the "fundamental building block" of #MeToo? Is not so much of this unwanted or unpleasant workplace sex ostensibly consensual? A lot of the sex is not (assaults, groping, forced kissing), but a lot of it is (requests for peculiar sexual services or naked selfies). Mayer wants consent to divide the good sex from the bad, wanted from unwanted, an equalizing buffer against the unequal workplace; except that sometimes women "consent to their misery," which does not make it any less of a political problem (West 2000, 161).

Reconsider the crash-and-burn of comedian Louis C.K., who is on the bad man list primarily for masturbating in front of other women comedians or associates. If we lived in a sex-equal world the news reports of his conduct might instead read: Louis C.K. *requests the affirmative consent* of two women comedians before proceeding to masturbate in front of them; Louis C.K. *does not masturbate* in front of a woman after she denies his request; another young woman *agrees to watch* Louis C.K. masturbate; a woman performer listens to Louis C.K. masturbate on the phone for several minutes and does not hang up (Ryzik, Buckley, and Kantor 2017).

In the cases so documented (and with the caveat, again, that we were not there), Louis C.K. does not physically contact, let alone penetrate, the complainants; he does not force himself upon them or coerce them into sex; he does not, as far as we know, condition job promotion or demotion on sex; in short, he verbally requests verbal consent to jerk off. Is he not the fantasy man of satirized university sexual misconduct codes?

A lot of sex that is consented to and agreed upon, even affirmatively, is no doubt immiserating or unpleasant or the pleasure is one-sided (for him; Traister 2015; West 2000). It is also sex that can instantiate inequality, affirmation that affirms sex hierarchy. In these lights, every time the young woman on the set of *The Chris Rock Show* reluctantly permits Louis C.K. to masturbate in front of her, she ratifies, to him, her subordination—*I am your cum rag.* Her *yes*-saying says *yes* to his superordination and entitlement. That problem cannot be fixed through redefining consent, providing consent education, or saying *yes* ever more boldly (with regrets, one more time, to Gigi Engle, Jane Mayer, and the Consent Is Sexy campaign). That problem is braided from three others—enculturation (*I should demur, I should not cause a scene*), fear of repercussions (getting fired or badmouthed in a close-knit industry), and lack of alternatives (*Where will I get a gig now?*)—and is structural, which does not mean it is irresolvable. A promise of #MeToo is to lift the curtain enough times on men, on men in positions of power, on whole industries and employment vectors, on everyday practices that should never have become just the way things are, in order to transform the conditions of our public lives, professional possibilities, and our intimacies.

Not everyone agrees that all the women consented to Louis C.K.'s masturbation rituals; some likely did not. But it also seems disingenuous and politically dangerous to claim that "asking someone if you can take out your penis [. . .] will often be enough to make her feel threatened," and that Louis C.K.'s "words alone—the words he claims he believed established consent—were a major part of his harassment" (Cauterucci 2017; but see Roiphe 2018). This sort of maneuver recodes the sex we find weird, nonnormative, and depressingly gendered as nonconsensual and assaultive, forsaking the difficult question *Why do women sometimes consent to unwanted sexual encounters?* and its more difficult complement *How do we create and maintain a democratically hedonic sexual culture so they don't, as much?*

And so a third problem of lumping #MeToo sex, along with Louis C.K.'s masturbation practices, as nonconsensual and thereby assaultive is predictably conservative blowback. It was this will to lump that nearly sounded the death knell for #MeToo, or so some critics had hoped (Bunch 2018; Peyser 2018), when the lifestyle website *babe* reported on a young woman's self-described "worst night of [her] life" with the comedian Aziz Ansari (Way 2018). The story describes a bullish Ansari unconcerned with or unaware of his date's disinterest-turned-noninterest in sex. The date, "Grace" (a pseudonym), coldly goes along with Ansari's initiatives, occasionally expresses her reluctance, acquiesces to his persistence, and then, months later, catalogs the experience as "sexual assault" (Way 2018).

Many critics and pundits, feminists included, were unwilling, in fact horrified, to classify Anzari's conduct as sexually assaultive, not least as a matter of strategy (Flanagan 2018; B. Weiss 2018). Indeed, renaming the celebrity's assertiveness as assaultiveness proved ample fodder for conservative commentators to decry #MeToo as overreaching, victimizing, carelessly *lumping* (Markowicz 2018; Peyser 2018). It is this sort of slippage—labeling bad sex sexual assault, not a rhetorical staple of social media but easily portrayed to be—that allowed Katie Roiphe (2018) to side-eye, "The need to differentiate between smaller offenses and assault is not interesting to a certain breed of Twitter feminist."

What is troubling to me is that Grace felt as if the only two classifications available for what happened that night, as she describes it, were "awkward sexual experience" or "sexual assault," and so chose the latter (Way 2018). But is there not a whole range of bad sex, really bad sex, that falls somewhere between awkward and assaultive, and should that not be a primary target for feminist and queer politics (see also Peterson 2008)? What binds together, if anything, really bad sex and assaultive sex if it is not nonconsent? Certainly, and if you are *lucky,* "you're gonna have so much unspecial sex in your life" (Gerwig 2017), but "unspecial" is not the same as "resolutely unpleasant"; moreover, it is the structural asymmetry of either that unspecialness or that unpleasantness that is rightfully a political problem. Put more plainly, really bad sex is typically really bad for just one partner, usually a woman (Loofbourow 2018).

SEX-DISCRIMINATING SEX?

Perhaps the real badness of the really bad sex called out by #MeToo is located not in assault but in discrimination and harassment. Perhaps what "unites these varied revelations isn't necessarily sexual harm, but *professional* harm and power abuse" (Traister 2017). This is the read tendered by feminist journalist Rebecca Traister, and it seems almost entirely right. In her smartly argued "This Moment Isn't (Just) about Sex; It's Really about Work" (2017), Traister takes to task, albeit sympathetically, lumping critics like Roiphe and Masha Gessen (2017; see also Traister 2018). #MeToo is not only or even primarily about sexual assault but also about sex, sexual innuendo, sexual advances, and sexual trespasses that constitute but one component of a larger discriminatory culture impeding women's equality and advancement in the workplace (see also Schultz 2003). Workplace "offers" and threats of sex, gossip about women's sexual behaviors and histories, and fears of retaliation for sexual rejection (or compliance) operate to sediment or reinstall gender hierarchy. "A focus on sex" alone, worries Traister (2017), "lets us off the hook," making #MeToo "about sex crimes" rather than about sexual harassment or sexism.

An account of this really bad sex, and sometimes sexual assault, as harassing and discriminatory seems far more compelling and politically potent than repackaging all that bad and unwanted sex as nonconsensual. I just want to add two amendments.

First, it seems unlikely that in every case of powerful celebrity men leveraging their power and celebrity to exact sex from women (and sometimes men, girls, or boys), the women's professional possibilities were or even could be jeopardized. Certainly this was not the case with "Grace" and Aziz Ansari, and even if you believe there is no *there* there, there are other #MeToo moments in which professional futures were not in peril. Consider Suki Kim's (2017) uncomfortable exchanges with journalist John Hockenberry, or some of the inebriated, aggressive passes by journalist Glenn Thrush at uninterested women (Ember 2017). Maybe the exceptions prove the rule. Nevertheless, it strikes me that it is not just discrimination, harassment, and fear of employment repercussions that compel (indexically) women to endure unwanted sex. It is also about not wanting to make a scene, cause embarrassment, "create" awkwardness. And men like Louis C.K., John Hockenberry, Harvey Weinstein, (maybe) Aziz Ansari, and too many others capitalize on precisely this, banking on women's socialization to be demure, especially in matters of sex (A. Jones 2018; Silman 2018; Traister 2015; see also Roupenian 2017).

And so, second, might we keep a "focus on sex" even if the sex is not criminal? By drawing our attention to work and power rather than to sex and (hetero)sexuality, Traister (2017) wants to make #MeToo about women's equality and "professional autonomy." She wants to make sex a little less special. But as in chapter 3, where I suggest that the "transgender deception" cases should prompt us to take stock not only of transgender equality but also transgender sexual autonomy, here too I want to suggest that what unites the #MeToo stories are denials of women's sexual autonomy. They are stories of men arranging social and intimate life so the pleasure is all one-sided, their-sided. They are stories of undemocratic hedonism, maximizing sexual gratification or one's access to sexual gratification, by denying anyone else's. Katie Roiphe (2018) rebuts: "It is easier to think, for instance, that [. . .] a man said something awful and sexual to us while we were working on a television show, and we got depressed and could never again achieve what we might have. And yet do we really in our hearts believe that is the whole story?"

But must it be the whole story? Can it not be just part of the story? Even if her depression was not exhaustively a function of his "awful," "sexual" comment, why should she have to endure it? The comment is not only an impingement (however slight) on the employee's "professional autonomy" but also (again, however slight) on her sexual autonomy. The nasty comment, as but a small part of a constellation of "systemic disadvantaging of a gender in the public and professional sphere" (Traister 2017), grants him access to her while denying her access to the sexual worlds and experiences she might otherwise choose.

This moment "isn't (just) about sex," but neither is it "*really* about work*" (Traister 2017; emphasis added). It is "*really* about" sex too, (indexically) women's sexual autonomy and access. Or, as Traister puts it elsewhere, "we still can't talk easily about the disgusting sexism that makes our sexual interactions—even the consensual ones—unequal and often ultimately unsatisfying for women" (Traister and Douthat 2017; see also Traister 2015).

So while some of the #MeToo incidents do not or well might not involve issues of harassment, discrimination, or even nonconsent, they share a scaffold of undemocratic hedonism and sexual one-sidedness that structures the more violent, nonconsensual, harassing, and discriminatory behaviors of men in power.

#MEFIRST: UNDEMOCRATIC HEDONISM

I end this conclusion where I began it: what if these men—the Weinsteins and everyone not *as* bad—are more like Nicolas Radke, the failed corpse fucker, and Kenneth Pinyan, the dead horse fucker, than we might initially suppose? What if Ansari, and even Harvey Weinstein, is less like the monstrous German Cannibal (chapter 1) than like mothers' boyfriends (chapter 2) or weirdly straightish men (chapter 4)? What if these #MeToo stories are not just stories of men abusing their power but also of men whose only card is their power? The power is a prop against the rejection and judgment of live women. The Washington and Wisconsin men took themselves out of homosocial competition by switching out a typical hetero object choice with less resistant substitutes (or, in former senator Al Franken's case, a sleeping woman could not push him away; Garber 2017; see also Berlant 2017). The Hollywood men, though, safeguard against the risks of failed masculinity and heterosexuality by structuring their sexual encounters and leveraging their power and status to minimize the possibility of woman's refusal and to barricade against the possibility that she might choose otherwise. So, in this sense, the Hollywood men are also like child pornographers, not pathological perverts, but as Suzanne Ost (2009) explains (quoted earlier), exploiters exploiting "a situation or context in which an individual takes unfair advantage of someone else for his own ends" (139). The Hollywood men's sexual advances and trespasses threaten women's equality, usually. But by exploiting women's (and young people's and sometimes other men's) subordinated positions, they also sexually gratify themselves by curtailing women's sexual autonomy, impeding women's capability to co-determine their sexual and intimate relationships.

In chapter 5, Hilary O'Connell and I turn to a case of sexual assault involving a woman with significant physical and cognitive disabilities in order to ask and propose provisional answers to the questions: How might we promote sexual autonomy across the spectrum of ability, beyond consent? What kinds of institutional arrangements and world building, beyond the consent paradigm, facilitate access to sex and democratically hedonic culture? Our proposals resonate with what disability scholars famously call the "dignity of risk," the normative premise that, ceteris paribus, it is better for persons with disabilities to try, experiment, and risk, maybe to fail but hopefully to succeed, than to be cloistered from the world and its perturbations (Perske 1972).

The #MeToo men insure against risks of rejection; they maintain positions of gendered dominance by extracting sex and pleasure from exploited subordinates. But what the #MeToo men also deny is *women's* (and sometimes other men's) risk, their "dignity of risk"; that is, risking sex on any terms other than the terms men set through power. How do we facilitate access for people less privileged by power to risk more and then to "demand better" (A. Jones 2018)? How might we democratize sexual culture?

Perpetrator-Victim Relationships in Sexual Assault Cases

Connecticut, Michigan, and Wisconsin, 2010–2016

TABLE A1   PERPETRATOR-VICTIM RELATIONSHIPS IN CONNECTICUT APPELLATE COURT SEXUAL ASSAULT CASES, 2010–2016

		No.	%
Case descriptions[1]	Sexual assault	195	N/A
	Unique victims[2]	222	N/A
Case type	State of CT v. Defendant	139	71.3
	Appellant v. Commissioner of Correction[3]	55	28.2
	Other	1	0.5
No. of crimes[4]	Single	87	44.6
	Multiple	108	55.4
Specific crimes involved[5]	Sexual assault in the 1st degree	111	56.9
	Sexual assault in the 2nd degree	35	17.9
	Sexual assault in the 3rd degree	18	18.4
	Sexual assault in the 4th degree	37	19.0
	Sexual assault in a spousal/ cohabiting relationship	9	4.6
	Risk of injury to a child	123	63.1
	Sexual assault, degree not specified	5	2.6
		No.	%
No. of victims[6]	Single	175	89.7
	Multiple	20	10.3
	2	14	7.2
	3	6	3.1
	>3	0	0

Ages of perpetrators and victims	Age of perpetrator	Adult (18+)	21	10.8
		Minor (<18)	1	0.5
		Not specified[7]	173	88.7
		Total	195	100
	Age of victim	Adult (18+)	6	2.7
		Minor (<18)	148	66.7
		Not specified[8]	65	29.3
		Police officer posing as minor	3	1.4
		Total[9]	222	100.1
Relationship between perpetrators and victims	Relationship classification			
	Intimate relationship		13	5.9
		Spouse[10]	5	2.3
		Former spouse	1	0.5
		Partner (excl. spouse)	3	1.4
		Former partner (excl. spouse)	4	1.8
	Familial or semifamilial relationship		73	32.9
		Father[11]	28	12.6
		Uncle[12]	8	3.6
		Grandfather[13]	5	2.3
		Other family member	6	2.7
		Other legal guardian	0	0
		Stepfather	7	3.2
		Mother's boyfriend/ intimate partner[14]	19	8.6%
	Caretaking relationship		13	5.9
		Babysitter	2	0.9
		Teacher or Coach	5	2.3
		Other Caretaker	6	2.7
	Other relationship		65	29.3
		Co-worker or Employer	4	1.8
		Family friend	12	5.4
		Parent of a friend	5	2.3
		Friend of a friend	3	1.4
		Other personal acquaintance or known individual[15]	41	18.5
	No prior relationship		20	9.0
		Client (for sex workers)	1	0.5
		Stranger	16	7.2
		Police officer (posing as teen girl online)	3	1.4
	Relationship not specified		38	17.1
Total[16]			222	100.1

Genders of perpetrators and victims	Perpetrators	Male	194	99.5
		Female	1	0.5
		Unspecified	0	0
		N/A	0	0
	Victims	Male	23	10.4
		Female	169	76.1
		Unspecified	27	12.2
		N/A[17]	3	1.4

[1] We coded all cases from a LexisNexis search of appellate sexual assault cases decided between January 1, 2010, and September 18, 2016.

[2] One victim is assumed when the number is not specified. If it is known that there were multiple victims, but the specific number is not known, two victims are assumed. If it is known that there were more than two victims, but the specific number is not known, three victims are assumed. If there was only one victim of the charged sexual assault, it is coded as one victim, even if there were other victims of non-sex-related charges in the same case.

[3] "Appellant v. Commissioner of Correction" refers to cases involving an appellate plea for a writ of habeas corpus.

[4] Crimes are coded as single if the perpetrator was found guilty in a trial case of one or more charges of the same crime and that crime was one of those specified in the "Specific crimes involved" section below.

[5] This table includes only crimes with which defendants were charged and found guilty in a trial court, unless a case had not yet gone to trial and some aspect of the case was on appeal pretrial. It includes attempted and aggravated crimes, but not accessory charges. In addition to the categories of crimes specified here, perpetrators may have been found guilty of additional crimes. The % column here contains the percentage of total cases resulting in a conviction for this crime.

[6] See footnote 2.

[7] Perpetrators whose age is "not specified" in the appeal are likely over 18, given the other facts of these cases.

[8] Victims whose age is "not specified" in the appeal are likely over 18, given the other facts of these cases. If the perpetrator was charged with "risk of injury to a child," a child victim was assumed. If a victim had his or her 18th birthday during the period of abuse, he or she was coded as a minor.

[9] This number slightly exceeds 100% because all calculations were rounded to the nearest 10th.

[10] "Spouse" includes common-law spouses, including those who are separated.

[11] "Father" includes biological and adoptive fathers.

[12] "Uncle" includes uncles by marriage and aunts' live-in boyfriends.

[13] "Grandfather" includes step-grandfathers and grandmothers' live-in boyfriends.

[14] In State v. Carlos C., 165 Conn. App. 195 (2016), the perpetrator was first the victim's mother's boyfriend and then the victim's stepfather during the period of sexual abuse. The perpetrator was coded as the victim's mother's boyfriend/intimate partner.

[15] In 13 of the cases coded as "other personal acquaintance or known individual," the perpetrator is likely the mother's boyfriend or intimate partner, based on the circumstances described (e.g., he lives in the household with the victim and his or her mother, or sometimes sleeps over).

[16] This number slightly exceeds 100% because all calculations were rounded to the nearest 10th.

[17] In these cases, police officers posed as teen girls online.

TABLE A2   PERPETRATOR-VICTIM RELATIONSHIPS IN MICHIGAN APPELLATE
COURT SEXUAL ASSAULT CASES, 2010–2016

			No.	%
Case descriptions[1]		Sexual assault	200	N/A
		Unique victims[2]	230	N/A
Case type		State of MI v. Defendant	198	99
		Appellant v. Commissioner of Correction[3]	0	0
		Other	2	1
No. of crimes[4]		Single	140	70
		Multiple	60	30
Specific crimes involved[5]		Criminal sexual conduct in the 1st degree	128	64
		Criminal sexual conduct in the 2nd degree	75	37.5
		Criminal sexual conduct in the 3rd degree	36	18
		Criminal sexual conduct in the 4th degree	17	8.5
		Criminal sexual conduct, degree not specified	1	0.5
		Assault with intent to commit criminal sexual conduct	9	4.5
No. of victims[6]	Single		180	90
	Multiple		20	10
		2	14	7
		3	6	3
		>3	0	0
Ages of perpetrators and victims	Age of perpetrator	Adult (18+)	12	6
		Minor (<18)	3	1.5
		Not specified[7]	185	92.5
		Total	200	100

Age of victim	Adult (18+)	10	4.3
	Minor (<18)	154	70.0
	Not specified[8]	66	28.7
	Police officer posing as minor	0	0
	Total	230	
Relationship between perpetrators and victims	Relationship classification		
Intimate relationship	Spouse[9]	1	0.4
	Former spouse	0	0
	Partner (excl. spouse)	3	1.3
	Former partner (excl. spouse)	2	0.9
Familial or semifamilial relationship	Father[10]	18	7.8
	Uncle[11]	6	2.6
	Grandfather[12]	8	3.5
	Other family member, or unspecified family member	13	5.7
	Other legal guardian	0	0
	Stepfather	11	4.8
	Mother's boyfriend/ intimate partner[13]	11	4.8
Caretaking relationship	Babysitter[14]	2	0.9
	Teacher or coach	3	1.3
	Other caretaker[15]	8	3.5
Other relationship	Coworker or employer	1	0.4
	Family friend	8	3.5
	Parent of a friend	1	0.4
	Friend of a friend	4	1.7
	Other personal acquaintance or known individual	29	12.6
No prior relationship	Client (for sex workers)	0	0
	Stranger	20	8.7
	Police officer (posing as teen girl online)	0	0
Relationship not specified		81	35.2
	Total	230	

			No.	%
Genders of perpetrators and victims	Perpetrators	Male	198	99
		Female	2	1
		Unspecified	0	0
		N/A	0	0
	Victims	Male	12	5.2
		Female	196	85.2
		Unspecified	22	9.6
		N/A	0	0

[1] We sampled and coded every seventh case from a LexisNexis search of appellate sexual assault cases decided between January 1, 2010, and September 14, 2016.

[2] One victim is assumed when the number is not specified. If it is known that there were multiple victims, but the specific number is not known, two victims are assumed. If it is known that there were more than two victims, but the specific number is not known, three victims are assumed. If there was only one victim of the sexual assault charges, it is coded as one victim, even if there were other victims of non-sex-related charges in the same case.

[3] "Appellant v. Commissioner of Correction" refers to cases involving an appellate plea for a writ of habeas corpus.

[4] Crimes are coded as single if the perpetrator was found guilty in a trial case of one or more charges of the same crime and that crime was one of those specified in the "specific crimes involved" section below.

[5] This table includes only crimes with which defendants were charged and found guilty in a trial court, unless a case had not yet gone to trial and some aspect of the case was on appeal pretrial. It includes attempted and aggravated crimes, but not accessory charges. In addition to the categories of crimes specified here, perpetrators may have been found guilty of additional crimes. The % column here contains the percentage of total cases resulting in a conviction for this crime.

[6] See footnote 2.

[7] Perpetrators whose age is "not specified" in the appeal are likely over 18, given the other facts of these cases.

[8] Victims whose age is "not specified" in the appeal are likely over 18, given the other facts of these cases. If the perpetrator was charged with "risk of injury to a child," a child victim was assumed. If a victim had her or his 18th birthday during the period of abuse, she or he was coded as a minor.

[9] "Spouse" includes common-law spouse, including those who are separated.

[10] "Father" includes biological and adoptive fathers.

[11] "Uncle" includes uncles by marriage and aunts' live-in boyfriends.

[12] "Grandfather" includes step-grandfathers and grandmothers' live-in boyfriends.

[13] In two cases, the perpetrator was likely the mother's boyfriend, given the facts provided, but a definitive determination could not be made. These cases were coded as "relationship not specified."

[14] A perpetrator who was both a babysitter and a family friend was coded as babysitter since the first of multiple assaults occurred in the context of babysitting. A day care worker was coded as "babysitter."

[15] Cases include doctor-patient relationships.

		No.	%
Case descriptions[1]	Sexual assault	200	N/A
	Unique victims[2]	230	N/A
Case type	State of WI v. Defendant	187	93.5
	Appellant v. Commissioner of Correction[3]	0	0
	Other	13	6.5
No. of crimes[4]	Single	174	87
	Multiple	26	13
Specific crimes involved[5]	Sexual assault in the 1st degree	10	5
	Sexual assault in the 2nd degree	39	19.5
	Sexual assault in the 3rd degree	12	6
	Sexual assault in the 4th degree	8	4
	Sexual assault, degree not specified	7	3.5
	Sexual Assault of a child in the 1st degree	51	25.5
	Sexual Assault of a child in the 2nd degree	46	23
	Sexual Assault of a child in the 4th degree	1	0.5
	Sexual assault of a child, degree not specified	12	6
	Sexual assault of a child by a school staff person or a person who works or volunteers with children	1	0.5
	Engaging in repeated acts of sexual assault with the same child	32	16
	Sexual intercourse with a child age 16 or older	3	1.5
	Incest	3	1.5
	Incest with a child	5	2.5

			No.	%
No. of victims[6]	Single		179	89.5
	Multiple		21	10.5
		2	16	8
		3	1	0.5
		> 3	4	2
Ages of	Age of perpetrator	Adult (18+)	10	5
perpetrators		Minor (<18)	10	5
and victims		Not specified[7]	180	90
		Total	200	100
	Age of victim	Adult (18+)	8	3.5
		Minor (<18)	153	66.5
		Not specified[8]	68	29.6
		Police officer posing as minor	1	0.4
		Total	230	100
Relationship between perpetrators and victims	Relationship classification			
	Intimate relationship	Spouse[9]	0	0
		Former spouse	0	0
		Partner (excl. spouse)	6	2.6
		Former partner (excl. spouse)	3	1.3
	Familial or semifamilial relationship	Father[10]	11	4.8
		Uncle[11]	5	2.2
		Grandfather[12]	3	1.3
		Other family member, or unspecified family member	11	4.8
		Other legal guardian	0	0
		Stepfather	6	2.6
		Mother's boyfriend/ intimate partner	12	5.2
	Caretaking relationship	Babysitter	1	0.4
		Teacher or coach	1	0.4
		Other caretaker[13]	10	4.3
	Other relationship	Co-worker or employer	2	0.9
		Family friend	5	2.2
		Parent of a friend	0	0
		Friend of a friend	0	0

		Other personal acquaintance or known individual	28	12.2
	No prior relationship	Client (for sex workers)	0	0
		Stranger	15	6.5
		Police officer (posing as teen girl online)	1	0.4
	Relationship not specified		110	47.8
		Total	230	
Genders of perpetrators and victims	Perpetrators	Male	199	99.5
		Female	1	0.5
		Unspecified	0	0
		N/A	0	0
	Victims	Male	14	6.1
		Female	153	66.5
		Unspecified	63	27.4
		N/A	0	0

[1] We sampled and coded every fourth case from a LexisNexis search of appellate sexual assault cases decided between January 1, 2010, and September 14, 2016.

[2] One victim is assumed when the number is not specified. If it is known that there were multiple victims, but the specific number is not known, two victims are assumed. If it is known that there were more than two victims, but the specific number is not known, three victims are assumed. If there was only one victim of the charged sexual assault, it is coded as one victim, even if there were other victims of non-sex-related charges in the same case.

[3] "Appellant v. Commissioner of Correction" refers to cases involving an appellate plea for a writ of habeas corpus.

[4] Crimes are coded as single if the perpetrator was found guilty in a trial case of one or more charges of the same crime and that crime was one of those specified in the "specific crimes involved" section below.

[5] This table includes only crimes with which defendants were charged and found guilty in a trial court, unless a case had not yet gone to trial and some aspect of the case was on appeal pretrial. It includes attempted and aggravated crimes, but not accessory charges. In addition to the categories of crimes specified here, perpetrators may have been found guilty of additional crimes. The % column here contains percentages of total cases resulting in a conviction for this crime.

[6] There were multiple victims in roughly 10% of sampled cases from Wisconsin. See note 2.

[7] Perpetrators whose age is "not specified" in the appeal are likely over 18, given the other facts of these cases.

[8] Victims whose age is "not specified" in the appeal are likely over 18, given the other facts of these cases. If the perpetrator was charged with "risk of injury to a child," a child victim was assumed. If a victim had his or her 18th birthday during the period of abuse, he or she was coded as a minor.

[9] "Spouse" includes common-law spouses, including those who are separated.

[10] "Father" includes biological and adoptive fathers.

[11] "Uncle" includes uncles by marriage and aunts' live-in boyfriends.

[12] "Grandfather" includes step-grandfathers and grandmothers' live-in boyfriends.

[13] Defendants in these cases include a school bus driver, a doctor, and a correctional officer.

Sex, Law, and Status Relations

Fifty State Survey

TABLE B1 SEX, LAW, AND STATUS RELATIONS

State	Parent	Stepparent	Intimate partner of parent	Sibling	Biological aunt/uncle	Nonbiological aunt/uncle	Teacher & student	Teacher & student age specifications:	Psychotherapist
AL	Y**[1]	Y[2]	N	Y*[3]	Y*[4]	N	Y[5]	Student is under 19.	N
AK	Y**^^[6]	Y[7]	Y[8]	Y*[9]	Y[10]	N	Y[11]	Student is under 16.	N[12]
AZ	Y[13]	Y^[14]	Y^[15]	Y[16]	Y[17]	N	Y^[18]	Student is 15–18.	Y[19]
AR	Y**[20]	Y[21]	Y^[22]	Y*[23]	Y[24]	N	Y[25]	Student is under 21.	N
CA	Y[26]	N	N	Y*[27]	Y[28]	Y[29]	N	N/A	N
CO	Y**[30]	Y[31]	Y^[32]	Y*[33]	Y[34]	N	Y^[35]	Student is under 18.	Y[36]
CT	Y^^[37]	Y^[38]	N	N	N	N	Y[39]	No age specifications	N[40]
DE	Y**[41]	Y[42]	Y^[43]	Y[44]	Y***[45]	N	Y^[46]	Student is under 18.	Y^[47]
FL	Y[48]	Y^[49]	N	Y[50]	Y[51]	Y[52]	Y^[53]	Student is under 18.	Y[54]
GA	Y[55]	Y[56]	N	Y*[57]	Y[58]	Y[59]	Y[60]	No age specifications	Y[61]
HI	Y[62]	N	N	Y*[63]	Y[64]	Y[65]	Y[66]	Student is 16–18.	Y[67]
ID	Y[68]	N	N	Y*[69]	Y[70]	Y[71]	N	N/A	Y[72]
IL	Y**[73]	Y[74]	Y^[75]	Y*[76]	Y[77]	Y[78]	Y^[79]	Student is 13–18.	Y^[80]
IN	Y[81]	N	N	Y[82]	Y[83]	N	N	N/A	N
IA	Y[84]	Y[85]	Y[86]	Y*[87]	Y[88]	Y[89]	Y[90]	No age specifications[91]	Y[92]
KS	Y**[93]	Y[94]	N	Y*[95]	Y[96]	N	Y[97]	Student is over 15.	N[98]
KY	Y**[99]	Y[100]	Y^[101]	Y*[102]	Y[103]	N	Y^[104]	Student is under 18.	Y[105]
LA	Y**[106]	Y[107]	N	Y*[108]	Y[109]	N	Y[110]	Student is 17–21.[111]	N
ME	Y^^[112]	Y[113]	Y[114]	Y[115]	Y[116]	N	Y[117]	Student is under 18.	Y[118]
MD	Y[119]	Y[120]	N	Y[121]	Y[122]	N	Y^[123]	Student is under 18.[124]	N
MA	Y**[125]	N	N	Y*[126]	Y***[127]	N	Y[128]	Student is under 16.	Y[129]
MI	Y[130]	Y^[131]	Y^[132]	Y[133]	Y[134]	Y[135]	Y[136]	Student is 13–17.[137]	Y[138]
MN	Y[139]	Y[140]	Y^[141]	Y*[142]	Y*[143]	Y[144]	Y[145]	Student is 13–17.	Y[146]
MS	Y**[147]	Y[148]	Y[149]	Y*[150]	Y***[151]	N	Y[152]	Student is under 18.	Y^[153]

MO	Y**[154]	Y[155]	N	Y*[156]	Y[157]	N	Y[158]	No age specifications[159]	N
MT	Y**[160]	Y[161]	N	Y*[162]	Y[163]	N	N	N/A	N
NE	Y[164]	Y[165]	N	Y*[166]	Y***[167]	Y***[168]	N	N/A	N
NV	Y[169]	N	N	Y*[170]	Y[171]	N	Y[172]	Student is over 15.[173]	N
NH	Y**[174]	Y[175]	Y^[176]	Y*[177]	Y[178]	N	Y^[179]	Student is 13–17.	Y[180]
NJ	Y^^[181]	Y[182]	N	Y[183]	Y[184]	Y[185]	Y^[186]	Student is 13–18.[187]	N
NM	Y[188]	N	N	Y*[189]	Y[190]	N	Y[191]	Student is under 19.[192]	Y[193]
NY	Y[194]	Y[195]	N	Y*[196]	Y[197]	Y[198]	N	N/A	N[199]
NC	Y**^^[200]	Y[201]	Y[202]	Y*[203]	Y[204]	Y[205]	Y[206]	No age specifications[207]	N
ND	Y^^[208]	N	Y[209]	Y*[210]	Y***[211]	N	Y[212]	Student is 15–18.	Y[213]
OH	Y**^^[214]	Y[215]	N	N	N	N	Y[216]	Student is under 19.	N[217]
OK	Y[218]	Y[219]	N	Y*[220]	Y***[221]	N	N	N/A	N
OR	Y[222]	N	N	Y*[223]	Y[224]	N	N	N/A	N
PA	Y**[225]	N	N	Y*[226]	Y[227]	N	Y[228]	No age specifications	N
RI[229]	N	N	N	N	N	N	N	N/A	N
SC	Y[230]	Y[231]	N	Y[232]	Y***[233]	Y***[234]	Y[235]	Student is over 15.[236]	N
SD	Y**[237]	Y[238]	N	Y*[239]	Y***[240]	Y***[241]	N	N/A	Y[242]
TN	Y**[243]	Y[244]	N	Y*[245]	Y[246]	Y[247]	Y^[248]	Student is 13–17.[249]	N
TX	Y**[250]	Y[251]	N	Y*[252]	Y[253]	Y[254]	Y[255]	No age specifications	Y[256]
UT	Y**[257]	Y[258]	Y^[259]	Y*[260]	Y[261]	Y[262]	Y^[263]	Student is under 14.[264]	Y^[265]
VT	Y**^^[266]	Y[267]	Y[268]	Y[269]	Y[270]	N	Y[271]	Student is under 19.[272]	N
VA	Y[273]	Y[274]	N	Y*[275]	Y***[276]	N	N	N/A	N
WA	Y**[277]	Y[278]	N	Y*[279]	Y[280]	N	Y[281]	Student is 16–21.[282]	N[283]
WV	Y**[284]	Y[285]	N	Y[286]	Y[287]	N	N	N/A	N
WI	Y**[288]	Y[289]	N	Y*[290]	Y[291]	N	Y[292]	Student is over 15.	Y[293]
WY	Y**[294]	Y[295]	Y^[296]	Y*[297]	Y[298]	N	Y^[299]	Student is under 18.[300]	N
Total	49	39	18	47	47	17	38	30	22
% Y	98	78	36	94	94	34	76	80[301]	44

KEY

* Relevant relationship is one of the "whole or half blood."

^ Relevant relationship is one of trust or authority, as defined by state law.

^^ Law proscribing sex with a parent explicitly proscribes legal guardians.

** Law proscribing sex with a parent explicitly proscribes adoptive parents.

*** Law proscribes sex between aunts and nephews and between uncles and nieces.

Y Primary relevant law located under sexual assault and offenses of criminal code

Y Primary relevant law located under domestic/family relation or morals/decency offense of criminal code

Y Primary relevant law located under other subsection of the criminal code

[1] Code of Alabama §13A-13-3.

[2] Code of Alabama §13A-13-3; as long as the stepparent is married to the victim's parent at the time of the offense.

[3] Code of Alabama §13A-13-3.

[4] Code of Alabama §13A-13-3.

[5] Code of Alabama §§13A-6-80, 13A-6-82.

[6] Alaska Statute §§11.41.434, 11.41.450. Incest statute applies to persons age 18 or older.

[7] Alaska Statute §§11.41.434.

[8] Alaska Statute §§11.41.434.

[9] Alaska Statute §11.41.450. Incest statute applies to persons age 18 or older.

[10] Alaska Statute §11.41.450. Incest statute applies to persons age 18 or older.

[11] Alaska Statute §§11.41.434.

[12] Alaska Statutes §§11.41.410, 11.41.420, 11.41.470. This statute applies to conduct that occurs during the course of treatment and when the victim is unaware that sexual activity is occurring. Sex is therefore not categorically proscribed in such patient-doctor relationships.

[13] Arizona Revised Statutes §§13-3608, 25-101. Incest statute applies to persons age 18 or older.

[14] Arizona Revised Statutes §13-1405; if victim is a minor. Section of law specifically regarding relationships of trust applies to victims at least 15, but less than 18.

[15] Arizona Revised Statutes §13-1405; if victim is a minor. Section of law specifically regarding relationships of trust applies to victims at least 15, but less than 18.

[16] Arizona Revised Statutes §§13-3608, 15-101. Incest statute applies to persons age 18 or older.

[17] Arizona Revised Statutes §§13-3608, 15-101. Incest statute applies to persons age 18 or older.

[18] Arizona Revised Statutes §13-1405. Section of law specifically regarding relationships of trust applies to victims at least 15, but less than 18.

[19] Arizona Revised Statutes §13-1418.

[20] Arkansas Code §§5-26-202, 5-14-101. Incest statute applies to persons age 16 or older.

[21] Arkansas Code §§5-26-202, 5-14-101. Incest statute applies to persons age 16 or older.

[22] Arkansas Code §§5-14-124, 5-14-101, if the victim is a minor. These statutes proscribe those in positions of power from leveraging their authority to procure sex with the victim. Sex is therefore not categorically proscribed in such patient-actor relationships.

[23] Arkansas Code §§5-26-202, 5-14-101. Incest statute applies to persons age 16 or older.

[24] Arkansas Code §§5-26-202, 5-14-101. Incest statute applies to persons age 16 or older.

[25] Arkansas Code §§5-14-110, 5-14-124.

[26] California Penal Code §285, Family Code §§2200–2201. Incest statute applies to persons age 14 or older.

[27] California Penal Code §285, Family Code §§2200–2201. Incest statute applies to persons age 14 or older.

[28] California Penal Code §285, Family Code §§2200–2201. Incest statute applies to persons age 14 or older.

[29] California Penal Code §285, Family Code §§2200–2201. Incest statute applies to persons age 14 or older.

[30] Colorado Criminal Code §18-6-301. Incest statute applies to persons age 21 or older.

[31] Colorado Criminal Code §18-6-301. Incest statute applies to persons age 21 or older.

[32] Colorado Criminal Code §18-3-405.3; if victim is a minor.

[33] Colorado Criminal Code §18-6-301. Incest statute applies to persons age 21 or older.

[34] Colorado Criminal Code §18-6-301. Incest statute applies to persons age 21 or older.

[35] Colorado Criminal Code §18-3-405.3.

[36] Colorado Criminal Code §18-3-405.5.

[37] Connecticut General Statutes §53a-71a. Law stipulates that the perpetrator "is such person's [the victim's] guardian or otherwise responsible for the general supervision of such person's welfare."

[38] Connecticut General Statutes §53a-71a.

[39] Connecticut General Statutes §§53a-71, 53a-65.

[40] Connecticut General Statutes §§53a-71, 53a-65, if the victim is "a patient or former patient of the actor and the sexual intercourse occurs by means of therapeutic deception." Sex is therefore not categorically proscribed in such patient-actor relationships.

[41] Delaware Criminal Code §766.

[42] Delaware Criminal Code §766.

[43] Delaware Criminal Codes §§778, 761; if the victim is a minor.

[44] Delaware Criminal Code §766.

[45] Delaware Criminal Code §766.

[46] Delaware Criminal Code §§778, 761.

[47] Delaware Criminal Code §§778, 761, if the victim is a minor. Delaware Criminal Code §761 applies also to therapeutic deception, but sex is not categorically proscribed in such patient-doctor relationships.

[48] Florida Statutes §826.04.

[49] Florida Statutes §794.011; if the victim is a minor.

[50] Florida Statutes §826.04.

[51] Florida Statutes §826.04.

[52] Florida Statutes §826.04.

[53] Florida Statutes §794.011; if the victim is a minor.

[54] Florida Statutes §491.0112.

[55] Georgia Code §16-6-22.

[56] Georgia Code §16-6-22.

[57] Georgia Code §16-6-22.

[58] Georgia Code §16-6-22.

[59] Georgia Code §16-6-22.

[60] Georgia Code §16-6-5.1.

[61] Georgia Code §16-6-5.1; if the victim is someone "who the actor knew or should have known is the subject of the actor's actual or purported treatment or counseling or the actor uses the treatment or counseling relationship to facilitate sexual contact between the actor and such individual."

[62] Hawaii Revised Statutes §§707-741, 572-1.

[63] Hawaii Revised Statutes §§707-741, 572-1.

[64] Hawaii Revised Statutes §§707-741, 572-1.

[65] Hawaii Revised Statutes §§707-741, 572-1.

[66] Hawaii Revised Statutes §§707-731, 707-732, 707-733. The actor must be "contemporaneously acting in a professional capacity to instruct, advise, or supervise the minor."

[67] Hawaii Revised Statutes §§707-731, 707-732, 707-733. The actor must be "contemporaneously acting in a professional capacity to instruct, advise, or supervise the minor."

[68] Idaho Code §§18-6602, 32-205.

[69] Idaho Code §§18-6602, 32-205.

[70] Idaho Code §§18-6602, 32-205.

[71] Idaho Code §§18-6602, 32-205.

[72] Idaho Code §§18-919.

[73] Illinois Criminal Statutes §§5/11-11, 5/11-0.1, 5/11-1.20. Incest statute applies to persons age 18 or older, but sexual assault statute has no age specifications.

[74] Illinois Criminal Statutes §§5/11-11, 5/11-0.1, 5/11-1.20. Incest statute applies to persons age 18 or older, but sexual assault statute has no age specifications.

[75] Illinois Criminal Statutes §5/11-1.20. Law regarding relationships of trust or authority applies to victims at least 13 but less than 18.

[76] Illinois Criminal Statutes §§5/11-11, 5/11-0.1, 5/11-1.20. Incest statute applies to persons age 18 or older, but sexual assault statute has no age specifications.

[77] Illinois Criminal Statutes §§5/11-11, 5/11-0.1, 5/11-1.20. Incest statute applies to persons age 18 or older, but sexual assault statute has no age specifications.

[78] Illinois Criminal Statutes §§5/11-11, 5/11-0.1, 5/11-1.20. Incest statute applies to persons age 18 or older, but sexual assault statute has no age specifications.

[79] Illinois Criminal Statute §5/11-1.20. Law regarding relationships of trust or authority applies to victims at least 13 but less than 18.

[80] Illinois Criminal Statute §5/11-1.20. Law regarding relationships of trust or authority applies to victims at least 13 but less than 18.

[81] Indiana Code §35-46-1-3. Incest statute applies to persons age 18 or older.

[82] Indiana Code §35-46-1-3. Incest statute applies to persons age 18 or older.

[83] Indiana Code §35-46-1-3. Incest statute applies to persons age 18 or older.

[84] Iowa Code §§726.2, 702.5. Incest statute applies to persons age 14 or older.

[85] Iowa Code §709.4(3b); if the victim is 14–15.

[86] Iowa Code §709.4(3a/3c); if the victim is 14–15.

[87] Iowa Code §§726.2, 702.5. Incest statute applies to persons age 14 or older.

[88] Iowa Code §§726.2, 702.5. Incest statute applies to persons age 14 or older.

[89] Iowa Code §§726.2, 702.5. Incest statute applies to persons age 14 or older.

[90] Iowa Code §709.15.

[91] Student and teacher must have been attending the same primary or secondary school within 30 days of the alleged conduct.

[92] Iowa Code §709.15.

[93] Kansas Statutes §21-5604. Incest statute applies to persons age 18 or older. Aggravated incest statute applies to persons at least age 16 but under 18.

[94] Kansas Statutes §21-5604. Incest statute applies to persons age 18 or older. Aggravated incest statute applies to persons at least age 16 but under 18.

[95] Kansas Statutes §21-5604. Incest statute applies to persons age 18 or older. Aggravated incest statute applies to persons at least age 16 but under 18.

[96] Kansas Statutes §21-5604. Incest statute applies to persons age 18 or older. Aggravated incest statute applies to persons at least age 16 but under 18.

[97] Kansas Statutes §21-5512.

[98] Kansas Statutes §21-5503 proscribes "sexual intercourse with a victim when the victim's consent was obtained through a knowing misrepresentation made by the offender that the sexual intercourse was a medically or therapeutically necessary procedure." Sex is therefore not categorically proscribed in such patient-actor relationships.

[99] Kentucky Revised Statutes §530.020.

[100] Kentucky Revised Statutes §530.020.

[101] Kentucky Revised Statutes §§510.060, 532.045; if the victim is a minor.

[102] Kentucky Revised Statutes §530.020.

[103] Kentucky Revised Statutes §530.020.

[104] Kentucky Revised Statutes §§510.060, 532.045.

[105] Kentucky Revised Statutes §§510.060, 532.045; if the victim is a minor.

[106] Louisiana Revised Statutes §14:89.

[107] Louisiana Revised Statutes §14:89.1; if the victim is a minor.

[108] Louisiana Revised Statutes §14:89.

[109] Louisiana Revised Statutes §14:89.

[110] Louisiana Revised Statutes §14:81.4.

[111] The age difference must be more than four years; and the perpetrator must be assigned, employed, or working in the same school as the victim.

[112] Maine Statutes §556. Incest statute applies to persons age 18 or older.

[113] Maine Statutes §253; if the victim is a minor.

[114] Maine Statutes §253; if the victim is a minor and if the actor is "responsible for the long-term care or welfare of the child."

[115] Maine Statutes §556. Incest statute applies to persons age 18 or older.

[116] Maine Statutes §556. Incest statute applies to persons age 18 or older.

[117] Maine Statutes §253.

[118] Maine Statutes §253.

[119] Maryland Criminal Code §3-323; Maryland Family Code §2-202. The law criminalizes vaginal intercourse between such persons.

[120] Maryland Criminal Code §3-323; Maryland Family Code §2-202. The law criminalizes vaginal intercourse between such persons.

[121] Maryland Criminal Code §3-323, Maryland Family Code §2-202. The law criminalizes vaginal intercourse between such persons.

[122] Maryland Criminal Code §3-323, Maryland Family Code §2-202. The law criminalizes vaginal intercourse between such persons.

[123] Maryland Criminal Code §3-308.

[124] The perpetrator must be over 20.

[125] Massachusetts General Laws, Chapter 272 §17, Chapter 207 §1.

[126] Massachusetts General Laws, Chapter 272 §17, Chapter 207 §1.

[127] Massachusetts General Laws, Chapter 272 §17, Chapter 207 §1.

[128] Massachusetts General Laws, Chapter 265 §265-23A, Chapter 119 §21.

[129] Massachusetts General Laws, Chapter 265 §265-23A, Chapter 119 §21; if the victim is under 16.

[130] Michigan Penal Code §750.520e.

[131] Michigan Penal Code §750.520b; if victim is 13–15.

[132] Michigan Penal Code §750.520b if victim is 13–15.

[133] Michigan Penal Code §750.520e.

[134] Michigan Penal Code §750.520e.

[135] Michigan Penal Code §750.520b; if victim is 13–15.

[136] Michigan Penal Code §750.520b & e; if victim is 13–15 or 16–18, respectively.

[137] 2nd degree sexual assault if victim is 13–15; 3rd/4th degree sexual assault if victim is 16–17.

[138] Michigan Penal Code §750.520e.

[139] Minnesota Statutes §609.365.

[140] Minnesota Statutes §609.345. "Significant relationship" includes stepparents. Law regarding significant relationships applies to victims at least 16 but less than 18.

[141] Minnesota Statutes §609.345. Law specifically regarding relationships of trust or authority applies to victims at least 13 but less than 18. If the victim is at least 16, but less than 18, the "position of authority" may not be invoked unless the perpetrator is more than 48 months older.

[142] Minnesota Statutes §609.365.

[143] Minnesota Statutes §609.365.

[144] Minnesota Statutes §§609.345, 609.341. "Significant relationship" includes nonbiological aunts and uncles. Law regarding significant relationships applies to victims at least 16 but less than 18.

[145] Minnesota Statutes §§609.343, 609.344; if victim is 13–15 or 16–17, respectively.

[146] Minnesota Statutes §609.344.

[147] Mississippi Code §§97-29-27, 93-1-1.

[148] Mississippi Code §§97-29-27, 93-1-1.

[149] Mississippi Code §97-5-41; if the actor is cohabiting and if the victim is over 14 and under 18.

[150] Mississippi Code §§97-29-27, 93-1-1.

[151] Mississippi Code §97-29-27.

[152] Mississippi Code §97-5-24.

[153] Mississippi Code §97-5-23; if the victim is a minor.

[154] Missouri Revised Statutes §568.020.

[155] Missouri Revised Statutes §568.020; as long as stepparent is married to the victim's parent at the time of the offense.

[156] Missouri Revised Statutes §568.020.

[157] Missouri Revised Statutes §568.020.

[158] Missouri Revised Statutes §566.086.

[159] Student must be in grades K–12.

[160] Montana Code §45-5-507.

[161] Montana Code §45-5-507. "Consent is a defense under this section to incest with or upon a stepson or stepdaughter, but consent is ineffective if the victim is less than 18 years old."

[162] Montana Code §45-5-507.

[163] Montana Code §45-5-507.

[164] Nebraska Code §§28-702, 28-703.

[165] Nebraska Code §§28-702, 28-703; if the victim is under 19.

[166] Nebraska Codes §§28-702, 28-703.

[167] Nebraska Codes §§28-702, 28-703.

[168] Nebraska Codes §§28-702, 28-703.

[169] Nevada Revised Statutes §§201.180, 122.025.

[170] Nevada Revised Statutes §§201.180, 122.025.

[171] Nevada Revised Statutes §§201.180, 122.025.

[172] Nevada Revised Statutes §§201.540, 201.550.

[173] The teacher must be 21 or older.

[174] New Hampshire Revised Statutes §§639-2, 53a-71. New Hampshire Revised Statutes §53a-71 covers legal guardian relationships.

[175] New Hampshire Revised Statutes §639-2.

[176] New Hampshire Revised Statutes §632-A:2. Section of law regarding relationships of authority applies to victims at least 13 but less than 18 and proscribes those in positions of power from leveraging their authority to procure sex with the victim. Sex is therefore not categorically proscribed in such patient-actor relationships. However, the law also proscribes sex between minors at least 13 but less than 16 and perpetrators who are members of the "same household."

[177] New Hampshire Revised Statutes §639-2.

[178] New Hampshire Revised Statutes §639-2.

[179] New Hampshire Revised Statutes §632-A:2. Law proscribes those in positions of power from leveraging their authority to procure sex with the victim. Sex is therefore not categorically proscribed in such patient-actor relationships.

[180] New Hampshire Revised Statutes §632-A:2.

[181] New Jersey Statutes §2C:14-2; if the victim is a minor.

[182] New Jersey Statutes §2C:14-2; if the victim is a minor.

[183] New Jersey Statutes §2C:14-2; if the victim is a minor.

[184] New Jersey Statutes §2C:14-2; if the victim is a minor.

[185] New Jersey Statutes §2C:14-2; if the victim is a minor.

[186] New Jersey Statutes §2C:14-2; if the victim is a minor.

[187] Aggravated sexual assault if student is 13–15; sexual assault if student is 16–17. Students under 13 are covered by age of consent statutes.

[188] New Mexico Statutes §30-10-3.

[189] New Mexico Statutes §30-10-3.

[190] New Mexico Statutes §30-10-3.

[191] New Mexico Statutes §30-9-13; if the victim is a minor. Section of law specifically regarding relationships of authority applies to victims at least 13 but less than 19 and proscribes those in positions of power from leveraging their authority to procure sex with the victim. Sex is therefore not categorically proscribed in such patient-actor relationships.

[192] The teacher must be at least 18 and at least 4 years older than the victim.

[193] New Mexico Statutes §§30-9-10, 30-9-11.

[194] New York Penal Law §255.25.

[195] New York Penal Law §255.25.

[196] New York Penal Law §255.25.

[197] New York Penal Law §255.25.

[198] New York Penal Law §255.25.

[199] New York Penal Law §130.05. "The act of sexual conduct [must occur] ... during a treatment session, consultation, interview, or examination." Sex is therefore not categorically proscribed in such patient-doctor relationships.

[200] North Carolina General Statutes §§14-178, 14-27.

[201] North Carolina General Statutes §14-178.

[202] North Carolina General Statutes §14-27.31. This statute refers to "a Defendant who has assumed the position of a parent in the home of a minor victim."

[203] North Carolina General Statutes §14-178.

[204] North Carolina General Statutes §14-178.

[205] North Carolina General Statutes §14-178.

[206] North Carolina General Statutes §14-27.32.

[207] If the teacher is 4 or more years older than the student, the crime is a Class G felony; if the teacher is less than 4 years older than the student, the crime is a Class I felony.

[208] North Dakota Century Code §§12.1-20-07, 12.1-20-11, 14-03-03.

[209] North Dakota Century Code §12.1-20-07.

[210] North Dakota Century Code §§12.1-20-11, 14-03-03.

[211] North Dakota Century Code §§12.1-20-11, 14-03-03.

[212] North Dakota Century Code §12.1-20-07. Law stipulates that the perpetrator is "responsible for general supervision of the other person's welfare."

[213] North Dakota Century Code §12.1-20-06.1.

[214] Ohio Revised Code §2907.03.

[215] Ohio Revised Code §2907.03.

[216] Ohio Revised Code §2907.03.

[217] Ohio Revised Code §2907.03. The perpetrator must induce "the other person to submit by falsely representing to the other person that the sexual conduct is necessary for mental health treatment purposes." Sex is therefore not categorically proscribed in such patient-doctor relationships.

[218] 21 Oklahoma Statutes §885; 43 Oklahoma Statutes §2.

[219] 21 Oklahoma Statutes §885; 43 Oklahoma Statutes §2.

[220] 21 Oklahoma Statutes §885; 43 Oklahoma Statutes §2.

[221] 21 Oklahoma Statutes §885; 43 Oklahoma Statutes §2.

[222] Oregon Revised Statutes §§163.525, 163.375.

[223] Oregon Revised Statutes §§163.525, 163.375.

[224] Oregon Revised Statutes §163.525.

[225] Pennsylvania Consolidated Statutes §18-4302.

[226] Pennsylvania Consolidated Statutes §18-4302.

[227] Pennsylvania Consolidated Statutes §18-4302.

[228] Pennsylvania Consolidated Statutes §18-3124.2.

[229] In Rhode Island, incestuous marriages are prohibited but not incestuous sex.

[230] South Carolina Code §§16-15-20, 16-3-655 (B2). South Carolina Code §16-3-655 (B2) covers legal guardians if the victim is 14–15. The language of South Carolina Code §16-15-20 is gendered, reading in part that "carnal intercourse" is proscribed for "[a] man with his mother, grandmother, daughter, granddaughter, stepmother, sister, grandfather's wife, son's wife, grandson's wife, wife's mother, wife's grandmother, wife's daughter, wife's granddaughter, brother's daughter, sister's daughter, father's sister or mother's sister" and including similar language for a woman with her father, etc.

[231] South Carolina Code §§16-15-20, 16-3-655 (B2).

232 South Carolina Code §§16-15-20, 16-3-655 (B2).

233 South Carolina Code §§16-15-20, 16-3-655 (B2).

234 South Carolina Code §16-3-655 (B2). Victim must be 14–15 "and the actor [. . .] in a position of familial, custodial, or official authority to coerce the victim to submit or is older than the victim. However, a person may not be convicted of a violation of the provisions of this item if he is eighteen years of age or less when he engages in consensual sexual conduct with another person who is at least fourteen years of age."

235 South Carolina Code §16-3-755.

236 Felony if student is 16 or 17 and there was no aggravated coercion or aggravated force; misdemeanor if student is 18 or older and the same conditions applied. Felony if student 18 or older and perpetrator has direct supervisory authority over the student.

237 South Dakota Codified Law §§22-22A-2, 22-22A-3, 25-1-6.

238 South Dakota Codified Law §22-22A-3; if the victim is a minor.

239 South Dakota Codified Law §§22-22A-2, 22-22A-3, 25-1-6.

240 South Dakota Codified Law §§22-22A-2, 22-22A-3, 25-1-6.

241 South Dakota Codified Law §§22-22A-2, 22-22A-3, 25-1-6.

242 South Dakota Codified Law §§22-22-27, 22-22-28, 22-22-29. Victim must be "a patient who is emotionally dependent on the psychotherapist at the time of contact."

243 Tennessee Code §§39-15-302, 39-13-509. Tennessee Code §39-13-509 covers legal guardian relationships if victim is 13–17 and the guardian is at least 4 years older.

244 Tennessee Code §39-15-302.

245 Tennessee Code §39-15-302.

246 Tennessee Code §39-15-302.

247 Tennessee Code §39-15-302.

248 Tennessee Code §§39-13-509, 39-13-532. These statutes proscribe those in positions of power from leveraging their authority to procure sex with the victim.

249 The teacher must be at least 4 years older than the student.

250 Texas Penal Code §25.02.

251 Texas Penal Code §25.02.

252 Texas Penal Code §25.02.

253 Texas Penal Code §25.02.

254 Texas Penal Code §25.02.

255 Texas Penal Code §21.12.

256 Texas Penal Code §22.011. Mental health care provider must cause the victim "to submit or participate by exploiting the other person's emotional dependency on the actor."

257 Utah Code §§76-7-102, 76-5-406.10, 76-5-404.1. Utah Code §76-5-404.1 covers legal guardian relationships.

258 Utah Code §§76-7-102, 76-5-406.10; as long as stepparent is married to the victim's parent at the time of the offense.

259 Utah Code §§76-5-404.1, 76-5-406.10; if the victim is a minor.

260 Utah Code §76-7-102.

261 Utah Code §76-7-102.

262 Utah Code §76-5-404.1.

263 Utah Code §76-5-404.1.

264 The teacher must be at least 18 years old.

265 Utah Code §§76-5-404.1, 76-5-406, if the victim is a minor. Utah Code §76-5-406 covers cases in which the act "is committed under the guise of providing professional diagnosis, counseling, or treatment, and at the time of the act the victim reasonably believed that the act was for medically or professionally appropriate diagnosis, counseling, or treatment to the extent that resistance by the victim could not reasonably be expected to have been manifested." Sex is therefore not categorically proscribed in such patient-doctor relationships.

266 13 Vermont Statutes §§205, 3252; 15 Vermont Statute §511. 13 Vermont Statutes §3252 covers legal guardian relationships if the victim is a minor.

267 13 Vermont Statutes §§205, 3252; 15 Vermont Statutes §511.

268 13 Vermont Statutes §3252; if "the actor is at least 18 years of age, resides in the victim's household, and serves in a parental role with respect to the victim."

269 13 Vermont Statutes §205; 15 Vermont Statutes §511.

270 13 Vermont Statutes §205; 15 Vermont Statutes §511.

271 13 Vermont Statutes §3258.

[272] Teacher must be at least 48 months older than the student.

[273] Virginia Code §§18.2-366, 20-38.1. Virginia Code §20-38.1 likely extends the statute to cover relationships by adoption. The language of Virginia Code §18.2-366 is gendered, reading in part, "Any person who commits adultery or fornication with his daughter or granddaughter, or with her son or grandson, or her father or his mother, shall be guilty of a Class 5 felony."

[274] Virginia Code §18.2-366.

[275] Virginia Code §§18.2-366, 20-38.1.

[276] Virginia Code §§18.2-366, 20-38.1.

[277] Revised Code of Washington §9A.64.020. This statute covers relationships by adoption if victim is under 18.

[278] Revised Code of Washington §9A.64.020, if victim is under 18.

[279] Revised Code of Washington §9A.64.020.

[280] Revised Code of Washington §9A.64.020.

[281] Revised Code of Washington §9A.44.093.

[282] If the student is "not married to the employee, if the employee is at least sixty months older than the student."

[283] Revised Code of Washington §§9A.44.050, 9A.44.100. Client must be unaware that the conduct is not "for the purpose of treatment," and sexual contact or intercourse must occur during a "treatment session, consultation, interview, or examination."

[284] West Virginia Code §61-8-12.

[285] West Virginia Code §61-8-12.

[286] West Virginia Code §61-8-12.

[287] West Virginia Code §61-8-12.

[288] Wisconsin Code §§944.06, 765.03, 948.06.

[289] Wisconsin Code §948.06; if the victim is a minor.

[290] Wisconsin Code §§944.06, 765.03.

[291] Wisconsin Code §§944.06, 765.03.

[292] Wisconsin Code §948.095.

[293] Wisconsin Code §940.22.

[294] Wyoming Statutes §§6-4-402, 6-2-314, 6-2-315. Wyoming Statutes §§6-2-314, 6-2-315 cover legal guardian relationships and minor victims.

[295] Wyoming Statutes §6-4-402.

[296] Wyoming Statutes §§6-2-301, 6-2-303. These statutes proscribe those in positions of power from leveraging their authority to procure sex with the victim. Sex is therefore not categorically proscribed in such patient-actor relationships.

[297] Wyoming Statutes §6-4-402.

[298] Wyoming Statutes §6-4-402.

[299] Wyoming Statutes §§6-2-314, 6-2-315, 6-2-316, 6-2-317.

[300] 1st or 2nd degree sexual assault if student is under 16 and teacher is 18 or older; 3rd or 4th degree sexual assault if student is 16–17 and at least 4 years younger than teacher, and the teacher is over 19.

[301] To capture the percentage of states with prohibitions on teacher-student relationships that also include age specifications, this percentage takes a denominator of 38, not 50.

Notes

1. *Oxford English Dictionary* (www.oed.com), s.v. "screw."

2. In the book's conclusion I discuss in further detail why, from a feminist sexual justice perspective, it may be more costly than beneficial to classify Aziz Ansari's alleged conduct with "Grace" as "sexual assault." See Way (2018).

3. Title IX of the Education Amendments of 1972, 20 USC §§1681–88 (2012): "No person in the United States shall, on the basis of sex, be excluded from participation in, be denied the benefits of, or be subjected to discrimination under any education program or activity receiving Federal financial assistance."

4. In spring 2016, ALI members rejected a proposal to redefine consent affirmatively in the sexual assault provisions of the Model Penal Code. See Rotunda (2016).

5. According to Yale University's sexual misconduct policy, "Sexual activity requires consent, which is defined as positive, unambiguous, and voluntary agreement to engage in specific sexual activity throughout a sexual encounter." "Sexual Misconduct Response," Yale University, http://smr.yale.edu/sexual-misconduct-policies-and-definitions.

6. The University of Wyoming brochure, titled "Where Is Your Line: Consent Is Sexy," is no longer in use and no longer available online. See note 15.

7. For the definition of consent in the sexual misconduct policy at the University of Wyoming, see "Sexual Misconduct Policies and Procedures Document for Faculty, Staff, and Students," September 2014, http://www.uwyo.edu/dos/sexualmisconduct/sexual%20misconduct%20policy.pdf; at Gordon College, see "Sexual Misconduct Policy," January 2018, http://www.gordon.edu/sexualmisconduct-policy; at Elon University, see "Consent, Coercion, and Incapacitation," http://elon.smartcatalog.co/en/2015–2016/Student-Handbook/Interpersonal-Violence-Including-Sexual-Violence/Consent-Coercion-and-Incapacitation; at Georgia

Southern University, see "Code of Student Conduct," 2018–2019, https://students
.georgiasouthern.edu/conduct/files/2018-2019-Code-of-Student-Conduct-
FINAL-1.pdf.

8. Email correspondence with Whitney Gregory, Assistant Dean of Students,
Elon University, July 25, 2017; email correspondence with Megan Selheim,
STOP Violence Program Coordinator, Dean of Students Office, University of
Wyoming, July 26, 2017; email correspondence with Diane Shertz, Equal
Opportunity and Title IX Staff Assistant, Georgia Southern University, August
3, 2017; email correspondence with Jennifer Jukanovich, Vice President for Student Life, Gordon College, August 11, 2017 (all correspondence in author's
possession). However, Vice President Jukanovich informed me that while the
college briefly (from October 2014 to May 2015) incorporated an expansively
affirmative definition of consent in its sexual misconduct policies, administrators have since revised the definition so that it now aligns with common affirmative consent standards at other colleges and universities. See note 7.

9. California Senate Bill No. 967 (2014), https://leginfo.legislature.ca.gov
/faces/billNavClient.xhtml?bill_id=201320140SB967.

10. Consent Is Sexy, http://www.consentissexy.net/poster-07/.

11. Consent Is Sexy, http://www.consentissexy.net/.

12. Poster 1, "Do You Get It?" Consent Is Sexy, http://www.consentissexy
.net/poster-01/.

13. That consent is a checkbox does not mean it is easily defined or interpreted. For discussion of the "factual," "legal," "prescriptive," "expressive,"
and "imputed" dimensions of consent, see generally Westen (2004).

14. The Consent Project, https://www.facebook.com/consentproject; Project
Consent, http://www.projectconsent.com; Yale CCE [Communication and Consent Educators] Program, http://cce.yalecollege.yale.edu/; Consent Is Sexy, http://
consentissexy.net; #Consentiseverything, http://www.consentiseverything.com/.

15. Email correspondence with Megan Selheim, STOP Violence Program
coordinator, Dean of Students Office, University of Wyoming, July 26, 2017 (in
author's possession).

16. Oxford English Dictionary, s.v. "screw."

17. State v. Grunke (2008).

18. State v. Fourtin (2012).

CHAPTER 1

1. I use BDSM and kink interchangeably throughout this chapter to connote
sexual practices and sexual communities that (a) are avowedly nonnormative
and (b) eroticize power exchange. As Margot Weiss (2011) explains, "BDSM is
of relatively recent (and, many suggest, Internet) coinage. It is an amalgamation
of three acronyms: B & D (bondage and discipline), D/s (domination/submis-
sion), and SM (sadomasochism)" (vii). The terms initialed by BDSM are not
much more illuminating than the initials themselves but at least map out the
erotic territory I am surveying.

2. Yet, extending insights from Butler (1982) and Weiss, Cruz argues that
consent can function as an alibi for smuggling violence and inequalities into sex

that consent ostensibly neutralizes (see also Weiss 2011, 221–22). Consent inflates the sovereignty of the sexual subject, privileging by disencumbering "choice" from its social (and therefore sexist and racist) coordinates (Cruz 2016, 44–49; see also Butler 1982, 172–73).

3. "Consent Counts Project Description," National Coalition for Sexual Freedom, https://www.ncsfreedom.org/key-programs/consent-counts-64083/consent-counts-44979.

4. For homophobia, see the statement of Lord Lowry: "Sado-masochistic homosexual activity cannot be regarded as conducive to the enhancement or enjoyment of family life or conducive to the welfare of society. A relaxation of the prohibitions in sections 20 and 47 can only encourage the practice of homo-sexual sado-masochism and the physical cruelty that it must involve (which can scarcely be regarded as a 'manly diversion') by withdrawing the legal penalty and giving the activity a judicial imprimatur" (R. v. Brown 1994, 255).

For AIDS panic, see Lord Templeman's opinion: "Prosecuting counsel informed the trial judge [. . .] that although the appellants had not contracted AIDS, two members of the group had died from AIDS and one other had contracted an HIV infection although not necessarily from the practices of the group. Some activities involved excrement. The assertion that the instruments employed by the sadists were clean and sterilized could not have removed the danger of infection, and the assertion that care was taken demonstrates the possibility of infection" (R. v. Brown 1993, 51; see also Khan 2014, 233).

5. Or as law professor Cheryl Hanna writes, "Just as hard cases make bad law, hard cases show us why the law is hard" (2001, 263).

6. In Gaspar, the Supreme Court of Rhode Island vacated Shane Gaspar's con-viction of sexual assault against Sally Smith (a pseudonym), holding certain wit-ness testimony in the trial court as prejudicial and therefore inadmissible. Note-worthy in this case, though, as opposed to other cases involving allegedly kinky sex, is that Gaspar was permitted to put up a (she-liked-it-rough) consent defense. Because the alleged conduct—fellatio, gagging, biting, inter alia—were juridically rendered "sexual," "the issue was more consent," as the on-duty sergeant reported.

Gaspar dramatizes the conflict for feminists and sex-positive legal scholars: had Gaspar been charged with assaulting, not sexually assaulting, Sally Smith, his conviction would not hinge on her consent. Yet disallowing a consent defense enables the targeting of sexual minorities and authorizes vindictive ex-partners.

Gaspar agrees with Smith about several of the activities that occurred on the evening of the encounter (e.g., biting and rough fellatio) but disagrees about whether or not Smith consented to them; however, Gaspar tellingly denies vagi-nally fisting Smith. Vaginal fisting would likely qualify simply as assault, not sexual assault, for which consent would not have been a defense. Thus, when sexual violence looks more like "sex," the defendant claims consent; when the sexual violence looks more like "violence," the defendant denies it outright. See R.I. Gen L §11–5-2 (2016). I thank Alexa Derman for elaborating this point.

7. The phrase is credited to david stein (n.d.), who agrees he is the likely author; it first appeared in a 1983 statement from the Gay Male S/M Activists (GMSMA). Stein's insightful retrospective essay on SSC is published in the

newsletter *VASM Scene* (September–October 2003), but I am citing a version available on stein's website, www.boybear.us.

8. The Model Penal Code defines "serious bodily injury" as "bodily injury which creates a substantial risk of death or which causes serious, permanent disfigurement, or protracted loss or impairment of the function of any bodily member or organ." Model Penal Code §210.0(3).

9. Thanks to Grace Paine.

10. The title of this section is adapted from Cheryl Hanna's "Sex is Not Sport: Consent and Violence in Criminal Law" (2001).

11. It seems to me that the Model Penal Code exemption is an irresponsible tautology. By bracketing out consent as a defense to serious injuries sustained during an "activity not forbidden by law," the MPC disavows its own influence in determining the very lawfulness of an activity. It is the exemption itself that—via statutory codification and judicial interpretation—then determines the unlawfulness of an activity, like kinky consensual sex.

12. But see the National Coalition for Sexual Freedom, https://www.ncsfreedom.org/; and the National Leather Association International, http://www.nla-international.com/home.html.

13. Lord Templeton opines, "There is a difference between violence which is incidental and violence which is inflicted for the indulgence of cruelty" (*R. v. Brown* 1994, 236). Templeton overlooks the fact that in contact sports, in contrast to BDSM, violence is sometimes inflicted *in order to remove a player from the game* (Almond 2014, 140–42). Of course, American football is not a point of comparison for the British lords, but boxing is. It is preposterous (or just normatively gendered; see Khan 2014, 232) that violence is construed as incidental to boxing (and football) yet elemental to kink (Kaplan 2014, 127–28).

Dennis Baker's Kantian criticism of kink (2009; 121) inclines him toward indicting boxing as consensual violence that should be criminalized. I am far more sympathetic toward banning boxing outright than banning kink outright; Baker takes the latter position, however immanently contradictory to his own arguments (120).

14. As Marx observed (2000 [1844], 118), "The effect of ugliness, its power of repulsion, is annulled by money."

15. That the NFL dropped it tax-exempt status seemed more calculated to placate critics than to substantively redistribute earnings (Pinsker 2015).

16. I take the idea of human doing and being in the world as an ethical benchmark of social and political institutions from Martha Nussbaum's capabilities approach (2001, 5; 2006, 73); although, as I intimate in the following section and make explicit elsewhere (Fischel and McKinney, forthcoming), I believe one can and should distinguish human doing and being from human dignity as a principle of justice.

17. However, youth football appears to be undergoing serious reform to address growing concerns for boys' health (Belson 2017).

18. Is such a proposition ableist? I do not think so, although it is avowedly normative. I have argued that human beings should not be unequivocally permitted to impair themselves or others in any possible way simply and summarily by virtue of their (imagined) consent. And I will argue, in the remainder of

this chapter, that doing-and being in the world (see note 16) is a more defensible ethical barometer for consensual human conduct than either degrees of physical injury or of violations of dignity.

The proposition does not claim to govern, for example, a deaf person who forgoes a (highly time-consuming) cochlear implant and whose life and relationships are enriched and facilitated by deaf culture, communication, and community (Bauman and Murray 2010; see also Mauldin 2016). Yet the proposition does imply that we should be a degree more concerned about a hearing person who elects to become deaf. At the very least, we should ask whether the objective and subjective benefits outweigh the costs of diminishment. They might (and analogies to transgender identification and gender-affirming medical procedures are instructive; see Baril 2015). All things considered, the costs of erotic cannibalism, and more important, the costs of American football, are too high. I thank an anonymous reader for UC Press for raising the ableism question.

19. On the limited influence of the feminist-led movement of the 1970s and 1980s to reform the policing, prosecuting, and convicting of sexual assault, see Schulhofer (1998); Caringella (2009); and Corrigan (2013).

20. For Bergelson, a consent defense may be permissible for serious physical injury incurred during sexual activity provided the injury neither sets back the welfare interests of the submissive nor violates his or her dignity (2007, 220). I discuss the dignity prong of Bergelson's proposal later in this section.

Unlike Bergelson and Egan, Haley (2015) would permit a consent defense to serious bodily injury sustained during sexual activity, but with "a presumption of nonconsent combined with a high burden of proof" (654).

21. The notion of corporanormativity may be seen as a self-contradiction, given the ink spilt by critical theorists of all stripes who lament the degradation of the body in the Western philosophical canon, or who aim to dissolve mind-body dualism altogether. Iris Young (2005), for example, in her accounting of menstruation as associated with impurity and abjection, describes our culture as "somatophobic" (108). Can a culture be both corporanormative and somatophobic? Perhaps both societal disgust at (gendered) bodily processes and the legal indexing of seriousness with physicality hyperbolize corporeality.

22. Haley's protestations that the Nebraska Supreme Court "explicitly refused to extend *Lawrence* to cases involving BDSM" (2015, 646) and that "the jury did not have the opportunity to consider whether the activities were consensual" (638) are overstated. The Court refused to extend *Lawrence* to cases involving assault specifically, not BDSM generally. And the jury did have the opportunity consider whether the sex between Van and J.C.G. was consensual, and determined it was not.

23. Under law professor Jed Rubenfeld's proposed solution to rape law (see chapter 3), force would include "not only an assault of any kind, but physical restraint of any kind [like] locking the victim up." (2013b, 389).

24. Solitary confinement undoubtedly impacts the body too (Guenther 2013), and insofar as obstructions to human flourishing always also impact the bodies of humans so affected, the binary I draw between nth-degree physical injury and impediments to human flourishing—to autonomy and access—is necessarily an analytic one. One might object that my notion of corporanormativity rests on a

simplistic, dualistic, and tiresomely modern account of the human body as defined and isolable by the physical boundaries of a particular human (Ramachandran 2009, 10–13; Frost 2016, 119–25; Solomon 2016, 9). I would counter that it is the simplistic, dualistic, modern concept of the body adopted by the Model Penal Code, assault law, and many legal critics that I am in fact criticizing. I hope to draw our attention to other modes of injury and impediment that may or may not be helpfully reconstructed as corporeal, once "corporeal" is more expansively imagined. I thank Ann Cahill for helping me clarify this point.

25. The Nebraska Supreme Court did not address Van's constitutional attack on the state's assault statutes since Van had not challenged the laws in the district court.

26. Egan might reply that her exemption is specific to kink scenes and does not cross over to medical practices principled by patient nonmaleficence and beneficence. And while her clarification (2007, 164on199) that the "seriousness" of serious physical injury is scaled to capability diminishment and function impairment, the inclusion of "disfigurement" would, I think, render unlawful kink practices like scarification and branding.

27. Thus, Bergelson also sees her project as distancing itself from what I am calling corporanormativity. Hanna (2001) raises dignity as a limit to consent's moral force, but the reference is gestural: "The social goals of promoting human dignity are better served by limiting, not extending, the doctrine of violent consent" (248).

28. Bergelson argues that the difference between killing Brandes, a competent adult with a future worth having, and killing a terminally ill Kevorkian patient with no prospect of a meaningful future is a difference of dignity: killing Brandes is undignified, while killing the terminally ill patient is dignified (226). I think this is not right. The morally critical issue is not dignity (is the taking of a life really ever dignified?) but, again, interest. Brandes, presumably, has some welfare or long-term interests that a liberal democratic state has a defensible claim in protecting and promoting. The terminally ill patient has no such interests; or if he or she does, those welfare interests may be reasonably counterbalanced against a subjective interest in a peaceful end of life with minimal suffering.

29. From this perspective, and to take an analytic recess from BDSM, the fraternity initiate need not argue that his consent to hazing was polluted by "peer pressure"; nor are the physical injuries of hazing ipso facto necessarily the most serious affront to the hazed. In fact, "extreme sleep deprivation," however consented to, brought on by late-night hazing rituals, seems far more egregious, even if not as undignified, as sitting in a garbage can of human excrement. The former may affect the long-term health and "academic performance" of the initiate; the latter is just smelly (Weinberg 2016, 102–3).

30. Baker (2009) is willing to entertain the possibility that the dignity violation of an HIV-negative woman having unprotected sex with an HIV-positive man might be worth the trade-off of a child (114). This is reproductive futurism to a nearly comical extreme (Edelman 2004).

31. In Bauer's (2014) ethnographic investigation, a top refusing to heed the enthusiastic if self-destructive requests of a novice bottom registers as an example of "working," as opposed to "pseudo," consent (89). Refusing the ill-

advised demands of an excited submissive may be ethically praiseworthy, but naming that refusal a form of consent seems peculiar if not contradictory.

32. "The objective of aftercare is to meet the post-scene needs of the bottom (and sometimes, but never only, of the top). Typically this involves caressing, stroking, cuddling with, or rocking the bottom. [. . .] It is also widely accepted that, because the bottom's judgment and functioning may be impaired to some degree, the top is even more responsible for the welfare of the bottom at this point" (Newmahr 2011, 76).

CHAPTER 2

1. Georgia Code §16-6-3.

2. While the court majority in *Fourtin* (2012), along with disability rights activists, chastised Connecticut state attorneys for not prosecuting Fourtin under a law proscribing sex with someone who is "mentally defective" rather than "physically helpless," it is far from clear that the state would have succeeded had it pursued the latter alternative. For further elaboration, see Fischel and O'Connell 2015, 479.

3. Connecticut General Statutes §53a-191; §53a-71; see also appendix A, this volume. The state's incest laws proscribe marriage, not sex, across specified relations.

4. For all three states, we defined appellate cases as "sexual assault" cases if the defendant had been tried for a sexual assault offense in a lower court and was appealing an element of the sexual assault conviction.

5. For Wisconsin, we sampled every fourth case from a LexisNexis search of appellate sexual assault cases decided between January 1, 2010, and September 14, 2016. For Connecticut, we coded all cases from a LexisNexis search of appellate sexual assault cases decided between January 1, 2010, and September 18, 2016. For Michigan, we sampled and coded every seventh case from a LexisNexis search of appellate sexual assault cases decided between January 1, 2010, and September 14, 2016. Our search terms were the words or phrases each respective state uses to codify sexual assault (e.g., rape, *sexual assault,* or *criminal sexual conduct*).

6. Michigan Penal Code §750.520b; see also appendix A, this volume; Buchhandler-Raphael 2011, 224–25.

7. Connecticut General Statutes §§53a-70-72. Although Connecticut defines fourth-degree sexual assault as, in part, "sexual contact without [. . .] consent," the charge is rarely used by the state, usually for less serious crimes like groping, according to a state attorney (Connecticut General Statutes §53a-73a(a)(2); author interview with Susann E. Gill, Supervisory Assistant State's Attorney, Connecticut State's Attorney's Office, October 16, 2014).

8. Wisconsin Statutes §940.225(4).

9. Sex was unspecified for 30 percent of victims in the Wisconsin appellate sexual assault cases. Based on the victim sex ratio from the other cases, we can assume most such victims are female.

10. Regarding "his victim(s)": In the 200 sexual assault cases surveyed, only 1 alleged perpetrator was a woman. See appendix A. Roughly 10 percent of the

sampled cases from Wisconsin involved multiple victims. One victim was assumed if the number of victims was not specified. If there were multiple victims, but the specific number was unreported, two victims were assumed. If there were more than two victims, but the specific number was unreported, three victims were assumed.

11. Five perpetrator-victim relationships from the Wisconsin cases involved a "family friend." In twenty-eight of the specified relationships, the defendant was a personal acquaintance or person otherwise known to the victim. See appendix A.

12. Sex was unspecified for 12 percent of victims in the Connecticut appellate sexual assault cases. Based on the victim-sex ratio from the other cases, we can assume most such victims are female. In the 195 sexual assault cases surveyed, only one alleged perpetrator was a woman. There were multiple victims in just over 10 percent of sampled cases from Connecticut, and multiple victims were coded as they were with Wisconsin cases (see note 10). In addition to the 80 relationships in these cases entailing explicitly vertical status differences, 12 involved relationships with family friends, and 41 involved relationships with a perpetrator who was a personal acquaintance or was otherwise known to the victim. See appendix A.

13. Sex was unspecified for 10 percent of victims in the Michigan appellate sexual assault cases. Based on the victim-sex ratio from the other cases, we can assume most such victims are female. In the 200 sexual assault cases surveyed, only two alleged perpetrators were women. There were multiple victims in 10 percent of sampled cases from Michigan, and multiple victims were coded as they were with Wisconsin cases (see note 10). In addition to the 67 relationships in these cases entailing explicitly vertical status differences, 8 involved relationships with family friends, and 29 involved relationships with a perpetrator who was a personal acquaintance or was otherwise known to the victim. See appendix A.

14. For example, the age of consent in Arkansas is sixteen (with an age span provision and a marriage exemption), but sexual contact between school employees and students is proscribed if the student is under eighteen; Arkansas Code §514–103(A); § 5–14–125(a)(4)(A)(3). See appendix A.

15. Interestingly, Michigan categorically proscribes sex between students under eighteen and teachers and other school staff, but does not categorically proscribe sex between a seventeen-year-old and her mother's boyfriend. Michigan Penal Code §750.520e(1)(f)(i); §750.520b(1)(b)(iii–iv). See appendix A.

16. Mississippi Code §97–5–41; North Carolina Statutes §14–27.31; see appendix A.

17. Virginia and South Carolina, too, gender-specify sex across other incestuous relations (for example, between father and daughter). Virginia Code §18.2–366(B); South Carolina Code §16–15–20(1–2). See appendix A.

18. Delaware and Kentucky, for example, specify age requirements in their proscriptions of sex between health professionals and their patients. Delaware Criminal Code § 761(e)(4); § 778; Kentucky Revised Statutes § 510.060; § 532.045(1)(a). See appendix A.

19. *Lawrence* does not, and should not, authorize sexual activity that is life ending or that seriously or permanently impedes human capabilities. See chapter 1.

20. Michigan Penal Code §750.520b; Florida Statutes 826.04.

21. Criminal Code RSC 1985, c. C-46, s. 153(1–2), s. 153.1(1).

22. Criminal Code RSC. 1985, c. C-46, s. 273.1(1).

23. Criminal Code RSC. 1985, c. C-46, s. 155(1).

24. Criminal Code RSC. 1985, c. C-46, s. 159(1).

25. Sexual Offences Act, 2003, c. 42, s. 16–17, s. 25, s. 27.

26. The subheading for this section (and the concerns it telegraphs) can also be found in Collier 2014; Dreisinger 2016; Talvi 2007; and Zakaria 2012.

27. While Buchhandler-Raphael's examples of sexual abuse of power by superordinates within vertical relationships tend to entail the superordinate threatening to make the subordinate less well off, the subjective elements in her accounting of abuse of power—"placing victims in *fear* of professional and economic harm" (2011, 204; emphasis added); a complainant's *belief* that no alternative choices were available (191; emphasis added)—could expand the law's capture considerably.

Given that Buchhandler-Raphael's discussion of sex across age differences involves only instances in which the older, superordinate person explicitly leverages his authority (217–19, 224–25), it may be too speculative to say she would not criminalize such sex absent explicit leveraging.

28. *Status* and *power*, though, are not synonyms. Power inequality can in no simple way be inferred from status difference, and sex and desire scramble any orderly accounting of who is dependent upon whom, or who is vulnerable. Commenting on a soured relationship between a female philosophy graduate student and male philosophy professor, Laura Kipnis (2017b) writes,

> [E]verything I learned about this relationship [. . .] throws into question all easy assumptions about institutional roles alone determining who has more power in romantic entanglements. For instances, it's a well-known fact that if you're in two relationships simultaneously [. . .] you alter the balance of power in your favor. It's a well-known fact that whoever's more in love has less power. Youth and attractiveness may also offset the weight of institutional standing and higher degrees; so do calculations about who's more likely to end things. (94)

Or consider that intern Monica Lewinsky had a lot to gain, and President Bill Clinton had a lot to lose, by embarking on their affair (see also Gallop with Berlant 2001). Of course, a teenage stepchild and an adult graduate student are situated differently, and not merely by age alone but by available exit options and post hoc legal remedies (the stepchild may have none). Consent proffered by the stepchild is exponentially more suspect than consent proffered by the graduate student, although, in either case, status difference can leverage power difference in distinctive and distinctively troubling ways—distinguishable in kind and not just degree from leveraging youth or beauty. A professor may do dumb things—even risk professional suicide—because he is smitten. But thinking and acting with your heart—or other parts of your body—is a conventional and reasonably expected "cost" of intimacy. Jeopardizing your food, shelter, or academic job prospects should not be. The difference about such "moralized baselines" probably augurs for criminal law to intervene in cases of mothers' boyfriends and the mothers' minor children, but for university policy to intervene in cases of sexual or romantic relationships between professors and students under their direct supervision (for example, by a disclosure rule or relinquishment of an advisory position, or both). On conditioning another's moralized baseline by sex, see Wertheimer (2003, 167).

29. See End the Backlog, www.endthebacklog.org.

CHAPTER 3

1. Like Alex Sharpe (2014, 208–9), I use female pronouns to refer to McNally since she "now apparently identifies as female." In her relationship with M, though, McNally expressed herself as a man and "made reference to her desire for gender reassignment surgery" when M's mother outed her as female.

2. If M had indeed expressed such doubts and remained with McNally, this would attest to both the fetishistic and regulatory force of heteronormativity, and to "divided belief," knowing and not knowing, latticed by desire and social prohibition. See Eng (2001, 137–66).

3. McNally appealed her conviction on the grounds that she received ineffective counsel; she appealed the sentence of the lower court on several grounds.

4. I use the gender-neutral pronoun *their* because the gender identification of defendants varies both within and across cases.

5. In fact, in nearly all cases, defendants are charged not with "rape" but with a lesser form of sexual assault. In the United Kingdom, this is in part because a necessary element of "rape," the gravest sexual offense, is penetration with a penis. Sexual Offences Act 2003(1)(a).

6. I use *butch* to refer "to those female-born people who think of themselves as masculine but not necessarily male and certainly not as female," while cautioning that *butch* "cannot adequately bridge the categorical gap between lesbian and transsexual" (Halberstam 2005, 50; see also Halberstam 1998). Like Jack Halberstam, I recognize that people's gender identifications range in salience and may or may not be permanent.

7. For a similar argument regarding how and why to penalize nonconsensual condom removal during sex, see Brodsky 2017.

8. Parts of the remaining sections of this chapter have been published in revised form elsewhere. See Fischel and O'Connell 2016; Fischel 2016; 2017.

Given the undeniable and undeniably variable social and legal construction of race, I will simply speculate without fully arguing that it is probably also in the category of the unanswerable as an explicit condition for sex. The coordinates of racial classification in the United States are manifold, often contradictory, and historically supremacist. *Are you white?* or *Are you black?* are answerable, socially and politically speaking. Erotically and juridically speaking, these questions seem so overburdened by history, blood, lineage, supremacy, experience, and even self-identification as to be impossible to answer (López 1996; Reed 2015; Cooper 2017; Tuvell 2017). By rendering the question *Are you white?* legally unanswerable for purposes of criminalizing sexual conduct, we undermine the fiction of correspondence across racial identification, racialized experience, and skin color.

9. *Cisgender* refers to people whose gender identity corresponds exclusively to their assigned sex at birth. The term is used to denaturalize all gender signi-

fications of "sex," such that neither cisgender nor transgender people enjoy privileged status as "men" or "women" by virtue of genitals or any other criteria. The political payoff of the neologism probably makes the term worth its coinage, but I worry that *cisgender* inadvertently renaturalizes, by stabilizing and individualizing, the sex-gender correspondence for nontransgender people. For example, I am not transgender, but my identification as a "man" is not without deep ambivalence. Nor, though, does personal ambivalence in any way undercut the fact that I am a beneficiary of impersonalized male privilege. *Cisgender* risks depoliticizing social ascriptions and stratifications of gender as matters of preference.

10. For earlier discussions of sexual deception, its potential vitiation of consent, and whether and when it should constitute rape (or another legal wrong), see, for example, Chamallas 1988, 830–35; Schulhofer 1998, 152–59; Herring 2005; McGregor 2005, 181–90; Wertheimer 2003, 193–214.

11. Justine McNally took the name "Scott Hill" in her communications with M. "Scott Hill" is also the name of a boy who attended McNally's school. *McNally* (2013); see also A. Gross 2009, 177–79.

12. Brodsky takes a harder stance against criminalizing rape by deception and reproductive misrepresentation than against nondisclosure of sexually transmitted infections, but the larger point is that rendering nonconsensual condom removal nonconsensual on the basis of unanticipated risk enhancement rather than violation of an explicit conditional invites state overreach.

It should also be noted that the Israeli rape-by-deception case Brodsky cites (2017, 194) as a "Jewish Israeli woman's horror to learn she had slept with an Arab man," while much discussed in these terms, likely did not occur this way. In *Kashur v. State of Israel* (2012), the defendant, Kashur, was initially charged with forcible rape against a woman he had not previously known. He met the complainant on the street and shortly thereafter they had sex (or he sexually assaulted her) on the top floor of a nearby building. But because the victim was reluctant to testify, Kashur was prosecuted under a lesser sexual offense of sex by deception. It appears that counsels for the defense and prosecution, as well as the judge, cofabricated the story of Kashur falsely representing himself as a Jew. So while the attorneys and court did indeed "operationalize bigotry" in conjuring an Arab man deceptively seducing a Jewish woman, it was the state's bigotry that was operationalized, not the woman's (Brodsky 2017, 194). See A. Gross (2015, 19–21).

13. On the gendered, erotic, and subcultural value of bareback sex for some gay men, whether or not consciously gauged, see Dean 2009.

14. Such "deal breakers," as Dougherty calls them (2013b, 719), need not be made through "explicit communication" if the deal-breaking facts are outside a "common ground" of expectations (735-36n40). If I allow you to bring your dog into my apartment, I rightly assume the dog is not rabid. Nonetheless, I do not believe my "explicit conditional" requirement for rendering deceptive sex legally wrong contravenes Dougherty's thesis. For elsewhere in his article, and referenced above, Dougherty argues that we ought to treat people's particular sexual preferences as morally important and deliberate infractions of those preferences as morally wrong, whatever those preferences may be. But Chloe

would have no way of knowing Victoria's preference for sex with and only with peaceniks unless Victoria explicitly expresses the preference (728). Likewise, if a transgender man and a woman agree to "have sex," it is in fact *not* "common ground" between the two parties that the sex will involve penetration with a human penis. It is "common ground," perhaps, that whatever object penetrates the receptive partner is not coated with arsenic.

CHAPTER 4

Epigraphs: Roach and Limbaugh quotations from Devor (2007); Wexler quotation from Aniello (2016).

1. However, although Peter Beirne rests his definition of "interspecies sexual assault" on the presumptive inability of animals to proffer "genuine consent" (1997, 325), his typology of such assaults emphasizes human mens rea over animal welfare (328–32). He would likely classify a man being topped by a horse as interspecies sexual assault (committed by the man against the horse) before classifying gelding as such. Martha Nussbaum (2007, 395–96) makes a brief but compelling argument that, under certain circumstances, animal sterilization is morally permissible, especially if sterilization facilitates or at least does not impede the animal's flourishing.

2. Neil Levy (2003, 446) refers to these animal "behavioral analogue[s]" as "consent*."

3. The capabilities approach inquiry would be: Does interspecies sex diminish animals' species-specific capacity for flourishing, unduly limiting their "opportunities for excellence" (Nussbaum 2007, 378)?

4. The bioethicist Jessica Pierce (2016, 128–35) concludes her investigation of human-animal sex by categorically condemning such sex as exploitative (135), though *exploitation* remains undefined. Her account demonstrates how easily disgust can overpower careful analysis. For despite initially asking her readers to heed the varieties of human-animal sex and intimacy (129), and despite her documenting zoos' own insistence on treating animals with love and respect (131–32), she nevertheless marshals graphic, horrific veterinary records of animal sexual abuse to reject the view of "zoophilia as a relatively benign activity" (132). Any subcultural group, sexual or not, can be tarnished by substituting a part for the whole.

5. Washington Rev. Code §16.52.205(6). For a sustained, excellent treatment of the legal and cultural distinctions between bestiality and animal husbandry, see Rosenberg (2017).

6. In a preliminary hearing, Nicholas Grunke's lawyer objected to the district attorney's use of "her" and "she" in reference to the corpse: "There is no 'her' or 'she,' anymore—there's human remains in that grave." "Preliminary Hearing in Necrophile Case," YouTube, uploaded by Dreamin' Demon, July 10, 2008, https://www.youtube.com/watch?v=91_YdX7jNRg.

7. Moreover, if for Aristotle (1999) questions of justice and injustice are pegged to human voluntariness and nonvoluntariness (79–85), then it is not unjust to penetrate human remains, though it may be unnatural, diseased, or nonrational (106–9).

8. Pierce (2016) reports that in online chat rooms men having sex with animals advise each other to train the animals to "show signs of pleasure, interest, [and] willingness" in sex (134). To Pierce, "this blurring of the line between consent and coercion is deeply problematic," but I think posing the issue this way is untenable and ultimately uninteresting (135). Is a dog "coerced" into enjoying a game of fetch, or into not peeing on the rug?

9. Both sex with animals and sex with corpses may qualify as property damage. Another reason sex with beasts is allegedly wrong is that it dehumanizes *us*. The argument is propounded by Neil Levy (2003, 453–54), who posits that sex with animals may be irrational, though not categorically immoral; interspecies sex potentially plunges us outside the category of *human*. For Singer (2001), the argument is "speciesist," our aversion a disavowal of human (libidinal) commonalities with animals.

A presumption of this chapter is that liberals' opposition to sex with animals (or sex with corpses) is likely lodged in consent. Traditional, more conservative opposition to sex with animals is that such sex is against nature, which locates us squarely on antigay terrain. Not coincidentally, in the same textual passages where Aristotle (1999, 106) and Immanuel Kant (1963, 169–70) classify bestiality as diseased or unnatural, they also object to sex between men. It is the argument against nature, rather than the argument for gay sex, that turns out to be the slipperiest of slopes.

10. If key figures of this chapter were considered in reverse—children, corpses, horses—we would edge closer to confronting a moral atrocity greater in kind and degree than bestial or necrophilic sex: we raise children to eat so many dead animals whose mass-scale death requires mass-scale suffering and mass-scale environmental destruction. See Foer (2009).

11. Another presumption of this chapter, for the sake of argument, is that young children are incapable of consent. For my critique of the blanket classification of minors as sexually incompetent, see Fischel (2016).

12. See note 9.

13. The argument was repeated many years later by philosopher David Archard: "The key to the wrong of sexual abuse is that the child does not consent and does not because it *cannot*" (2004, 205). However, Archard's emphasis on the inequalities between children and adults—inequalities of power and understanding (206)—suggest not that such inequalities vitiate any token of consent, as he assumes, but that inequality, not consent, constitutes a core problem of adult-child sex.

14. Haugaard (2000) poses a related question that likewise underlines the ethical murkiness of incapacity: "At what age must a father stop bathing his daughter to avoid sexually abusing her—and why not the year before that age or the year after?" (1037).

15. Carol Adams paraphrases Frank Perdue's advertisements for his chicken.

16. In *Zoo* (Devor 2007), at least one of the zoos perceives his desires as innate and his orientation as zoophilic, not heterosexual.

17. This is not to deny that many people have enriching, spiritual, or otherwise deep intimate relationships with animals. For rather different shaves on those intimacies, see Dekkers (2000) and Rudy (2012).

18. More precisely, Ward (2015) demonstrates that for some populations of white straight men, sex practices with each other is elemental to, rather than a pause from or a contradiction of, their heterosexual masculinity.

CHAPTER 5

1. Connecticut General Statutes §53a-65(6).

2. Or almost nowhere. Many stakeholders rebuked the state attorneys for prosecuting Fourtin under two statutes that by precedent require total inability to communicate as proof of helplessness. Both the Connecticut Supreme Court and several commentators posited that the state attorney should have charged Fourtin under subsections of the Connecticut General Statutes that reference the sexual assault of victims determined "mentally defective." As Judge Palmer wrote for the *Fourtin* majority: "[T]his appears to be a case in which the state ultimately proceeded against the defendant under the wrong statute [. . .] By electing to prove that the victim was physically helpless rather than mentally defective, the state removed from the case all issues pertaining to the victim's mental capacity to consent to sex" (*Fourtin* 2012, 689n20). Judge Norcott, dissenting, agreed on the point: "[T]he state would have been far better advised" to charge Fourtin with violation of the sexual assault statutes, "which require a victim that is 'mentally defective'" (701n22; see also K. White 2012).

On the other hand, post hoc recriminations—locating someone to blame— may satisfy frustration more than fact of law. As Susann Gill, the lead prosecutor in *Fourtin* told us, case law delineating the parameters of the "mentally defective" subsection is even sparser than the pursued alternative, "physically helpless." L.K.'s demonstrated resistance classed her out of "helplessness"; it may just as well have classed her out of "defectiveness." This bind—too demonstratively abled to be "helpless," too disabled for force to be necessary—is nowhere more egregiously exemplified than in *State v. Hufford* (1987), discussed above. In that case the Connecticut Supreme Court overturned the conviction of an emergency medical technician for sexually assaulting a woman taped to a stretcher. Hufford "had no need to exert force to effect the sexual contact. The complainant had been rendered immobile for transport to the hospital and the defendant had only to open her blouse and pants to commit the sexual assault. We are unpersuaded by the state's argument that these actions constituted force" (*Hufford* 1987, 871). On the other hand, "[w]hile [the defendant's] testimony tends to show lack of consent, it contradicts the state's assertion that the complainant was unable to communicate her 'unwillingness to an act.' The record contains no evidence tending to show that the complainant was physically helpless" (873). While the Connecticut Supreme Court remanded the case "for a new trial limited to the issue of lack of consent," such a charge—violation of Connecticut General Statutes §53a-73a(a)(2)—is a misdemeanor, applicable only to sexual contact (not intercourse) and is hardly ever prosecuted but for unwanted gropes. Susann E. Gill, Supervisory Assistant State's Attorney, Connecticut State's Attorney's Office, interview with Fischel, October 16, 2014.

3. Senate Bill 247 (2012), Connecticut Legislature Regular Session (2013); Connecticut General Statutes §§53a-71(a)(4) (2013), 53a-73a(a)(1)(C).

4. We understand the reclaimed pejorative *crip* to signal practices and theories that put pressure on, while also countenancing the power effects of, the norms, determinants, and identity formations that orbit ability and disability. See McRuer (2006, 33–76); see also Kafer (2013, 15).

5. On "derealization" as an idiom and upshot of unjust sociolegal formations, see Butler (2006, 34).

Scholars have cautioned against the (often forcible) desexualization of disabled individuals (Clare 2015 [1999], 108–9; Garland-Thompson 2002, 16; Hahn 1994, 121–24; Siebers 2012; Wade 2002). In a variety of vernaculars and (inter)disciplines, these authors have advocated for the sexual autonomy of disabled persons—for the right to co-determine sexual relations and for that co-determination capability to be fostered.

6. Denno references Wolf Wolfensberger's "dignity of risk," which posits "a certain 'dignity' in allowing mentally retarded individuals to assume the same risks as nonretarded individuals" (Denno 1997, 359n277). Dignity, framed as such, lends itself to a presumption of noninterference and thus dedifferentiation regarding the legal treatment of persons with disabilities. Sexual autonomy and access, reconstructed, demand positive provisions for flourishing, and thus differentiation that compensates for extant social inequalities, asymmetric opportunities, and accidents of birth. See also Nussbaum (2006, 186–95); for a contiguous criticism of "human dignity" as a normative guidepost adjudicating kinky sex, see the section "The Dubiousness of Dignity" in chapter 1 of this volume.

7. Denno protests that "mentally retarded individuals" are preemptively disqualified from sex by the statutory codifications and judicial determinations of "mentally defective" (1997, 341–45; see also Gill 2015, 192–93). In this chapter, we use the now-more-acceptable language of "intellectual disability" or "cognitive disability" in reference to the same or similar populations as Denno refers to, aware that all such ascriptive and identitarian terms, including our own, are subject to changing and competing cultural norms. Sensitive terminology has no necessary correspondence to just policy. See Kulick and Rydström (2015, 37).

Denno describes how expansive interpretations of and determinative factors for "mentally defective" and "mental incapacity" have, by raising the consent standard unreachably high, rendered persons with intellectual disabilities unable to consent to sex (1997, 349). She argues that consent inquiries excessively emphasize the IQ and "mental age" of persons with intellectual disabilities, thereby wrongly assuming that intellectual (dis)ability is static, permanent, and unaltered by context (342, 355–56, 366; see also Gill 2015, 38). Moreover, such consent inquiries have historically provided cover for the moralistic containment of women's sexuality (say, to prevent disabled women from reproducing or to punish adultery or fornication; Denno 1997, 349–52). Of course, medical authorities have not always required the pretense of consent to intervene in the reproductive and sexual lives of women with disabilities. Sexual unruliness and "improvement" of the human population have long justified coercive sterilization and other eugenic policies. See, for example, Block (2000, 245).

Denno counteroffers a "contextual approach" to consent determinations, a strategy that would relieve persons with intellectual disabilities from "statutory isolation" (355–59, 343). Denno's approach, dissolving categorical exceptions like "physically helpless" or "mentally incapacitated," would instruct judges and juries to examine the many situational and circumstantial factors around a sexual encounter in order to determine consent. In her scheme, mental ability, more accurately assessed, might be one such factor, but neither primary nor summary (342–43, 394–95). For example, in the case of a gang rape of an intellectually disabled girl by a group of teenage boys, Denno soundly suggests that the boys' deception, manipulation, coercion, and threats of retaliation take judicial priority over locating, impossibly, an exact measurement or age equivalency of the girl's intellectual ability (360–76).

8. For our extended discussion of Kantian autonomy in relation to sex and social difference, see Fischel and O'Connell (2015, 446–56). Some scholars have proposed that sex is not as poisonous to autonomy as Kant assumes (Denis 2007, Halwani 2010, 200–225; Madigan 1998; Nussbaum 1999, 224–39).

9. However, we recognize that "self-determination" has served as a core political value for and rhetorical petition of the disability rights movement. See Charlton (2000, 17).

10. Nedelsky does not consider disability in much detail, but her relational reconstruction of autonomy comports with sociology professor Anna Yeatman's advocacy for persons with disabilities to participate more fully in their own lives (Nedelsky 2011, 27; Yeatman 2000). Like Nedelsky, Yeatman rejects the equivalence of autonomy with independence and rejects, too, independence as a prerequisite for participation. She suggests instead that "participation" "enables people to be and become autonomous individuals within their social worlds and connections" (182). *Participation*, as Yeatman understands it, refers to "whether an individual is invited to be and become his or her own agent" (183). Under this definition, all sorts of people can participate in the course of their own lives, including people "who cannot achieve independence [. . .] children and individuals whose level of intellectual disability means that they cannot reason on their own behalf" (183; see also Charlton 2000, 21–22). Yeatman argues that upping the participation level of persons with intellectual disabilities entails encouraging such persons to practice making choices; providing "support people" to offer "appropriate guidance and information for choice making"; and specialized interpreting of persons with disabilities' communicative behavior (which is too often rendered as nonsense; 190–92). Thus, social restructuring facilitates participation, participation facilitates autonomous action, and autonomous action "facilitate[s] the individuation of individuals"; individuation Yeatman takes as morally paramount (196). While Yeatman's chain of equivalences (participation = autonomy = individuality) is not philosophically substantiated as rigorously as Nedelsky's reworking of autonomy, both authors point to autonomy as a normative ideal predicated neither on independence nor on reason, but rather on creative capacity and participation. Nedelsky, though, cautions against collapsing autonomy into participation, as the latter can be purely procedural and the former is a "substantive value" (149, 151).

11. Nussbaum (2010) grounds her argument for political inclusion of persons with severe intellectual disabilities with recourse to "dignity" and "equal respect," not "autonomy," but the extant injustice she identifies registers as a

deprivation of autonomy, relationally reconstructed: "At present, a large group of citizens are simply disqualified from the most essential functions of citizenship. They do not count. Their interests are not weighed in the balance" (91).

12. When Nussbaum discusses persons with intellectual disabilities, she is concerned primarily with their educational, employment, and social accommodation and their political integration—not their erotic lives (2006, 195–216; 2010, 86–94; but see Kulick and Rydström 2015, 22).

13. In an otherwise sound synthesis of the CA and disability accommodations, Christopher Riddle performs just such a trivialization of sex and sexuality (2014, 77–85). Among other criticisms he levels at the CA, Riddle suggests that Nussbaum's list of central capabilities ought to be ranked by moral priority to give guidance to theorists and policy makers (42–44). If the denial of opportunities to realize certain capabilities leads to "corrosive disadvantage"—damaged functioning in other arenas of social life—those capabilities are more important than others (82). This may or may not be reasonable, but to evidence the point, Riddle characterizes "health" as a capability of highest moral importance (because unhealthiness infects so many other functions) and opportunities for sexual satisfaction as relatively morally unimportant (82–85). Given the ignominious history of degrading or denying the sexuality of persons with disabilities, one would think Riddle might have selected other examples.

14. The stipulation comports with Nussbaum's capabilities approach, which "recommends, as a necessary condition of social justice, bringing all citizens above a rather ample threshold on each of the ten capabilities, not complete equalizing of all the capabilities" (2010, 78).

15. But sometimes overprotected. See Denno (1997).

16. States with "force," "threat of force," "forcible compulsion," or "resistance" as threshold determinants for rape or sexual assault, or both, include Arkansas, Idaho, Illinois, Indiana, North Carolina, Ohio, Oklahoma, Pennsylvania, and South Carolina. See Arkansas Code §5–14–103 (a)(1); Idaho Statutes §18–6101(4); Illinois Compiled Statutes 720 ILCS 5/§11–1.20(a)(1); Indiana Code §35–42–4(a)(1); North Carolina General Statutes §14–27.21; Ohio Revised Code §2907.02(A)(2); Oklahoma Statutes §§21–1111(A)(3), (B); Pennsylvania Code §§3121(a)(1), (2); South Carolina Code §16–3–652(1)(a). In these states, nonconsent is not an issue of law for lesser sexual assault offenses, either, at least as codified. Case law may redefine "force" to include unconsented-to penetration; see, for example, *State in the Interest of M.T.S.* (1992).

17. Pressured by feminist and liberal legal advocates since the 1970s, states have eliminated the most affrontingly sexist elements of conventional rape law (e.g., the "utmost resistance" requirement, the marital rape exemption, and the corroboration requirement; see, for example, Bennice and Resick 2003; Chamallas 1987; Schwartz 1983). And since the 1980s, feminist legal activism and scholarship have helped shift the national conversation concerning sexual assault away from determinations of force and toward expressions of consent (see Caringella 2009, 14–15; but see Schulhofer 1998, 29–32). In some jurisdictions, resistance and force requirements have been relaxed or excised, replaced by nonconsent requirements (Caringella 2009, 76). However, like the replacement of "mentally defective" with "mentally incapacitated" in Connecticut,

statutory substitutions of force with nonconsent may be a codified distinction without a material difference: juries and judges often rely on evidence of resistance as proof of nonconsent (Caringella 2009, 106–7; Buchhandler-Raphael 2011, 156–60).

In Connecticut, while "lack of consent" has been read into the force element of sexual assault, the state court also made clear that, absent force, passiveness and silence register as consent. *State v. Smith* (1989).

18. The only subsection that criminalizes sexual conduct solely on the basis of nonconsent is sexual assault in the fourth degree. This subsection is hardly ever exercised by the state; when it is, it is used to reach comparatively less serious assaults like an unsolicited grope at a bar. Connecticut General Statutes §53a-73a(a)(2). Susann E. Gill, Supervisory Assistant State's Attorney, Connecticut State's Attorney's Office, interview with Fischel, October 16, 2014.

19. Connecticut General Statutes §§53a-70a(a)(1)(2)(3), -70b(b), -72a(a)(1)(A)(B), -72b(a).

20. See, for example, Wisconsin Statutes §940.225(4); California Senate Bill No. 967 (2014), https://leginfo.legislature.ca.gov/faces/billNavClient.xhtml?bill_id=201320140SB967; "Sexual Misconduct Response," Yale University, http://smr.yale.edu/sexual-misconduct-policies-and-definitions.

A nonconsent requirement, though preferable to requiring proof of resistance or force, may render permissible sex that is not agreed to, acquiesced to, or pursued with persons that are silent or frozen in fear. Saying *no* is not as easy as one might think, and many victims believe that expressed refusal will further endanger them (Kitzinger and Frith 1999; Schwartz 1982, 566–82; but see Marcus 1992).

21. Fourtin initially claimed at trial never to have had sexual contact with L.K. Gill, interview with Fischel, October 16, 2014.

22. Although critics lampoon affirmative consent standards by arguing that a legal requirement of a verbal *yes* to sex is too contractual, unsexy, or impractical, it should be evident to readers that this consent standard is a straw man (see Schulhofer 2015, 666–67). Neither states nor universities that have revised their sexual assault laws or sexual misconduct policies, respectively, require a verbal *yes*. Revised statutes and university policies typically require an indication of positive agreement, whether through speech, sounds, body language, gestures, or some combination of these. In any case, states and universities should not adopt a verbal standard, not only because people tend not to verbalize their agreement to wanted sex (Hall 1998), or only because young people report being uncomfortable expressing sexual desire (Humphreys 2004), or only because girls and women are taught to be demure, but also and perhaps more important, because such a standard would be plainly ableist. L.K. and anyone else who communicates nonverbally would be categorically prohibited from sex under such a verbal standard. The affirmative component of affirmative consent ought to be flexible enough to accommodate people across the spectrum of ability.

23. Connecticut General Statutes §§53a-70(a)(2),-71(a)(1), -73a(a)(1)(E).

24. Connecticut General Statutes §§53a-71(a)(4–10), -73a(a)(1–10). Connecticut General Statute §53a-72a(a)(2) prohibits sexual intercourse between persons who know that they are related within any of the following degrees:

parent, grandparent, child, grandchild, sibling, parent's sibling, sibling's child, stepparent, or stepchild. See appendix A.

25. Only one of the cases we surveyed involves a charge under Connecticut General Statutes §53a-71(a)(3), the "physically helpless" standard: *State v. Joseph* (2014). Another case involves Connecticut General Statute §§53a-71(a) (2), the former "mentally defective" standard, now the "impaired because of mental disability or disease" standard: *State v. Dickerson* (2014).

Three of the appellate cases we surveyed involve a victim whose disability is referenced in court decisions. In all three cases, the perpetrator was aware of the victim's disability. *State v. Carolina* (2013) (involving the assault of a teenage girl with unidentified "cognitive disabilities" by her nonbiological uncle); *State v. Dearing* (2012) (involving the assault of a nine-year-old girl with "pervasive developmental disorder not otherwise specified" by an adult family friend); *Di Teresi v. Stamford Health System, Inc.* (2013) (involving the assault of a ninety-two-year-old woman with "dementia, advanced Alzheimer's disease, Parkinson's disease, and other ailments" by a nurse's assistant while the victim was hospitalized at Stamford Hospital).

26. For example, disability service providers (e.g., personal care attendants, psychiatrists, residential care staff) constituted 27.7 percent of alleged perpetrators, specialized transportation providers 5.4 percent, and specialized foster parents 4.3 percent.

27. For example, family members constituted 16.8 percent of alleged perpetrators, paid service providers (e.g., babysitters) 9.8 percent, and step-family members 2.2 percent.

28. In the United Kingdom, sex between a caretaker and a dependent with a "mental disorder" is lawful if a sexual relationship predated the caretaking. Sexual Offences Act 2003, c. 42, s. 44.

For a similar argument regarding sex between minors (for which affirmative consent would provide an affirmative defense), see Kitrosser (1996, 330–31). Of course, this solution would not solve the problem if the caretaker accused of sexual assault is the person facilitating the alleged victim's affirmative consent. See Engber (2015); see also Boni-Saenz (2015, 1239, 1245).

29. Michael Oliver maintains that the social model is best understood as a "practical tool" rather than a "concept" or "idea" (2004, 30, cited in Shakespeare 2006, 199). For a succinct but illuminating political history of "access" in the disability rights movement, see Williamson (2015).

30. Other criticisms of the social model are not as germane to, or as potentially conflictual with, our argument for access. See, for example, Kafer (2013, 6–10); Terzi (2004); Tremain (2002); Shakespeare and Watson (2002); Shildrick (2009, 1–16).

31. "The British social model is arguably the most powerful form which social approaches to disability have taken," comments Tom Shakespeare (2006, 199), yet he concludes his brief overview of the social model of disability with the caution that it "has become a barrier to further progress," in part because of its unilateralism and separatism (202).

32. Traversing the arguments of this chapter, the documentary *Best and Most Beautiful Things* (Zevgetis 2016) chronicles Michelle Smith, a legally

blind young woman with Asperger's syndrome who discovers in BDSM communities experiences of access and autonomy she is denied or deferred in everyday life. "Age play" allows her to enact a fantasy of adulthood by distancing herself from the little girl she performs. See also Weinstein (2016).

33. The social model is also positioned against a charity model of disability, which understands disabled persons as recipients of beneficence and requires no corresponding institutional reforms for people's participation in social life (Oliver 2013, 1026).

34. As Anne Finger (1992), Russell Shuttleworth (2007b), Tobin Siebers (2012), and others have commented, the mainstream disabilities rights movement largely backgrounded issues of access to sex and intimacy in favor of access to education, employment, and transportation. The political calculation is understandable; integrationist agendas have historically been contained by the cultural imperative of respectability.

35. In a rebuke of philosopher Peter Singer's skepticism regarding the rational competencies of people with learning disabilities, Bérubé comments that it is this very skepticism, these lowered expectations, that deny the intellectually disabled access to learning and experiences that enrich their abilities. Low expectations are not just ableist but, more insidiously, self-fulfilling (Bérubé 2010, 105–6).

36. Some of these recommendations for democratizing sexual access refer to policies of group homes for intellectually disabled people. Insofar as they isolate disability, group homes are in a fundamental sense antithetical to the social model. Still, progressive group home policies and practices facilitate possibilities for, if not always realizations of, their residents' sex, sexuality, and intimacy.

37. Women with disabilities have disproportionately suffered suppression of their sexuality and continue to do so (Carlson 2009, 53–83; Finger 1992). In the past, medical and political authorities, motivated by eugenic fears of social degradation, sterilized women or otherwise curbed their sexuality (Denno 1997, 333–34). In the present, medical and political authorities restrict the sexual lives of women with disabilities out of concern for the caretaking responsibilities and financial burdens of their potential offspring (Kulick and Rydström 2015, 164–71). This concern also manifests in "menstrual manipulation"—the use of clinical methods, like contraceptives, to alter the symptoms and experiences associated with menstruation or to suppress menstruation altogether in young people with disabilities. In some cases, the young person may desire relief from menstrual inconveniences. However, clinical guidelines suggest that more commonly, caretakers' and parents' anxieties about the complications of menstruation and disability motivate menstrual manipulation. See American College of Obstetricians and Gynecologists (2009); Kirkham et al. (2014); Savasi et al. (2009). In one study, 40 percent of intellectually disabled women surveyed had never received any education regarding gynecologic or reproductive health (Kopac, Fritz, and Hold 1998).

38. As Kulick and Rydström (2015, 16) put it bluntly, persons with significant disabilities, often but not always intellectual, "write no poems" (primarily referencing Mark O'Brien [1990]) and "throw no balls" (primarily referencing the rugby players of *Murderball* [2005]). "These kinds of significantly disabled

adults," they insist, "are the ones who need the most help in exploring their sexuality" (2015, 3).

39. Prostitution is illegal across the United States, save in several counties in Nevada. However, sexual assistants hired under the auspices of therapy or surrogacy make the legality of such practices uncertain: "The legal status of surrogate partners is undefined in most of the United States and most countries around the world. This means that there are generally no laws regulating the profession" (International Professional Surrogates Association International Professional Surrogates Association, n.d.).

40. Sexual autonomy, relationally reconstructed, might be conceived as a "fertile functioning" that promotes other capabilities, like affiliation and imagination (Wolf and de-Shalit 2007, 133–54).

41. Denno (1997, 384–93) chronicles several cases in which assistants and social workers intervened to help persons with significant intellectual disabilities have sex. Caretakers continually gauged—and sometimes instructed patients how to legibly express—wantedness and unwantedness.

42. For a closer-to-home example of facilitating sex for the elderly (with or without diagnosed disabilities), see Belluck 2015; Dessel and Ramirez 1995.

43. Kulick and Rydström emphasize in their book (2015) that the population of persons with disabilities who directly purchase sexual services makes up a "tiny fragment" of all disabled people (24, 179). The authors suggest that such services receive disproportionate media and academic attention, reflecting a prejudiced presumption that the only way persons with significant disabilities could have sex is if they paid for it. This is untrue. Nonetheless, the private purchasing of sexual services occurs, and when done right, this sort of access to a sexual culture fosters the sexual autonomy of persons with disabilities while also protecting the rights and bodily integrity of sex workers, sexual assistants, and disabled persons themselves (196–200).

44. See, for example, University of California, Berkeley's Sexual Health Education Program, https://uhs.berkeley.edu/shep; Brown University's Sexual Health Awareness Group, https://www.brown.edu/campus-life/health/services/promotion/shag; and Wesleyan University's WesWell, http://www.wesleyan.edu/weswell/resources/Sexual%20Health.html.

45. On gender dynamics of oral sex among adolescents and college students, see, for example, Chambers 2007; Grigoriadis 2017, 50–51, 57; Lewis and Marston 2016.

46. Abstinence-plus education programs "aim to prevent, stop, or decrease sexual activity; however, programs also promote condom use and other safer-sex strategies as alternatives for sexually active participants. Abstinence-plus programs differ from abstinence-only interventions, which promote abstinence as the exclusive means of HIV prevention without encouraging safer sex" (Underhill, Montgomery, and Operario 2008, 2).

47. However, as Michael Gill (2015) points out, "[s]ex education that meaningfully incorporates a discussion of homosexuality, asexuality, and bisexuality is rare, especially in special education classrooms" (49).

48. In further corroboration of this point, Michael Gill attests to the rigidly gendered structure of sex education designed for persons with intellectual

disabilities, and describes how one of the more popular programs, premised on "harm reduction," is thematized around avoidance of pregnancy and the threat of stranger danger rather than around possibilities for polymorphous pleasures (2015, 56–57, 80–81). Programs that celebrate and teach masturbation practices for the intellectually disabled are also deployed to quash potential sexual relationships between the disabled or between the disabled and nondisabled (95). Michel Desjardins (2012) documents how young women with disabilities in Quebec are encouraged to trade in reproductive capacity for sexual activity; that is, they are permitted sexual interactions provided they agree to undergo sterilization procedures to avoid pregnancy and childbirth (2012). And Licia Carlson historicizes ways medical experts and institutions have arrogated power through variable constructions of the educable "idiot" (2009, 36–45).

CONCLUSION

1. Associate Editor, *Fortune* Magazine, email correspondence with author, November 10, 2017 (in author's possession).

2. "One of Spacey's accusers [. . .] says that when he was 14, he had an ongoing sexual relationship with the then-24-year-old rising actor. At first, the accuser was a consenting participant (or, as much as a minor can considered to be one), but he says the relationship ended when Spacey attempted to rape him" (Kornhaber 2017).

Court Cases Cited

Bowers v. Hardwick, 478 U.S. 186 (1986)
Di Teresi v. Stamford Health System, Inc., 63 A.3d 1011 (Conn. App. 2013)
Kashur v. State of Israel, CrimA 5734/10 (2012)
Lawrence v. Texas, 539 U.S. 558 (2003)
Martin v. Ziherl, 607 S.E.2d 367 (Va. 2005)
McNally v. R., EWCA Crim 1051 (2013). https://genderidentitywatch.files. wordpress.com/2013/06/mcnally-v-r.pdf.
Meritor Savings Bank v. Vinson, 477 U.S. 57 (1986)
Obergefell v. Hodges, 576 U.S. __ (2015)
Powell v. Georgia, 270 Ga. 327 (Ga. 1998)
R. v. Brown, 1 AC 212 (1994)
R. v. Wilson, Crim LR 573 (1996)
State in the Interest of M.T.S., 609 A.2d 122 (N.J. 1992)
State of Israel v. Alkobi, IsrDC 3341(3) (2003)
State v. Carolina, 69 A.3d 341 (Conn. App. 2013)
State v. Collier, 72 N.W.2d 303 (Iowa Ct. App. 1985)
State v. Dearing, 34 A.3d 1031 (Conn. App. 2012)
State v. Dickerson, 97 A.3d 15 (Conn. App. 2014).
State v. Fourtin, 982 A.2d 261 (Conn. App. 2009)
State v. Fourtin, 52 A.3d 674 (Conn. 2012)
State v. Gaspar, 982 A.2d 140 (R.I. 2009)
State v. Grunke, 752 N.W.2d 769 (Wis. 2008)
State v. Hufford, 533 A.2d 866 (Conn. 1987)
State v. Joseph, 93 A.3d 1174 (Conn. App. 2014)
State v. Smith, 554 A.2d 713 (Conn. 1989)
State v. Van, 688 N.W.2d 600 (Neb. 2004)

Bibliography

Abrams, Kathryn. 1999. "From Autonomy to Agency: Feminist Perspectives in Self-Direction." *William and Mary Law Review* 40:804–45.

Activist Mommy. 2017. "Mom Blogger Pulls Teen Vogue Magazine over Anal Sex Tutorial!" *YouTube*, July 14. https://www.youtube.com/watch?v=39Z5xC8rpQw.

Adams, Carol J. 1996. "Caring about Suffering: A Feminist Exploration." In *Beyond Animal Rights: A Feminist Caring Ethic for the Treatment of Animals.* Edited by Josephine Donovan and Carol J. Adams. New York: Continuum.

Adams, Carol J. 2015. *The Sexual Politics of Meat: A Feminist-Vegetarian Critical Theory.* New York: Continuum.

Adams, Carol J., and Josephine Donovan. 1996. *Beyond Animal Rights: A Feminist Caring Ethic for the Treatment of Animals.* New York: Continuum.

Alcoff, Linda. 1996. "Dangerous Pleasures: Foucault and the Politics of Pedophilia." In *Feminist Interpretations of Foucault.* Edited by Susan Hekman, 99–136. University Park: Pennsylvania State University Press.

Allen, Samantha. 2017. "Whatever Happened to the Transgender Tipping Point?" *Daily Beast*, March 3. http://www.thedailybeast.com/whatever-happened-to-the-transgender-tipping-point.

Almond, Steve. 2014. *Against Football: One Man's Reluctant Manifesto.* Brooklyn, NY: Melville House.

Altman, Matthew C. 2011. "Kant on Sex and Marriage: The Implications for the Same-Sex Marriage Debate." *Kant-Studien* 101:309–30.

American College of Obstetricians and Gynecologists. 2009. "Menstrual Manipulation for Adolescents with Disabilities: ACOG Committee Opinion No. 448." *Obstetrics and Gynecology* 114:1428–31.

American Council on Education. 2014. "New Requirements Imposed by the Violence Against Women Reauthorization Act." *American Council on*

Education, April 1. https://www.acenet.edu/news-room/Documents/VAWA-Summary.pdf.

Appel, Jacob M. 2010. "Sex Rights for the Disabled?" *Journal of Medical Ethics* 36:152–54.

Appell, Annette R. 2013. "Accommodating Childhood." *Cardozo Journal of Law and Gender* 19:715–80.

Appleton, Susan F., and Susan E. Stiritz. 2016. "The Joy of Sex Bureaucracy." *California Law Review Online* 7:49–65.

Aquinas, Thomas. 1999. *Selected Writings*. Edited by Ralph McInerny. London: Penguin Classics.

Archard, David. 2004. *Children: Rights and Childhood*. New York: Routledge.

Aristotle. 1999. *Nicomachean Ethics*. 2nd Edition. Translated by Terence Irwin. Indianapolis: Hackett.

Aristotle. 2017. *De Anima*. Translated by C. D. C. Reeve. Indianapolis: Hackett.

Assistant Secretary, Office for Civil Rights. 2011. "Dear Colleague Letter: Sexual Violence." *United States Department of Education Office for Civil Rights*. April 4. http://www2.ed.gov/about/offices/list/ocr/letters/colleague-201104 .pdf.

Baker, Dennis J. 2009. "The Moral Limits of Consent as a Defense in the Criminal Law." *New Criminal Law Review* 12:93–121.

Baker, Dennis J. 2014. "Should Unnecessary Harmful Nontherapeutic Cosmetic Surgery Be Criminalized?" *New Criminal Law Review* 17:587–630.

Balcombe, Jonathan. 2009. "Animal Pleasure and Its Moral Significance." *Applied Animal Behaviour Science* 118:208–16.

Ball, Carlos A. 2009. "This Is Not Your Father's Autonomy: Lesbian and Gay Rights from a Feminist and Relational Perspective." In *Feminist and Queer Legal Theories: Intimate Encounters, Uncomfortable Conversations*. Edited by Martha Fineman, Jack Jackson, and Adam Romero, 289–312. Aldershot, UK: Ashgate.

Baranetsky, Victoria. 2013. "Aborting Dignity: The Abortion Doctrine after *Gonzalez v. Carhart*." *Harvard Journal of Law and Gender* 36: 123–70.

Barcroft TV. 2016. "DOCS: Interview with a Cannibal." *YouTube*, February 4. https://www.youtube.com/watch?v=ym6TWmXw_fE.

Baril, Alexandre. 2015. "Needing to Acquire a Physical Impairment/Disability: (Re)Thinking the Connections between Trans and Disability Studies through Transability." *Hypatia* 30:30–48.

Bauer, Robin. 2014. *Queer BDSM Intimacies: Critical Consent and Pushing Boundaries*. Basingstoke: Palgrave MacMillan.

Bauman, H-Dirksen L., and Joseph J. Murray. 2010. "Deaf Studies in the 21st Century: 'Deaf-Gain' and the Future of Human Diversity." In *The Oxford Handbook of Deaf Studies, Language, and Education*, Vol. 2. Edited by Marc Marschark and Patricia Elizabeth Spencer, 210–25. Oxford: Oxford University Press.

Baumer, Eric P. 2004. "Temporal Variation in the Likelihood of Police Notification by Victims of Rape, 1973–2000." *National Institute of Justice Data Resources Program Project*, April 12. https://www.ncjrs.gov/pdffiles1/nij /grants/207497.pdf.

Beirne, Piers. 1997. "Rethinking Bestiality: Towards a Concept of Interspecies Sexual Assault." *Theoretical Criminology* 1:317–40.

Belluck, Pam. 2015. "Sex, Dementia, and a Husband on Trial at Age 70." *New York Times,* April 13. http://www.nytimes.com/2015/04/14/health/sex-dementia-and-a-husband-henry-rayhons-on-trial-at-age-78.html.

Belson, Ken. 2014. "Brain Trauma to Affect One in Three Players, N.F.L. Agrees." *New York Times,* September 12. https://www.nytimes.com/2014/09/13/sports/football/actuarial-reports-in-nfl-concussion-deal-are-released.html.

Belson, Ken. 2017. "Not Safe for Children? Football's Leaders Make Drastic Changes to Youth Game." *New York Times.* January 31. https://www.nytimes.com/2017/01/31/sports/youth-football-wants-to-save-the-game-by-shrinking-it.html.

Benderev, Chris. 2017. "#MeAt14 Reminds Internet 14-Year-Olds Are Innocent, Immature, Unable to Consent." *The Two-Way, National Public Radio,* November 11. https://www.npr.org/sections/thetwo-way/2017/11/11/563531559/-meat14-reminds-internet-14-year-olds-are-innocent-immature-unable-to-consent.

Bennet, Omalu, et al. 2005. "Chronic Traumatic Encephalopathy in a National Football League Player." *Neurosurgery* 57:128–34.

Bennice, Jennifer, and Patricia Resick. 2003. "Marital Rape: History, Research, and Practice." *Trauma, Violence, and Abuse* 4:228–46.

Bergelson, Vera. 2007. "The Right to Be Hurt: Testing the Boundaries of Consent." *George Washington Law Review* 75:165–263.

Bergelson, Vera. 2013. "Vice Is Nice but Incest Is Best: The Problem of a Moral Taboo." *Criminal Law and Philosophy* 7:43–59.

Berlant, Lauren. 2011. *Cruel Optimism.* Durham, NC: Duke University Press.

Berlant, Lauren. 2017. "The Predator and the Jokester." *The New Inquiry,* December 13. https://thenewinquiry.com/the-predator-and-the-jokester/.

Bernstein, Elizabeth. 2010. "Militarized Humanitarianism Meets Carceral Feminism: The Politics of Sex, Rights, and Freedom in Contemporary Antitrafficking Campaigns." *Signs: Journal of Women in Culture and Society* 36:45–71.

Bérubé, Michael. 1996. *Life As We Know It: A Father, a Family, and an Exceptional Child.* New York: Pantheon Books.

Bérubé, Michael. 2010. "Equality, Freedom, and/or Justice for All: A Response to Martha Nussbaum." In *Cognitive Disability and Its Challenge to Moral Philosophy.* Edited by Eva Kittay and Licia Carlson, 97–110. Malden, MA: Wiley-Blackwell.

Bérubé, Michael. 2016. *Life as Jamie Knows It: An Exceptional Child Grows Up.* Boston: Beacon Press.

Bettcher, Talia Mae. 2007. "Evil Deceivers and Make-Believers: On Transphobic Violence and the Politics of Illusion." *Hypatia* 22:43–65.

Bissinger, Buzz. 2015. "Caitlyn Jenner: The Full Story." *Vanity Fair,* July. http://www.vanityfair.com/hollywood/2015/06/caitlyn-jenner-bruce-cover-annie-leibovitz.

Block, Pamela. 2000. "Sexuality, Fertility, and Danger: Twentieth-Century Images of Women with Cognitive Disabilities." *Sexuality and Disability* 18:239–54.

Blue Seat Studios. 2015. "Tea Consent (Clean)." *YouTube,* May 13. https://
www.youtube.com/watch?v=fGoWLWS4-kU.

Boni-Saenz, Alexander A. 2015. "Sexuality and Incapacity." *Ohio State Law
Journal* 76:1201–55.

Bovsun, Mara. 2015. "Sicko German Cannibal Places a Personal Ad for a Well-
Built 18- to 30-Year-Old to be Slaughtered and Eaten—and He Finds a
Taker!" *New York Daily News,* February 7, 2015. http://www.nydailynews
.com/news/crime/sicko-finds-taker-slaughter-consume-personal-ad-article-
1.2106399.

Boyd, Melanie, and Joseph Fischel. 2014. "The Case for Affirmative Consent
(Or, Why You Can Stop Worrying That Your Son Will Go to Prison for Having Sex When He Gets to College)." *Huffington Post,* February 16. http://
www.huffingtonpost.com/melanie-boyd/the-case-for-affirmative-consent_
b_6312476.html.

Brodsky, Alexandra. 2017. "'Rape-Adjacent': Imagining Legal Responses to
Nonconsensual Condom Removal." *Columbia Journal of Gender and Law*
32:183–210.

Buchanan, Kim. 2015. "When Is HIV a Crime? Sexuality, Gender and Consent." *Minnesota Law Review* 99:1231–1342.

Buchhandler-Raphael, Michal. 2011. "The Failure of Consent: Re-conceptual-
izing Rape as Sexual Abuse of Power." *Michigan Journal of Gender and Law*
18:147–228.

Bunch, Sonny. 2018. "Babe's Aziz Ansari Piece Was a Gift to Anyone Who
Wants to Derail #MeToo." *Washington Post,* January 15. https://www
.washingtonpost.com/news/act-four/wp/2018/01/15/babes-aziz-ansari-piece-
was-a-gift-to-anyone-who-wants-to-derail-metoo/.

Burda, Jason P. 2015. "PrEP and Our Youth: Implications in Law and Policy."
Columbia Journal of Gender and Law 30:295–363.

Butler, Judith. 1982. "Lesbian S&M: The Politics of Dis-illusion." In *Against
Sadomasochism: A Radical Feminist Analysis.* Edited by Robin R. Linden,
Darlene R. Pagano, Diana E. H. Russell, and Susan L. Star, 169–75. Palo
Alto, CA: Frog in the Well.

Butler, Judith. 1990. *Gender Trouble: Feminism and the Subversion of Identity.*
New York: Routledge.

Butler, Judith, 1997. *Excitable Speech: A Politics of the Performative.* New
York: Routledge.

Butler, Judith, 2006. *Precarious Life: The Powers of Mourning and Violence.*
Brooklyn, NY: Verso.

Cahill, Ann J. 2001. *Rethinking Rape.* Ithaca, NY: Cornell University Press.

Cahill, Ann J. 2013. "Recognition, Desire, and Unjust Sex." *Hypatia* 29:303–19.

Cahill, Ann J. 2016. "Unjust Sex vs. Rape." *Hypatia* 31:746–61.

Califia, Pat. 1994 (1980). "Feminism and Sadomasochism." In *Public Sex: The
Culture of Radical Sex,* 168–80. San Francisco: Cleis Press.

Caringella, Susan. 2009. *Addressing Rape Reform in Law and Practice.* New
York: Columbia University Press.

Carlson, Licia. 2009. *The Faces of Intellectual Disability: Philosophical Reflections.* Bloomington: Indiana University Press.

Caron, Christina. 2017. "Students Look to Vending Machines for Better Access to Morning-After Pill." *New York Times,* September 18. https://www.nytimes.com/2017/09/28/us/plan-b-vending-machine.html.

Case, Mary A. 2003. "Of 'This' and 'That' in *Lawrence v Texas.*" *Supreme Court Review* 2003:75–142.

Case, Mary A. 2005. "Pets or Meat." *Chicago-Kent Law Review* 80:1129–50.

Casteel, Carri, et al. 2008. "National Study of Physical and Sexual Assault among Women with Disabilities." *Injury Prevention* 14:87–90.

Cauterucci, Christina. 2017. "Louis C.K.'s Public Statement Unnervingly Misunderstands the Concept of Consent." *Slate,* November 10. http://www.slate.com/blogs/xx_factor/2017/11/10/louis_c_k_s_masturbation_statement_unnervingly_misunderstands_the_concept.html.

Centers for Disease Control and Prevention. 2017. "HIV among Transgender People." *CDC,* August 3. https://www.cdc.gov/hiv/group/gender/transgender/index.html.

Cha, Ariana E. 2017. "Big City Health Officials Decry Trump Administration's Cuts to Teen Pregnancy Prevention Programs." *Washington Post,* August 9. https://www.washingtonpost.com/news/to-your-health/wp/2017/08/09/big-city-health-officials-decry-trump-administrations-cuts-to-teen-pregnancy-prevention-programs/?utm_term=.2e52e4ea3598.

Chamallas, Martha. 1987. "Consent, Equality, and the Legal Control of Sexual Conduct." *Southern California Law Review* 61:777–862.

Chambers, Wendy C. 2007. "Oral Sex: Varied Behaviors and Perceptions in a College Population." *Journal of Sex Research* 44:28–42.

Charlton, James I. 2000. *Nothing about Us without Us: Disability Oppression and Empowerment.* Berkeley: University of California Press.

Chemaly, Soraya. 2016. "How Police Still Fail Rape Victims." *Rolling Stone,* August 16. http://www.rollingstone.com/culture/features/how-police-still-fail-rape-victims-w434669.

Chozick, Amy. 2017. "Hillary Clinton Ignited a Feminist Movement: By Losing." *New York Times,* January 13. https://www.nytimes.com/2018/01/13/sunday-review/hillary-clinton-feminist-movement.html.

Clare, Eli. 2015 (1999). *Brilliant Imperfection: Grappling with Cure.* Durham, NC: Duke University Press.

Clare, Eli. 2017. *Exile and Pride: Disability, Queerness, and Liberation.* Durham, NC: Duke University Press.

Cleves, Rachel Hope, and Nicholas L. Syrett. 2017. "Roy Moore Is Not a Pedophile." *Washington Post,* November 19. https://www.washingtonpost.com/opinions/roy-moore-is-not-a-pedophile/2017/11/19/1a9ae238-cb21-11e7-aa96-54417592cf72_story.html?utm_term=.e0757631fea8.

Collier, Lorna. 2014. "Incarceration Nation." *Monitor on Psychology* 45:56–61.

Conly, Sarah. 2004. "Seduction, Rape, and Coercion." *Ethics* 115:96–121.

Contrera, Jessica. 2017. "Women Respond to Roy Moore Allegations by Reminding the World What It Looks Like to Be 14." *Washington Post,* November 13. https://www.washingtonpost.com/news/arts-and-entertainment/wp/2017/11/13/women-respond-to-roy-moore-allegations-by-reminding-the-world-what-it-looks-like-to-be-14/.

Cooper, Britney C. 2017. "Pussy Don't Fail Me Now: The Place of Vaginas in Black Feminist Theory and Organizing." *Crunk Feminist Collective*, January 23. http://www.crunkfeministcollective.com/2017/01/23/pussy-dont-fail-me-now-the-place-of-vaginas-in-black-feminist-theory-organizing/.

Corrigan, Rose. 2013. *Up against a Wall: Rape Reform and the Failure of Success*. New York: New York University Press.

Crenshaw, Kimberle. 1991. "Mapping the Margins: Intersectionality, Identity Politics, and Violence against Women of Color." *Stanford Law Review* 43:1241–99.

Cruz, Ariane. 2016. *The Color of Kink: Black Women, BDSM, and Pornography*. New York: New York University Press.

Currah, Paisley. 2016. "Transgender Rights without a Theory of Gender?" *Tulsa Law Review* 5:441–51.

Cuskelly, Monica, and Rachel Bryde. 2004. "Attitudes towards the Sexuality of Adults with an Intellectual Disability: Parents, Support Staff, and a Community Sample." *Journal of Intellectual and Developmental Disability* 29: 255–64.

De Beauvoir, Simone. 2010 (1949). *The Second Sex*. Translated by Constance Borde and Sheila Malovany-Chevallier. New York: Knopf.

De la Baume, Maïa. 2014. "Disabled People Say They, Too, Want a Sex Life and Seek Help in Attaining It." *New York Times*, July 4. http://www.nytimes.com/2013/07/05/world/europe/disabled-people-say-they-too-want-a-sex-life-and-seek-help-in-attaining-it.html.

De Waal, Frans. 2016. "What I Learned from Tickling Apes." *New York Times*, April 8. http://www.nytimes.com/2016/04/10/opinion/sunday/what-i-learned-from-tickling-apes.html.

Dean, Tim. 2009. *Unlimited Intimacy: Reflections on the Subculture of Barebacking*. Chicago: University of Chicago Press.

Dean, Tim. 2014. "Stumped." In *Porn Archives*. Edited by Tim Dean, Steven Ruszczycky, and David Squires, 420–40. Durham, NC: Duke University Press.

Dekkers, Midas. (1999) 2000. *Dearest Pet: On Bestiality*. Translated by Paul Vincent. Brooklyn, NY: Verso.

Denis, Lara. 2007. "Sex and the Virtuous Kantian Agent." In *Sex and Ethics: Essays on Sexuality, Virtue, and the Good Life*. Edited by Raja Halwani. New York: Palgrave Macmillan.

Denno, Deborah. 1997. "Sexuality, Rape, and Mental Retardation." *University of Illinois Law Review* 1997:315–434.

Desjardins, Michael. 2012. "The Sexualized Body of the Child: Parents and the Politics of 'Voluntary' Sterilization of People Labeled Intellectually Disabled." In *Sex and Disability*. Edited by Anna Mollow and Robert McRuer, 69–88. Durham, NC: Duke University Press.

Dessel, Robin, and Mildred Ramirez. 1995. "Policies and Procedures Concerning Sexual Expression at the Hebrew Home at Riverdale." August 1995. https://static1.squarespace.com/static/5520af09e4b0c878b5733095/t/56328f20e4b04afbbe92827d/1446154016232/sexualexpressionpolicy.pdf.

Devor, Robinson, dir. 2007. *Zoo*. New York: TH!NKFilm.

Donovan, Josephine. 2007. "Attention to Suffering: Sympathy as a Basis for Ethical Treatment of Animals." In *The Feminist Care Tradition in Animal Ethics: A Reader*. Edited by Carol J. Adams and Josephine Donovan, 174–97. New York: Continuum.

Dougherty, Tom. 2013a. "No Way around Consent: A Reply to Rubenfeld on 'Rape-by-Deception.'" *Yale Law Journal Online* 123:321–34. http://www.yalelawjournal.org/forum/no-way-around-consent-a-reply-to-rubenfeld-on-rape-by-deception.

Dougherty, Tom. 2013b. "Sex, Lies, and Consent." *Ethics* 123:717–44.

Downing, Lisa. 2004. "On the Limits of Sexual Ethics: The Phenomenology of Autassassinaphilia." *Sexuality & Culture* 8:3–17.

Dreisinger, Baz. 2016. *Incarceration Nations: A Journey to Justice in Prisons around the World*. New York: Other Press.

Du Toit, Louise. 2009. *A Philosophical Investigation of Rape: The Making and Unmaking of the Feminine Self*. Routledge Research in Gender and Society. Abingdon-on-Thames, UK: Routledge.

Dukes, Eileen, and Brian E. McGuire. 2009. "Enhancing Capacity to Make Sexuality-Related Decisions in People with an Intellectual Disability." *Journal of Intellectual Disability Research* 53:727–34.

Easterbrook, Gregg. 2013. "How the NFL Fleeces Taxpayers." *The Atlantic,* October. https://www.theatlantic.com/magazine/archive/2013/10/how-the-nfl-fleeces-taxpayers/309448/.

Eckardt, Andy. 2004. "Germany Awaits Verdict in 'Cannibal' Trial." *NBC News,* January 28. http://www.nbcnews.com/id/4039034/ns/world_news/t/germany-awaits-verdict-cannibal-trial/.

Egan, Kelly. 2006. "Morality-Based Legislation Is Alive and Well: Why the Law Permits Consent to Body Modification but Not Sadomasochistic Sex." *Albany Law Review* 70:1615–42.

Edelman, Lee. 2004. *No Future: Queer Theory and the Death Drive*. Durham, NC: Duke University Press.

Ember, Sydney. 2017. "Glenn Thrush, *New York Times* Reporter, Accused of Sexual Misconduct." *New York Times,* November 20. https://www.nytimes.com/2017/11/20/business/media/glenn-thrush-sexual-misconduct.html.

Eng, David L. 2001. *Racial Castration: Managing Masculinity in Asian America*. Durham, NC: Duke University Press.

Engber, Daniel. 2015. "The Strange Case of Anna Stubblefield." *New York Times,* October 20. http://www.nytimes.com/2015/10/25/magazine/the-strange-case-of-anna-stubblefield.html?_r=0.

Engle, Gigi. 2017. "Anal Sex: What You Need to Know." *Teen Vogue,* July 7, 2017. http://www.teenvogue.com/story/anal-sex-what-you-need-to-know/.

Eskridge, William, Jr. 1995. "The Many Faces of Sexual Consent." *William and Mary Law Review* 37:47–68.

Estrich, Susan. 1988. *Real Rape*. Cambridge, MA: Harvard University Press.

European Disability Forum. 2008. "A World Made for Disabilities." *YouTube,* January 30. https://www.youtube.com/watch?v=RsuKxY_9f_8.

Falk, Patricia J. 1998. "Rape by Fraud and Rape by Coercion." *Brooklyn Law Review* 64:39–180.

Falk, Patricia J. 2013. "Not Logic, but Experience: Drawing on Lessons from the Real World in Thinking about the Riddle of Rape-by-Fraud." *Yale Law Journal Online* 123:353–70.

Fausset, Richard. 2017. "Bathroom Law Repeal Leaves Few Pleased in North Carolina." *New York Times*, March 30. https://www.nytimes.com/2017/03/30/us/north-carolina-senate-acts-to-repeal-restrictive-bathroom-law.html.

Fausto-Sterling, Anne. 1993. "The Five Sexes: Why Male and Female Are Not Enough." *The Sciences*, March–April.

Fickling, David. 2006. "Cannibal Killer Gets Life Sentence." *The Guardian*, May 9. https://www.theguardian.com/uk/2006/may/09/ukcrime.world.

Fields, Jessica. 2008. *Risky Lessons: Sex Education and Social Inequality*. New Brunswick, NJ: Rutgers University Press.

Fine, Michelle, and Sara McClelland. 2006. "Sexuality Education and Desire: Still Missing after All These Years." *Harvard Educational Review* 76:297–338.

Fineman, Martha. 2004. *The Autonomy Myth: A Theory of Dependency*. New York: The New Press.

Fineman, Martha. 2008. "The Vulnerable Subject: Anchoring Equality in the Human Condition." *Yale Journal of Law and Feminism* 20:1–24.

Finger, Anne. 1992. "Forbidden Fruit." *New Internationalist*, July 5. https://newint.org/features/1992/07/05/fruit.

Finkelhor, David. 1979. "What's Wrong with Sex between Adults and Children? Ethics and the Problem of Sexual Abuse." *American Journal of Orthopsychiatry* 49:692–97.

Fischel, Joseph J. 2016. *Sex and Harm in the Age of Consent*. Minneapolis: University of Minnesota Press.

Fischel, Joseph J. 2017. "Sodomy's Penumbra." *Journal of Homosexuality Online* 65:1–27.

Fischel, Joseph J., and Claire McKinney. Forthcoming. "Capability without Dignity."

Fischel, Joseph J., and Hilary R. O'Connell. 2015. "Disabling Consent, or Reconstructing Sexual Autonomy." *Columbia Journal of Gender and Law* 30:428–528.

Flanagan, Caitlin. 2018. "The Humiliation of Aziz Ansari." *The Atlantic*. January 14. https://www.theatlantic.com/entertainment/archive/2018/01/the-humiliation-of-aziz-ansari/550541/.

Flannery, Mary Ellen. 2016. "Affirmative Consent: 'Yes Means Yes' in Sex on Campus." *neaToday*, November 17, 2016. http://neatoday.org/2016/11/17/affirmative-consent/.

Foer, Jonathan. 2009. *Eating Animals*. New York: Back Bay Books.

Foley, Douglas E. 1990. "The Great American Football Ritual: Reproducing Race, Class, and Gender Inequality." *Sociology of Sport Journal* 7:111–35.

Ford, Matt. 2017. "Jeff Sessions Reinvigorates the Drug War." *The Atlantic*, May 12. https://www.theatlantic.com/politics/archive/2017/05/sessions-sentencing-memo/526029/.

Ford, Zack. 2017. "CDC Joins Consensus on HIV That 'Undetectable = Untransmittable.'" *Think Progress*, September 28. https://thinkprogress.org /cdc-hiv-undetectable-3a7d331dfda1/.

Foucault, Michel. 1988. *Politics, Philosophy, Culture: Interviews and Other Writings, 1977–1984.* Edited by Lawrence D. Kritzman. New York: Routledge.

Foucault, Michel. 1990 (1976). *The History of Sexuality: An Introduction.* Translated by Robert Hurley. New York: Vintage Books.

Foucault, Michel. 1997. "Sex, Power, and the Politics of Identity." In *Ethics: Subjectivity and Truth: Essential Works of Michel Foucault.* Edited by Paul Rabinow, 163–74. New York: The New Press.

Frank, Gillian. 2015. "Stalling Civil Rights: Conservative Sexual Thought Has Been in the Toilet since the 1940s." *Notches*, November 9. http://notchesblog .com/2015/11/09/stalling-civil-rights/.

Franke, Katherine M. 2002. "Putting Sex to Work." In *Left Legalism/Left Critique.* Edited by Wendy Brown and Janet Halley, 290–336. Durham, NC: Duke University Press.

Franke, Katherine M. 2004. "The Domesticated Liberty of *Lawrence v. Texas.*" *Columbia Law Review* 104:1399–1426.

Fraser, Nancy. 1996. *Justice Interruptus: Critical Reflections on the "Postsocialist" Condition.* Abingdon-on-Thames, UK: Routledge.

Freedman, Estelle B. 2013. *Redefining Rape: Sexual Violence in the Era of Suffrage and Segregation.* Cambridge, MA: Harvard University Press.

Freud, Sigmund. 1990 (1920). *Beyond the Pleasure Principle.* Edited by James Strachey. New York: W. W. Norton.

Freud, Sigmund. 2000 (1905). *Three Essays on the Theory of Sexuality.* Edited and translated by James Strachey. New York: Basic Books.

Friedman, Jaclyn, and Jessica Valenti, eds. 2008. *Yes Means Yes! Visions of Female Sexual Power and a World without Rape.* Berkeley, CA: Seal Press.

Friedman, Marilyn. 2003. *Autonomy, Gender, Politics.* Oxford: Oxford University Press.

Frost, Samantha. 2016. *Biocultural Creatures: Toward a New Theory of the Human.* Durham, NC: Duke University Press.

Gallop, Jane, with Lauren Berlant. 2001. "Loose Lips." In *Our Monica, Ourselves: The Clinton Affair and the National Interest.* Edited by Lauren Berlant and Lisa Duggan, 246–67. New York: New York University Press.

Aniello, Lucia. 2016. "Game Over." *Broad City*, Season 3. Show created by Ilana Glazer and Abbi Jacobson. Aired March 2.

Gamson, Joshua. 1995. *Freaks Talk Back: Tabloid Talk Shows and Sexual Nonconformity.* Chicago: University of Chicago Press.

Garber, Megan. 2017. "Al Franken, That Photo, and Trusting the Women." *The Atlantic.* November 17. https://www.theatlantic.com/entertainment /archive/2017/11/al-franken-that-photo-and-trusting-the-women/545954/.

Garcia, Belkys. 2005. "Reimagining the Right to Commercial Sex: The Impact of *Lawrence v. Texas* on Prostitution Statutes." *City University of New York Law Review* 9:161–82.

Garland-Thomson, Rosemarie. 2002. "Integrating Disability, Transforming Feminist Theory." *NWSA Journal* 14:1–32.

Gassó, Jordi. 2011. "Yale Not Alone in Title IX Probe." *Yale Daily News,* April 15. http://yaledailynews.com/blog/2011/04/15/yale-not-alone-in-title-ix-probe/.

Gavey, Nicola. 2005. *Just Sex? The Cultural Scaffolding of Rape.* Abingdon-on-Thames, UK: Routledge.

Gersen, Jacob, and Jeannie Suk. 2016. "The Sex Bureaucracy." *California Law Review* 104:881–948.

Gerwig, Greta, dir. 2017. *Lady Bird.* Scott Rudin Productions.

Gessen, Masha. 2017. "When Does a Watershed Become a Sex Panic?" *New Yorker,* November 14. https://www.newyorker.com/news/our-columnists/when-does-a-watershed-become-a-sex-panic.

Gibbs, Lindsay, and Casey Quinlan. 2017. "The Trump Administration Is Systematically Dismantling Title IX." *Think Progress,* June 23. https://thinkprogress.org/how-the-trump-administration-is-systematically-attacking-title-ix-21bde2f73fc6.

Gill, Michael. 2015. *Already Doing It: Intellectual Disability and Sexual Agency.* Minneapolis: University of Minnesota Press.

Golladay, Michelle. 2013. "Legislation Would Close 'Gap' in Sex Assault Law Involving Disabled." *Golladay Portfolio,* March 29. https://golladayportfolio.wordpress.com/2013/04/29/legislation-would-close-gap-in-sex-assault-law-involving-disabled/.

Goodley, Daniel, and Rebecca Lawthom. 2011. "Disability, Deleuze, and Sex." In *Deleuze and Sex.* Edited by Frida Beckman, 89–105. Edinburgh: Edinburgh University Press.

Graybill, Rhiannon. 2017. "Critiquing the Discourse of Consent." *Journal of Feminist Studies in Religion* 33:175–76.

Green, Stuart P. 2017. "How to Criminalize Incest." *Social Science Research Network,* May 11. https://papers.ssrn.com/sol3/papers.cfm?abstract_id=2967280.

Grigoriadis, Vanessa. 2017. *Blurred Lines: Rethinking Sex, Power, and Consent on Campus.* Boston: Houghton Mifflin Harcourt.

Grose, Rose, Shelly Grabe, and Danielle Kohfeldt. 2014. "Sexual Education, Gender Ideology, and Youth Sexual Empowerment." *Journal of Sex Research* 51:742–53.

Gross, Aeyal. 2009. "Gender Outlaws before the Law: The Courts of the Borderland." *Harvard Journal of Law and Gender* 32:165–231.

Gross, Aeyal. 2015. "Rape by Deception and the Policing of Gender and Nationality Borders." *Tulane Journal of Law and Sexuality* 24:1–33.

Gross, Terry. 2017. "For Years, Anita Hill Was a 'Canary in the Coal Mine' for Women Speaking Out." *Fresh Air, National Public Radio,* November 30. https://www.npr.org/2017/11/30/567430106/for-years-anita-hill-was-a-canary-in-the-coal-mine-for-women-speaking-out.

Gruber, Aya. 2015. "Not Affirmative Consent." *University of the Pacific Law Review* 47:683–707.

Gruber, Aya. 2016. "Anti-Rape Culture." *Kansas Law Review* 64:1027–56.

Guenther, Lisa. 2013. *Solitary Confinement: Social Death and Its Afterlives.* Minneapolis: University of Minnesota Press.

Haas, Ann P., Philip L. Rodgers, and Jody L. Herman. 2014. "Suicide Attempts among Transgender and Gender Non-conforming Adults: Findings of National Transgender Discrimination Survey." *American Foundation for Suicide Prevention,* January. https://williamsinstitute.law.ucla.edu/wp-content/uploads/AFSP-Williams-Suicide-Report-Final.pdf.

Haberland, Nicole A. 2015. "The Case for Addressing Gender and Power in Sexuality and HIV Education: A Comprehensive Review of Evaluation Studies." *International Perspectives on Sexual and Reproductive Health* 41:31–42.

Hahn, Harlan. 1994. "Feminist Perspectives, Disability, Sexuality, and Law: New Issues and Agendas." *Southern California Review of Law and Women's Studies* 4:97–144.

Haidt, Jonathan. 2001. "The Emotional Dog and Its Rational Tail: A Social Intuitionist Approach to Moral Judgment." *Psychological Review* 108:814–34.

Haidt, Jonathan, Silvia Helena Koller, and Maria G. Dias. 1993. "Affect, Culture, and Morality: Or Is It Wrong to Eat Your Dog?" *Journal of Personality and Social Psychology* 65:613–28.

Halberstam, Judith. 1998. *Female Masculinity.* Durham, NC: Duke University Press.

Halberstam, Judith. 2005. *In a Queer Time and Place: Transgender Bodies, Subcultural Lives.* New York: New York University Press.

Haley, Daniel. 2014. "Bound by Law: A Roadmap for the Practical Legalization of BDSM." *Cardozo Journal of Law and Gender* 21:631–56.

Hall, David S. 1998. "Consent for Sexual Behavior in a College Student Population." *Electronic Journal of Human Sexuality* 1:1–16.

Halley, Janet. 2002. "Sexuality Harassment." In *Left Legalism/Left Critique.* Edited by Wendy Brown and Janet Halley, 80–104. Durham, NC: Duke University Press.

Halley, Janet. 2006. *Split Decisions: How and Why to Take a Break from Feminism.* Princeton: Princeton University Press.

Halley, Janet. 2008. "Rape at Rome: Feminist Interventions in the Criminalization of Sex-Related Violence in Positive International Law." *Michigan Journal of International Law* 30:1–123.

Halley, Janet. 2015. "The Move to Affirmative Consent." *Signs: Journal of Women in Culture and Society* 42:257–79.

Halperin, David M. 1995. *Saint Foucault: Towards a Gay Hagiography.* Oxford: Oxford University Press.

Halwani, Raja. 2007. *Sex and Ethics: Essays on Sexuality, Virtue, and the Good Life.* New York: Palgrave Macmillan.

Halwani, Raja. 2010. *Philosophy of Love, Sex, and Marriage: An Introduction.* New York: Routledge.

Hanna, Cheryl. 2001. "Sex Is Not a Sport: Consent and Violence in Criminal Law." *Boston College Law Review* 42:239–90.

Harcourt, Bernard E. 1999. "The Collapse of the Harm Principle." *Journal of Criminal Law and Criminology* 90:109–94.

Harding, Luke. 2003. "Victim of Cannibal Agreed to Be Eaten." *The Guardian,* December 3. https://www.theguardian.com/world/2003/dec/04/germany.lukeharding.

Harding, Luke. 2004. "Cannibal Who Fried Victim in Garlic Is Cleared of Murder." *The Guardian,* January 30. https://www.theguardian.com/world/2004/jan/31/germany.lukeharding.

Haugaard, Jeffrey J. 2000. "The Challenge of Defining Child Sexual Abuse." *American Psychologist* 55:1036–39.

Hayashi, Mayumi, Mikako Arakida, and Kazutomo Ohashi. 2011. "The Effectiveness of a Sex Education Program Facilitating Social Skills for People with Intellectual Disability in Japan." *Journal of Intellectual and Developmental Disability* 1:11–19.

Hefling, Kimberly. 2014. "Justice Department: Majority of Campus Sexual Assault Goes Unreported to Police." *PBS Newshour,* December 11. http://www.pbs.org/newshour/rundown/four-five-acts-campus-sexual-assault-go-unreported-police/.

Henkin, William A. 2007. "Some Beneficial Aspects of Exploring Personas and Role Play in the BDSM Context." In *Safe, Sane, and Consensual: Contemporary Perspectives on Sadomasochism.* Edited by Darren Langdridge and Meg Barker. Basingstoke, UK: Palgrave Macmillan.

Herman, Jody L. 2013. "Gendered Restrooms and Minority Stress: The Public Regulation of Gender and Its Impact on Transgender People's Lives." *Journal of Public Management and Social Policy* 19:65–80.

Herring, Jonathan. 2005. "Mistaken Sex." *Criminal Law Review* 511–24.

Higdon, Michael J. 2011. "To Lynch a Child: Bullying and Gender Nonconformity in Our Nation's Schools." *Indiana Law Journal* 86:828–78.

Honig, Bonnie. 1993. "Rawls on Politics and Punishment." *Political Research Quarterly* 46:99–125.

Hörnle, Tatjana. 2014. "Consensual Adult Incest: A Sex Offense?" *New Criminal Law Review* 17:76–102.

Howard, Jacqueline. 2017. "Bo Jackson Opens Up about Football's CTE Risk." *CNN,* January 20. http://www.cnn.com/2017/01/13/health/bo-jackson-football-cte-bn/.

Huffer, Lynne. 2013. *Are the Lips a Grave? A Queer Feminist on the Ethics of Sex.* New York: Columbia University Press.

Humphreys, Terry P. 2004. "Understanding Sexual Consent: An Empirical Investigation of the Normative Script for Young Heterosexual Adults." In *Making Sense of Sexual Consent.* Edited by Mark Cowley and Paul Reynolds, 209–26. Aldershot, UK: Ashgate.

Hurd, Heidi M. 1996. "The Moral Magic of Consent." *Legal Theory* 2:121–46.

Hurd, Heidi M. 2005. "Blaming the Victim: A Response to the Proposal That Criminal Law Recognize a General Defense of Contributory Responsibility." *Buffalo Criminal Law Review* 8:503–22.

"Inbred Obscurity: Improving Incest Laws in the Shadow of the 'Sexual Family.'" 2006. *Harvard Law Review* 119:2464–85.

INCITE! Women of Color Against Violence. 2016. *Color of Violence: The INCITE! Anthology.* Durham, NC: Duke University Press.

Ingold, John. 2017. "Colorado Sex Ed Program Closes after Trump Administration Cuts Federal Grant." *Denver Post,* September 20. http://www

.denverpost.com/2017/09/20/colorado-sex-ed-program-closes-after-trump-administration-cuts-federal-grant/.

International Professional Surrogates Association. N.d. "Legal Status: Legal and Ethical." *IPSA*. http://www.surrogatetherapy.org/what-is-surrogate-partner-therapy/legal-status/.

James, E. L. 2011. *Fifty Shades of Grey*. New York: Vintage Books.

Jefferson, Cord. 2010. "The Dementia Bonus: Football as Black Servitude." *The Awl*, August 11. https://theawl.com/the-dementia-bonus-football-as-black-servitude-ebde584cca82.

Jones, Angela. 2018. "#DemandBetter Straight Sex!" *Bully Bloggers*, January 21. https://bullybloggers.wordpress.com/2018/01/21/demandbetter-straight-sex-by-angela-jones/.

Jones, Maggie. 2018. "What Teenagers Are Learning from Online Porn." *New York Times Magazine*, February 7. https://www.nytimes.com/2018/02/07/magazine/teenagers-learning-online-porn-literacy-sex-education.html.

Kafer, Alison. 2013. *Feminist, Queer, Crip*. Bloomington: Indiana University Press.

Kant, Immanuel. 1963. *Lectures on Ethics*. Translated by Louis Infield. Indianapolis: Hackett.

Kaplan, Margo. 2014. "Sex-Positive Law." *New York University Law Review* 87:89–165.

Kendall, Nancy. 2013. *The Sex Education Debates*. Chicago: University of Chicago Press.

Khan, Ummni. 2014. *Vicarious Kinks: S/M in the Socio-Legal Imaginary*. Toronto: University of Toronto Press.

Kim, Suki. 2017. "Public-Radio Icon John Hockenberry Accused of Harassing Female Colleagues." *The Cut: New York Magazine*, December 1. https://www.thecut.com/2017/12/public-radio-icon-john-hockenberry-accused-of-harassment.html.

Kingkade, Tyler. 2014. "Fewer Than One-Third of Campus Sexual Assault Cases Result in Expulsion." *Huffington Post*, September 29. http://www.huffingtonpost.com/2014/09/29/campus-sexual-assault_n_5888742.html.

Kincaid, James R. 1998. *Erotic Innocence: The Culture of Child Molesting*. Durham, NC: Duke University Press.

Kipnis, Laura. 2015. "My Title IX Inquisition." *Chronicle of Higher Education*, May 29. http://www.chronicle.com/article/My-Title-IX-Inquisition/230489.

Kipnis, Laura. 2017a. "Eyewitness to a Title IX Witch Trial." *Chronicle of Higher Education*, April 2. http://www.chronicle.com/article/Eyewitness-to-a-Title-IX-Witch/239634.

Kipnis, Laura. 2017b. *Unwanted Advances: Sexual Paranoia Comes to Campus*. New York: Harper.

Kirkham, Yolanda A., et al. 2014. "Menstrual Suppression in Special Circumstances." *Journal of Obstetrics and Gynaecology Canada* 36:915–24.

Kitrosser, Heidi. 1996. "Meaningful Consent: Toward a New Generation of Statutory Rape Laws." *Virginia Journal of Social Policy and the Law* 4:287–338.

Kittay, Eva. 1999. *Love's Labor: Essays on Women, Equality, and Dependency*. Thinking Gender series. New York: Routledge.

Kitzinger, Celia, and Hannah Frith. 1999. "Just Say No? The Use of Conversation Analysis in Developing a Feminist Perspective on Sexual Refusal." *Discourse and Society* 10:293–316.

Kopac, Catharine, Joni Fritz, and Robert Holt. 1998. "Gynecologic and Reproductive Services for Women with Developmental Disabilities." *Clinical Excellence for Nurse Practitioners: The International Journal of NPACE* 2:88–95.

Kornhaber, Spencer. 2017. "The Kevin Spacey Allegations, through the Lens of Power." *The Atlantic*, November 3. https://www.theatlantic.com/entertainment/archive/2017/11/unpacking-the-kevin-spacey-allegations/544685/.

Kreighbaum, Andrew. 2017. "Transgender Protections Withdrawn." *Inside Higher Ed*, February 23. https://www.insidehighered.com/news/2017/02/23/trump-administration-reverses-title-ix-guidance-transgender-protections.

Kulick, Don, and Jens Rydström. 2015. *Loneliness and Its Opposite: Sex, Disability, and the Ethics of Engagement*. Durham, NC: Duke University Press.

Lamb, Sharon. 2011. "The Place of Mutuality and Care in Democratic Sexuality Education: Incorporating the Other Person." *Counterpoints* 392:29–42.

Lamb, Sharon, Kelly Graling, and Kara Lustig. 2011. "Stereotypes in Four Current AOUM Sexuality Education Curricula: Good Girls, Good Boys, and the New Gender Equality." *American Journal of Sexuality Education* 6:360–80.

Lamb, Sharon, and Zoë D. Peterson. 2012. "Adolescent Girls' Sexual Empowerment: Two Feminists Explore the Concept." *Sex Roles* 66:703–12.

Landesman, Peter, dir. 2015. *Concussion*. Columbia Pictures.

Langdridge, Darren. 2007. "Speaking the Unspeakable: S/M and the Eroticisation of Pain." In *Safe, Sane, and Consensual: Contemporary Perspectives on Sadomasochism*. Edited by Darren Langdridge and Meg Barker, 85–97. Basingstoke, UK: Palgrave Macmillan.

Langdridge, Darren, and Meg Barker, eds. 2008. *Safe, Sane, and Consensual: Contemporary Perspectives on Sadomasochism*. Basingstoke, UK: Palgrave Macmillan.

Larson, Jane. 1993. " 'Women Understand So Little, They Call My Good Nature "Deceit" ': A Feminist Rethinking of Seduction." *Columbia Law Review* 93:374–472.

Laskas, Jeanne M. 2009. "Bennet Omalu, Concussions, and the NFL: How One Doctor Changed Football Forever." *GQ*, September 14. http://www.gq.com/story/nfl-players-brain-dementia-study-memory-concussions.

Lee, Cynthia, and Peter Kwan. 2014. "The Trans Panic Defense: Masculinity, Heteronormativity and the Murder of Transgender Women." *Hastings Law Journal* 66:77–132.

Lee, Youngjae. 2007. "Valuing Autonomy." *Fordham Law Review* 75:2972–88.

Levine, Judith. 2002. *Harmful to Minors: The Perils of Protecting Children from Sex*. New York: Thunder Mouth's Press.

Levintova, Hannah. 2017. "Trump Administration Guts Obamacare Birth Control Rule." *Mother Jones*, October 27. http://www.motherjones.com/politics/2017/10/trump-administration-guts-obamacare-birth-control-rule/.

Levy, Neil. 2003. "What (If Anything) Is Wrong with Bestiality?" *Journal of Social Philosophy* 34:444–56.

Lewinsky, Monica. 2018. "#MeToo and Me." *Vanity Fair,* March, 146–49, 176–78.

Lewis, Ruth, and Cicely Marston. 2016. "Oral Sex, Young People, and Gendered Narratives of Reciprocity." *Journal of Sex Research* 53:776–87.

Linden, Robin et al. 1982. *Against Sadomasochism: A Radical Feminist Analysis.* Palo Alto, CA: Frog in the Well.

Locke, John. 2003 (1689). *Two Treatises of Government and a Letter Concerning Toleration.* Edited by Ian Shapiro. New Haven: Yale University Press.

Locke, Kaitlyn. 2017. "Gloria Steinem Calls Trump the 'Sexual Harasser in Chief.'" *Boston Globe,* December 7. https://www.bostonglobe.com/metro/2017/12/06 /gloria-steinem-calls-trump-sexual-harasser-chief/pN1Te6RN1KN8nz7 Wbk2QeL/story.html.

Loofbourow, Lili. 2018. "The Female Price of Male Pleasure." *The Week,* January 25. http://theweek.com/articles/749978/female-price-male-pleasure.

López, Ian Haney. 1996. *White by Law: The Legal Construction of Race*: New York: New York University Press.

Lorde, Audre. 2007 (1984). *Sister Outsider: Essays and Speeches.* Berkeley, CA: Crossing Press.

Lowder, J. B. 2011. "16 Going on 17: Age-of-Consent Laws, Explained." *Slate,* February 22. http://www.slate.com/articles/news_and_politics/explainer/2011 /02/16_going_on_17.html.

Luke, Brian. 1996. "Justice, Caring, and Animal Liberation." In *Beyond Animal Rights.* Edited by Carol J. Adams and Josephine Donovan, 77–102. Basingstoke, UK: Palgrave Macmillan.

MacKinnon, Catharine A. 1983. "Feminism, Marxism, Method, and the State: Toward Feminist Jurisprudence." *Signs: Journal of Women in Culture and Society* 8:635–58.

MacKinnon, Catharine A. 1985. "Pornography, Civil Rights, and Speech." *Harvard Civil Rights–Civil Liberties Law Review* 20:1–70.

MacKinnon, Catharine A. 1989. *Toward a Feminist Theory of the State.* Cambridge, MA: Harvard University Press.

MacKinnon, Catherine A. 1991. "Reflections on Sex Equality under Law." *Yale Law Journal* 100:1281–1328.

MacKinnon, Catharine A. 1993. "Prostitution and Civil Rights." *Michigan Journal of Gender and Law* 1:13–32.

MacKinnon, Catherine A. 2007a. "Of Mice and Men: A Fragment on Animal Rights." In *The Feminist Care Tradition in Animal Ethics: A Reader.* Edited by Carol J. Adams and Josephine Donovan, 316–32. New York: Continuum.

MacKinnon, Catharine A. 2007b. *Women's Lives, Men's Laws.* Cambridge, MA: Harvard University Press

MacKinnon, Catharine A. 2016. "Rape Redefined." *Harvard Law and Policy Review* 10:431–77.

Madigan, Timothy J. 1998. "The Discarded Lemon: Kant, Prostitution, and Respect for Persons." *Philosophy Now* 21:14–16.

Mairs, Nancy. 1997. *Waist-High in the World: A Life among the Nondisabled.* Boston: Beacon Press.

Malone, Patrick, and Monica Rodriguez. "Comprehensive Sex Education vs. Abstinence-Only-Until-Marriage Programs." *Human Rights* 38:5–7.

Manson, Neil. 2017. "How Not to Think about the Ethics of Deceiving into Sex." *Ethics* 127:415–29.

Marcus, Sharon. 1992. "Fighting Bodies, Fighting Words: A Theory and Politics of Rape Prevention." In *Feminists Theorize the Political*. Edited by Judith Butler and Joan W. Scott, 386–403. New York: Routledge.

Markowicz, Karol. 2018. "Does the Aziz Ansari Sexual Misconduct Story Signal the End of the #MeToo Movement?" *Fox News*, January 15. http://www.foxnews.com/opinion/2018/01/15/does-aziz-ansari-sexual-misconduct-story-signal-end-metoo-movement.html.

Marran-Baden, Amelia. 2017. "College Students Want to Talk about Sex; They Just Don't Know How." *New York Times*, June 26. https://www.nytimes.com/2017/06/26/opinion/college-students-consent-sex-ed.html.

Martin, Jill. 2016. "NFL Acknowledges CTE Link with Football; Now What?" *CNN*, March 16. http://www.cnn.com/2016/03/15/health/nfl-cte-link/.

Martin, Sandra L., et al. 2006. "Physical and Sexual Assault of Women with Disabilities." *Violence Against Women* 12:823–37.

Marusic, Kristina. 2017. "North Carolina Woman Becomes 11th Transgender Person Killed in 2017." *NewNowNext*, May 22. http://www.newnownext.com/sherrell-faulkner-transgender-murder/05/2017/.

Marx, Karl. 2000 (1844). "Economic and Philosophical Manuscripts." In *Karl Marx: Selected Writings*. Edited by David McLellan, 83–121. Oxford: Oxford University Press.

Matsuda, Mari J. 1989. "Public Response to Racist Speech: Considering the Victim's Story." *Michigan Law Review* 87:2320–81.

Matsuda, Mari J., et al. 1993. *Words That Wound: Critical Race Theory, Assaultive Speech, and the First Amendment*. Boulder, CO: Westview Press.

Mauldin, Laura. 2016. *Made to Hear: Cochlear Implants and Raising Deaf Children*. Minneapolis: University of Minnesota Press.

McArthur, Neil. 2016. "Behind the Scenes of the Legal Group That Could Change America's Definition of Sexual Consent." *Vice*, October 20. https://www.vice.com/en_us/article/zn8yg5/behind-the-scenes-of-the-legal-group-that-could-change-americas-definition-of-sexual-consent.

McGregor, Joan. 2005. *Is It Rape? On Acquaintance Rape and Taking Women's Consent Seriously*. New York: Routledge.

McKee, Ann C., et al. 2009. "Chronic Traumatic Encephalopathy in Athletes: Progressive Tauopathy after Repetitive Head Injury." *Journal of Neuropathology and Experimental Neurology* 68:709–35.

McRuer, Robert. 2002. "Compulsory Able-Bodiedness and Queer/Disabled Existence." In *Disability Studies: Enabling the Humanities*. Edited by Rosemarie Garland-Thomson, Brenda Brueggemann, and Sharon Snyder. New York: Modern Language Association.

McRuer, Robert. 2006. *Crip Theory: Cultural Signs of Queerness and Disability*. New York: New York University Press.

McRuer, Robert. 2011. "Disabling Sex: Notes for a Crip Theory of Sexuality." *GLQ: A Journal of Lesbian and Gay Studies* 17:107–17.

McRuer, Robert, and Abby L. Wilkerson. 2003. "Introduction." In "Desiring Disability: Queer Theory Meets Disability Studies." Special issue, edited by Robert McRuer and Abby L. Wilkerson. *GLQ: A Journal of Lesbian and Gay Studies* 9:1–23.

Mingus, Mia. 2011. "Access Intimacy: The Missing Link." *Leaving Evidence*, May 5. https://leavingevidence.wordpress.com/2011/05/05/access-intimacy-the-missing-link/.

Mingus, Mia. 2017. "Access Intimacy, Interdependence, and Disability Justice." *Leaving Evidence*, April 12. https://leavingevidence.wordpress.com/2017/04/12/access-intimacy-interdependence-and-disability-justice/.

Mock, Janet. 2014. *Redefining Realness: My Path to Womanhood, Identity, Love, and So Much More*. New York: Atria Books.

Mollow, Anna. 2012. "Is Sex Disability? Queer Theory and the Disability Drive." In *Sex and Disability*. Edited by Robert McRuer and Anna Mollow, 286–312. Durham, NC: Duke University Press.

Moore, Antonio. 2015. "Football's War on the Minds of Black Men." *Vice*, December 24. https://sports.vice.com/en_us/article/footballs-war-on-the-minds-of-black-men.

Morris, Benjamin. 2014. "The Rate of Domestic Violence Arrests among NFL Players." *FiveThirtyEight*, July 31. https://fivethirtyeight.com/datalab/the-rate-of-domestic-violence-arrests-among-nfl-players/.

Moser, Charles, and J. J. Madeson. 1996. *Bound to Be Free: The SM Experience*. New York: Bloomsbury.

Movement Advancement Project et al. 2013. "A Broken Bargain for Transgender Workers." *MAP*, September. http://www.lgbtmap.org/file/a-broken-bargain-for-transgender-workers.pdf.

National Coalition for Sexual Freedom. 2013. "Statement on Consent." *NCSF*, February. https://www.ncsfreedom.org/images/stories/pdfs/Consent%20Counts/CC_Docs_New_011513/ConsentStatement.pdf.

National Coalition for Sexual Freedom. 2015. "Letter to ALI from NCSF." *NCSF*, January. https://ncsfreedom.org/images/stories/ALI/ALI%20Letter.pdf.

National Coalition for Sexual Freedom. n.d. "Consent Is a Defense." *NCSF*. https://www.ncsfreedom.org/images/stories/ALI/ALI_article.pdf.

National Coalition of Anti-Violence Programs. 2015. "Lesbian, Gay, Bisexual, Transgender, Queer, and HIV-Affected Hate Violence in 2014." *NCAVP*. https://avp.org/wp-content/uploads/2017/04/2014_HV_Report-Final.pdf.

National Health Care for the Homeless Council. 2014. "Gender Minority and Homelessness: Transgender Population." *Quarterly Research Review of the National HCH Council* 3:1–6.

National Institute of Justice. 2010. "Rape and Sexual Violence: Victims and Perpetrators." *NIJ*, October 26. https://www.nij.gov/topics/crime/rape-sexual-violence/Pages/victims-perpetrators.aspx.

NCSF. *See* National Coalition for Sexual Freedom.

Nedelsky, Jennifer. 2011. *Law's Relations: A Relational Theory of Self, Autonomy, and Law*. Oxford: Oxford University Press.

New, Jake. 2016. "Due Process and Sex Assaults." *Inside Higher Ed*, May 17. https://www.insidehighered.com/news/2016/05/17/professors-urge-department-education-revise-sexual-assault-guidance.

Newmahr, Staci. 2011. *Playing on the Edge: Sadomasochism, Risk, and Intimacy*. Bloomington: Indiana University Press.

New York Times. 2017. "Understanding Transgender Access Laws." February 24. https://www.nytimes.com/2017/02/24/us/transgender-bathroom-law.html.

Nosek, Margaret, et al. 2006. "Disability, Psychosocial, and Demographic Characteristics of Abused Women with Physical Disabilities." *Violence Against Women* 12:838–50.

Nunberg, Geoff. 2016. "Is Trump's Call for 'Law and Order' a Coded Racial Message?" *NPR*, July 28. http://www.npr.org/2016/07/28/487560886/is-trumps-call-for-law-and-order-a-coded-racial-message.

Nussbaum, Martha C. 1999. *Sex and Social Justice*. Oxford: Oxford University Press.

Nussbaum, Martha C. 2001. *Women and Human Development: The Capabilities Approach*. Cambridge: Cambridge University Press.

Nussbaum, Martha C. 2007. *Frontiers of Justice: Disability, Nationality, Species Membership*. Cambridge, MA: Harvard University Press.

Nussbaum, Martha C. 2010. "The Capabilities of People with Cognitive Disabilities." In *Cognitive Disability and Its Challenge to Moral Philosophy*. Edited by Eva Kittay and Licia Carlson, 75–96. Malden, MA: Wiley-Blackwell.

Nussbaum, Martha C. 2011. *Creating Capabilities: The Human Development Approach*. Cambridge, MA: Harvard University Press.

Oberman, Michelle. 2000. "Regulating Consensual Sex with Minors: Defining a Role for Statutory Rape." *Buffalo Law Review* 48:703–84.

Oberman, Michelle. 2001. "Girls in the Master's House: Of Protection, Patriarchy, and the Potential for Using the Master's Tools to Reconfigure Statutory Rape Law." *DePaul Law Review* 50:799–826.

O'Brien, Mark. 1990. "On Seeing a Sex Surrogate." *The Sun*, May. https://www.thesunmagazine.org/issues/174/on-seeing-a-sex-surrogate.

Oliver, Michael. 2004. "If I Had a Hammer: The Social Model in Action." In *Disabling Barriers, Enabling Environments*. Edited by Colin Barnes, Sally French, John Swain, and Carol Thomas, 7–12. London: Sage.

Oliver, Michael. 2013. "The Social Model of Disability, Thirty Years On." *Disability and Society* 28:1024–26.

Oliver, Michael, Bob Sapey, and Pam Thomas. 2012 (1983). *Social Work with Disabled People*. Basingstoke, UK: Palgrave MacMillan.

O'Regan, Deirdra. 2016. "The Very British Video Helping Americans Understand Sexual Consent." *Washington Post*, June 10. https://www.washingtonpost.com/news/worldviews/wp/2016/06/10/the-very-british-video-helping-americans-understand-sexual-consent/?utm_term=.a35720c632ae.

Ost, Suzanne. 2009. *Child Pornography and Sexual Grooming: Legal and Societal Responses*. Cambridge: Cambridge University Press.

Owens-Reid, Danielle, and Kristin Russo. 2014. "How to Talk to Your Gay Teen about Sex." *Time*. http://time.com/why-schools-cant-teach-sex-ed/#how-to-talk-to-your-gay-teen-about-sex.

Pa, Monica. 2001. "Beyond the Pleasure Principle: The Criminalization of Consensual Sadomasochistic Sex." *Texas Journal of Women and the Law* 11:51–92.

Pascoe, C. J. 2011. *Dude, You're a Fag: Masculinity and Sexuality in High School.* Berkeley: University of California Press.

Pateman, Carole. 1980. "Women and Consent." *Political Theory* 8:149–68.

Penny, Laurie. 2014. "What the 'Transgender Tipping Point' Really Means." *New Republic,* June 27. https://newrepublic.com/article/118451/what-transgender-tipping-point-really-means.

Perske, Robert. 1972. "The Dignity of Risk." In *The Principle of Normalization of Human Services.* Edited by Wolf Wolfensberger, 194–200. Toronto: National Institute on Mental Retardation.

Peters, Jeremy W., Jo Becker, and Julie Hirschfeld. 2017. "Trump Rescinds Rules on Bathrooms for Transgender Students." *New York Times,* February 22. https://www.nytimes.com/2017/02/22/us/politics/devos-sessions-transgender-students-rights.html.

Peterson, Latoya. 2008. "The Not-Rape Epidemic." In *Yes Means Yes! Visions of Female Sexual Power and a World without Rape.* Edited by Jaclyn Friedman and Jessica Valenti, 209–20. Berkeley, CA: Seal Press.

Pettit, Philip. 2013. *On the People's Terms: A Republican Theory and Model of Democracy.* Cambridge: Cambridge University Press.

Pew Research Center. 2015. "The American Family Today." *Pew Research Center,* December 17. http://www.pewsocialtrends.org/2015/12/17/1-the-american-family-today/.

Peyser, Andrea. 2017. "#MeToo Has Lumped Trivial In with Legitimate Sexual Assault." *New York Post,* November 17. https://nypost.com/2017/11/17/metoo-has-lumped-trivial-in-with-legitimate-sexual-assault/.

Peyser, Andrea. 2018. "The #MeToo Movement Has Officially Jumped the Shark." *New York Post.* January 15. https://nypost.com/2018/01/15/the-metoo-movement-has-officially-jumped-the-shark/.

Phipps, Charles A. 2002. "Misdirected Reform: On Regulating Consensual Sexual Activity between Teenagers." *Cornell Journal of Law and Public Policy* 12:373–445.

Pierce, Jessica. 2016. *Run, Spot, Run: The Ethics of Keeping Pets.* Chicago: University of Chicago Press.

Pinsker, Joe. 2015. "Why the NFL Decided to Start Paying Taxes." *The Atlantic,* April 28. https://www.theatlantic.com/business/archive/2015/04/why-the-nfl-decided-to-start-paying-taxes/391742/.

Plummer, Sara-Beth, and Patricia Findley. 2012. "Women with Disabilities' Experience with Physical and Sexual Abuse: Review of the Literature and Implications for the Field." *Trauma, Violence, and Abuse* 13:15–29.

Puar, Jasbir K. 2017. *The Right to Maim: Debility, Capacity, and Disability.* Durham, NC: Duke University Press.

Ramachandran, Gowri. 2009. "Against the Right to Bodily Integrity: Of Cyborgs and Human Rights." *Denver University Law Review* 87:1–57.

Ramachandran, Gowri. 2013. "Delineating the Heinous: Rape, Sex, and Self-Possession." *Yale Law Journal* 123:371–88.

Raymond, Janice. 1979. *The Transsexual Empire: The Making of the She-Male*. Boston: Beacon Press.

Reed, Adolph, Jr. 2015. "From Jenner to Dolezal: One Trans Good, the Other Not So Much." *Common Dreams*, June 15. https://www.commondreams.org/views/2015/06/15/jenner-dolezal-one-trans-good-other-not-so-much.

Regan, Tom. 2004. *The Case for Animal Rights*. Berkeley: University of California Press.

Rhoden, William C. 2011. "At Some N.F.L. Positions, Stereotypes Create Prototypes." *New York Times*, December 11. http://www.nytimes.com/2011/12/12/sports/football/at-some-nfl-positions-stereotypes-reign.html.

Rich, Adrienne. 1980. "Compulsory Heterosexuality and Lesbian Existence." *Signs: Journal of Women in Culture and Society* 5:631–60.

Riddle, Christopher. 2014. *Disability and Justice: The Capabilities Approach in Practice*. Lanham, MD: Lexington Books.

Roberts, Dorothy E. 1993. "Rape, Violence, and Women's Autonomy." *Chicago-Kent Law Review* 69:359–88.

Robertson, Stephen. 2010. "Shifting the Scene of the Crime: Sodomy and the American History of Sexual Violence." *Journal of the History of Sexuality* 19:223–42.

Rodríguez, Juana María. 2014. *Sexual Futures*. New York: New York University Press.

Rohleder, Poul, and Leslie Swartz. 2009. "Providing Sex Education to Persons with Learning Disabilities in the Era of HIV/AIDS." *Journal of Health Psychology* 14:601–10.

Roiphe, Katie. 2017. "The Other Whisper Network." *Harper's*, March. https://harpers.org/archive/2018/03/the-other-whisper-network-2/.

Rosenberg, Gabriel. 2017. "How Meat Changed Sex: The Law of Interspecies Intimacy after Industrial Reproduction." *GLQ: A Journal of Lesbian and Gay Studies* 23:473–507.

Rotunda, Ronald D. 2016. "Increased Controversy over the Future of American Law Institute." *Verdict*, June 20. https://verdict.justia.com/2016/06/20/increased-controversy-future-american-law-institute.

Roupenian, Kristen. 2017. "Cat Person." *New Yorker*, December 11. https://www.newyorker.com/magazine/2017/12/11/cat-person.

Rubenfeld, Jed. 2013a. "The Riddle of Rape-by-Deception and the Myth of Sexual Autonomy." *Yale Law Journal* 122:1372–1443.

Rubenfeld, Jed. 2013b. "Rape-by-Deception: A Response." *Yale Law Journal Online* 123:389–406. https://www.yalelawjournal.org/forum/rape-by-deceptiona-response.

Rubenfeld, Jed. 2014. "Mishandling Rape." *New York Times*, November 15. https://www.nytimes.com/2014/11/16/opinion/sunday/mishandling-rape.html.

Rubin, Gayle S. 1991. "The Catacombs: A Temple of the Butthole." In *Leatherfolk: Radical Sex, People, and Practice*. Edited by Mark Thompson, 119–41. Los Angeles: Daedalus.

Rubin, Gayle S. 1993 (1984). "Thinking Sex: Notes for a Radical Theory of the Politics of Sexuality." In *The Lesbian and Gay Studies Reader*. Edited by

Henry Abelove, Michèle A. Barale, and David M. Halperin, 3–44. New York: Routledge.

Rubin, Gayle S. 2011. "Blood under the Bridge: Reflections on 'Thinking Sex.'" *GLQ: A Journal of Lesbian and Gay Studies* 17:15–48.

Rubin, Henry A., and Dana A. Shapiro, dirs. 2005. *Murderball.* TH!NKFilm.

Rudd, Andy. 2013. "Schoolgirl Justine McNally Freed after Being Jailed for Three Years for Posing as Boy to Bed Girl." *Mirror*, June 12. https://www.mirror.co.uk/news/uk-news/schoolgirl-justine-mcnally-freed-after-1947851.

Rudy, Kathy. 2011. *Loving Animals: Toward a New Animal Advocacy.* Minneapolis: University of Minnesota Press.

Rudy, Kathy. 2012. "LGBTQ . . . Z?" *Hypatia* 27:601–15.

Ryzick, Melena, Cara Buckley, and Jodi Kantor. 2017. "Louis C.K. Is Accused by 5 Women of Sexual Misconduct." *New York Times,* November 9. https://www.nytimes.com/2017/11/09/arts/television/louis-ck-sexual-misconduct.html.

Sack, Kevin. 1998. "Georgia's High Court Voids Sodomy Law." *New York Times,* November 24. http://www.nytimes.com/1998/11/24/us/georgia-s-high-court-voids-sodomy-law.html.

Salamon, Gayle. 2010. *Transgender and Rhetorics of Materiality.* New York: Columbia University Press.

Sarrel, Philip M., and Lorna J. Sarrel. 1981. "Sexual Unfolding." *Journal of Adolescent Healthcare* 2:93–99.

Satz, Ani B. 2008. "Disability, Vulnerability, and the Limits of Antidiscrimination." *Washington Law Review* 83:513–68.

Saul, Stephanie, and Kate Taylor. 2017. "Betsy DeVos Reverses Obama-Era Policy on Campus Sexual Assault Investigations." *New York Times,* September 22. https://www.nytimes.com/2017/09/22/us/devos-colleges-sex-assault.html?_r=0.

Savasi, Ingrid, et al. 2009. "Menstrual Suppression for Adolescents with Developmental Disabilities." *Journal of Pediatric and Adolescent Gynecology* 22:143–49.

Schilt, Kristen, and Laurel Westbrook. 2009. "Doing Gender, Doing Heteronormativity: 'Gender Normals,' Transgender People, and the Social Maintenance of Heterosexuality." *Gender and Society* 23:440–64.

Schulhofer, Stephen J. 1992. "Taking Sexual Autonomy Seriously: Rape Law and Beyond." *Law and Philosophy* 11:35–94.

Schulhofer, Stephen J. 1998. *Unwanted Sex: The Culture of Intimidation and the Failure of Law.* Cambridge, MA: Harvard University Press.

Schulhofer, Stephen J. 2015. "Consent: What It Means and Why It's Time to Require It." *University of the Pacific Law Review* 47:665–81.

Schulman, Sarah. 2016. *Conflict Is Not Abuse: Overstating Harm, Community Responsibility, and the Duty of Repair.* Vancouver: Arsenal Pulp Press.

Schultz, Vicki. 2003. "The Sanitized Workplace." *Yale Law Journal* 112:2061–2193.

Schwartz, Susan. 1983. "An Argument for the Elimination of the Resistance Requirement from the Definition of Forcible Rape." *Loyola of Los Angeles Law Review* 16:567–602.

Scott, Joan W. 1991. "The Evidence of Experience." *Critical Inquiry* 17:773–97.

Sedgwick, Eve Kosofksy. 1985. *Between Men: English Literature and Male Homosocial Desire.* New York: Columbia University Press.

Sedgwick, Eve Kosofksy. 1990. *The Epistemology of the Closet.* Berkeley: University of California Press.

Sexuality Information and Education Council of the United States. 2018. "A History of Federal Funding For Abstinence-Only-Until-Marriage Programs." August 2011. https://siecus.org/wp-content/uploads/2018/08/A-History-of-AOUM-Funding-Final-Draft.pdf

Shakespeare, Tom. 2006. "The Social Model of Disability." In *The Disabilities Studies Reader.* Edited by Lennard J. Davis, 197–204. Abingdon-on-Thames, UK: Routledge.

Shakespeare, Tom, and Nicholas Watson. 2002. "The Social Model of Disability: An Outdated Ideology?" In *Research in Social Science and Disability.* Edited by Barbara Altman and Sharon Barnartt, 9–28. Bingley, UK: Emerald Group.

Sharpe, Alex. 2014. "Criminalising Sexual Intimacy: Transgender Defendants and the Legal Construction of Non-consent." *Criminal Law Review* 3:207–23.

Sharpe, Alex. 2015. "Sexual Intimacy, Gender Variance, and Criminal Law." *Nordic Journal of Human Rights* 33:380–91.

Shildrick, Margrit. 2009. *Dangerous Discourses of Disability, Subjectivity, and Sexuality.* Basingstoke, UK: Palgrave MacMillan.

Shor, Fran. 2014. "Racism, Football Follies, and the Killing of Michael Brown." *TruthOut,* August 25. http://www.truth-out.org/speakout/item/25794-racism-football-follies-and-the-killing-of-michael-brown.

Short, April M. 2014. "Michelle Alexander: White Men Get Rich from Legal Pot, Black Men Stay in Prison." *AlterNet,* March 16. http://www.alternet.org/drugs/michelle-alexander-white-men-get-rich-legal-pot-black-men-stay-prison.

Shuttleworth, Russell. 2007a. "Critical Research and Policy Debates in Disability and Sexuality Studies." *Sexuality Research and Social Policy* 4:1–14.

Shuttleworth, Russell. 2007b. "Disability and Sexuality: Toward a Constructionist Focus on Access in the Inclusion of Disabled People in the Sexual Rights Movement." In *Sexual Inequalities and Social Justice.* Edited by Niels Tunis and Gilbert Herd, 174–208. Berkeley: University of California Press.

Siebers, Tobin. 2012. "A Sexual Culture for Disabled People." In *Sex and Disability.* Edited by Robert McRuer and Anna Mollow, 37–53. Durham, NC: Duke University Press.

SIECUS. *See* Sexuality Information and Education Council of the United States

Siegel, Reva B. 2008. "Dignity and the Politics of Protection: Abortion Restrictions under *Casey/Carhart.*" *Yale Law Journal* 117:1694–1800.

Sifferlin, Alexandra. 2014. "Why Schools Can't Teach Sex Ed." *Time,* n.d. http://time.com/why-schools-cant-teach-sex-ed/.

Sifris, Dennis, and James Myhre. 2017. "The Real Reasons Why People Don't Use Condoms." *VeryWell,* July 17. https://www.verywell.com/the-real-reasons-why-people-dont-use-condoms-49669.

Silman, Ann. 2018. "Aziz Ansari, 'Cat Person,' and the #MeToo Backlash." *The Cut: New York Magazine.* January 16. https://www.thecut.com/2018/01/aziz-ansari-cat-person-and-the-metoo-backlash.html.

Simon, Carolyn. 2016. "Municipal Equality Index Shows Noteworthy Progress on Transgender Equality." *Human Rights Campaign Blog,* October 18. http://www.hrc.org/blog/municipal-equality-index-shows-noteworthy-progress-on-transgender-equality.

Singer, Peter. 2001. "Heavy Petting." *Nerve.* https://www.utilitarian.net/singer/by/2001----.htm.

Singer, Peter. 2009. *Animal Liberation.* New York: Harper.

Singer, Peter. 2014. "Should Adult Sibling Incest Be a Crime?" *Project Syndicate,* October 8. https://www.project-syndicate.org/commentary/should-adult-sibling-incest-be-a-crime-by-peter-singer-2014-10.

Smith, Christian. 2015. *To Flourish or Destruct: A Personalist Theory of Human Goods, Motivations, Failure, and Evil.* Chicago: University of Chicago Press.

Smith, S. E. 2015. "It's Not the BDSM That's Titillating in 'Fifty Shades of Grey'—It's All That Money." *xojane,* February 16. http://www.xojane.com/entertainment/fifty-shades-bdsm-money.

Sobsey, Dick, and Tanis Doe. 1991. "Patterns of Sexual Abuse and Assault." *Sexuality and Disability* 9:243–59.

Sokol, Zach. 2015. "The Strange, Sad Story of the Man Named Mr. Hands Who Died from Having Sex with a Horse." *Vice,* July 16. http://www.vice.com/read/ten-years-ago-mr-hands-got-fucked-to-death-by-a-horse-716.

Solomon, Harris. 2016. *Metabolic Living: Food, Fat, and the Absorption of Illness in India.* Durham, NC: Duke University Press.

Spade, Dean. 2003. "Resisting Medicine, Re/modeling Gender." *Berkeley Women's Law Journal* 18:15–39.

Spade, Dean. 2011. *Normal Life: Administrative Violence, Critical Trans Politics, and the Limits of Law.* Brooklyn, NY: South End Press.

Spade, Dean. 2013. "Intersectional Resistance and Law Reform." *Signs: Journal of Women in Culture and Society* 38:1031–55.

Spade, Dean, moderator. 2017. "Models of Futurity." In *Trap Door: Trans Cultural Production and the Politics of Visibility.* Edited by Reina Gossett, Eric A. Stanley, and Johanna Burton, 321–37. Cambridge, MA: MIT Press.

Spindelman, Marc. 2003. "Surviving *Lawrence v. Texas.*" *Michigan Law Review* 102:1615–67.

Stanley, Eric A. 2011. "Fugitive Flesh: Gender Self-Determination, Queer Abolition, and Trans Resistance." In *Captive Genders: Trans Embodiment and the Prison Industrial Complex.* Edited by Eric A. Stanley and Nat Smith, 1–14. Oakland, CA: AK Press.

Starnes, Todd. 2017. "Parents Outraged over Teen Vogue Anal Sex How-To Column (but Magazine Still Defends It)." *Fox News,* July 18. http://www.foxnews.com/opinion/2017/07/18/teen-vogue-defends-teaching-kids-how-to-engage-in-sodomy.html.

stein, david. 2002. "'Safe Sane Consensual: The Making of a Shibboleth." http://www.boybear.us/ssc.pdf.

Stein, Rob. 2010. "Obama Administration Launches a Sex-Ed Program." *Washington Post,* October 28. http://www.washingtonpost.com/wp-dyn/content/article/2010/10/27/AR2010102707471.html?sid=ST2010102800242.

Steinmetz, Katy. 2014. "The Transgender Tipping Point." *Time Magazine,* June 9. http://time.com/135480/transgender-tipping-point/.

Stepler, Renee. 2017. "Number of U.S. Adults Cohabiting with a Partner Continues to Rise, Especially among Those 50 and Older." *Pew Research Center,* April 6. http://www.pewresearch.org/fact-tank/2017/04/06/number-of-u-s-adults-cohabiting-with-a-partner-continues-to-rise-especially-among-those-50-and-older/.

Stryker, Susan. 2017. *Transgender History: The Roots of Today's Revolution.* New York: Seal Press.

Summers, Daniel. 2017. "Some Gay Men on PrEP May Stop Using Condoms: Does It Matter?" *Slate,* March 29. http://www.slate.com/blogs/outward/2017/03/29/do_some_gay_men_on_prep_stop_using_condoms.html.

Sunstein, Cass R. 1996. "On the Expressive Function of Law." *University of Pennsylvania Law Review* 144:2021–53.

Sunstein, Cass R. 2004. "Liberty after *Lawrence.*" *Ohio State Law Journal* 65:1059–80.

Swango-Wilson, Amy. 2008. "Caregiver Perceptions and Implications for Sex Education for Individuals with Intellectual and Developmental Disabilities." *Sexuality and Disability* 26:167–74.

Swango-Wilson, Amy. 2011. "Meaningful Sex Education Programs for Individuals with Intellectual/Developmental Disabilities." *Sexuality and Disability* 29:113–18.

Switch, Gary. 2002. "Origin of RACK: RACK vs. SSC." https://www.evilmonk.org/a/rack.cfm.

Talvi, Silja. 2007. "Incarceration Nation." *The Nation,* January 5. https://www.thenation.com/article/incarceration-nation/.

Tepfer, Daniel. 2012. "Supreme Court Sets Accused Rapist Free." *Connecticut Post,* October 1. http://www.ctpost.com/news/article/Supreme-Court-sets-accused-rapist-free-3910077.php.

Terzi, Lorella. 2004. "The Social Model of Disability: A Philosophical Critique." *Journal of Applied Philosophy* 21:141–57.

Thompson, Mark. 1991. *Leatherfolk: Radical Sex, People, Politics, and Practice.* Los Angeles: Daedalus.

Traister, Rebecca. 2015. "The Game Is Rigged." *The Cut: New York Magazine,* October 20. https://www.thecut.com/2015/10/why-consensual-sex-can-still-be-bad.html.

Traister, Rebecca. 2017. "This Moment Isn't (Just) about Sex: It's Really about Work." *The Cut: New York Magazine,* December 10. https://www.thecut.com/2017/12/rebecca-traister-this-moment-isnt-just-about-sex.html.

Traister, Rebecca. 2018. "No One Is Silencing Katie Roiphe." *The Cut: New York Magazine,* February 6. https://www.thecut.com/2018/02/rebecca-traister-on-katie-roiphe-harpers-and-metoo.html.

Traister, Rebecca, and Ross Douthat. 2017. "What Are the Lessons of the Post-Weinstein Moment?" *The Cut: New York Magazine,* November 21. https://www.thecut.com/2017/11/rebecca-traister-ross-douthat-post-weinstein-lessons.html.

Tralau, Jonah. 2013. "Incest and Liberal Neutrality." *Journal of Political Philosophy* 21:87–105.

Tremain, Shelley. 2002. "On the Subject of Impairment." In *Disability/Postmodernity: Embodying Disability Theory*. Edited by Mairian Corker and Tom Shakespeare, 32–47. London: Continuum.

Treleven, Ed. 2011. "Man Charged with Allegedly Having Sex with 14-Year-Old." *Wisconsin State Journal*, January 5. http://host.madison.com/wsj /news/local/crime_and_courts/man-charged-with-allegedly-having-sex-with--year-old/article_0552c24c-1908-11e0-a791-001cc4c002e0.html.

Tribe, Laurence H. 2004. "*Lawrence v. Texas*: The 'Fundamental Right' That Dare Not Speak Its Name." *Harvard Law Review* 117:1893–1956.

Truscott, Carol. 1991. "S/M: Some Questions and a Few Answers." In *Leatherfolk: Radical Sex, People, Politics, and Practice*. Edited by Mark Thompson, 15–36. Los Angeles: Daedalus Publishing.

Tuerkheimer, Deborah. 2013. "Sex without Consent." *Yale Law Journal* 123: 335–52.

Tuvel, Rebecca. 2017. "In Defense of Transracialism." *Hypatia* 32:263–78.

Underhill, Kristen, Paul Montgomery, and Don Operario. 2008. "Abstinence-Plus Programs for HIV Infection Prevention in High-Income Countries" (review). *Cochrane Database of Systematic Reviews*. January 23. http://www .cochrane.org/CD007006/HIV_abstinence-plus-programs-for-preventing-hiv-infection-in-high-income-countries-as-defined-by-the-world-bank.

US Department of Justice. 2016. "U.S. Departments of Justice and Education Release Joint Guidance to Help Schools Ensure the Civil Rights of Transgender Students." *U.S. Department of Education*, May 13. https://www.ed.gov /news/press-releases/us-departments-education-and-justice-release-joint-guidance-help-schools-ensure-civil-rights-transgender-students.

Vernacchio, Alfred. 2014. *For Goodness Sex: Changing the Way We Talk to Teens about Sexuality, Values, and Health*. New York: Harper.

Victor, Daniel. 2017. "Kevin Spacey Criticized for Using Apology to Anthony Rapp to Come Out." *New York Times*, October 30. https://www.nytimes .com/2017/10/30/arts/kevin-spacey-reaction.html.

Wade, Holly A. 2002. "Discrimination, Sexuality, and People with Significant Disabilities: Issues of Access and the Right to Sexual Expression in the United States." *Disability Studies Quarterly* 22:9–27.

Ward, Jane. 2015. *Not Gay: Sex between Straight White Men*. New York: New York University Press.

Wardenski, Joseph J. 2004. "A Minor Exception? The Impact of *Lawrence v. Texas* on LGBT Youth." *Journal of Criminal Law and Criminology* 95:1363–1410.

Waters, Mark, dir. 2004. *Mean Girls*. Paramount Pictures.

Way, Katie. 2018. "I Went on a Date with Aziz Ansari: It Turned into the Worst Night of My Life." *Babe*, January 13. https://babe.net/2018/01/13/aziz-ansari-28355.

Weinberg, Jill. 2016. *Consensual Violence: Sex, Sports, and the Politics of Injury*. Berkeley: University of California Press.

Weinstein, Michael M. 2016. "Becoming Disabled." *New Yorker,* December 22. https://www.newyorker.com/books/page-turner/becoming-disabled.

Weiss, Bari. 2018. "Aziz Ansari Is Guilty, of Not Being a Mind Reader." *New York Times,* January 15. https://www.nytimes.com/2018/01/15/opinion/aziz-ansari-babe-sexual-harassment.html?mtrref=www.thenation.com& assetType=opinion.

Weiss, Margot. 2011. *Techniques of Pleasure: BDSM and the Circuits of Sexuality.* Durham, NC: Duke University Press.

Weitz, Paul, and Chris Weitz, dirs. 1999. *American Pie.* Universal Pictures.

Wertheimer, Alan. 1996. *Exploitation.* Princeton: Princeton University Press.

Wertheimer, Alan. 2003. *Consent to Sexual Relations.* Cambridge: Cambridge University Press.

West, Robin. 2000. "The Difference in Women's Hedonic Lives: A Phenomenological Critique of Feminist Legal Theory." *Wisconsin Women's Law Journal* 15:149–215.

Westen, Peter. 2004. *The Logic of Consent: The Diversity and Deceptiveness of Consent as a Defense to Criminal Conduct (Law, Justice, and Power).* Abingdon-on-Thames, UK: Routledge.

White, Ken. 2012. "Frankly, I Don't Care about How Due Process Makes You Feel." *Popehat,* October 9. https://www.popehat.com/2012/10/09/frankly-i-dont-care-how-due-process-makes-you-feel/.

White, Patrick. 2003. "Sex Education; or, How the Blind Became Heterosexual. *GLQ: A Journal of Lesbian and Gay Studies* 9:133–4.

Whitehouse, Michelle A., and Marita P. McCabe. 1997. "Sex Education Programs for People with Intellectual Disability: How Effective Are They?" *Education and Training in Mental Retardation and Developmental Disabilities* 32:229–40.

Whittier, Nancy. 2009. *The Politics of Child Sexual Abuse: Emotion, Social Movements, and the State.* Oxford: Oxford University Press.

Wilkerson, Abby L. 2002. "Disability, Sex Radicalism, and Political Agency." *NWSA Journal* 14:33–57.

Williams, D. J., et al. 2014. "From 'SSC' and 'RACK' to the '4Cs': Introducing a new Framework for Negotiating BDSM Participation." *Electronic Journal of Human Sexuality* 17:1–10.

Williamson, Bess. 2015. "Access." In *Keywords for Disability Studies.* Edited by Rachel Adams, Benjamin Reiss, and David Serlin, 14–17. New York: New York University Press.

Wilson, Brenda. 2010. "Proven Sex-Ed Programs Get a Boost from Obama." *NPR,* June 6. http://www.npr.org/templates/story/story.php?storyId=127514185.

Wilson, Carlene, and Neil Brewer. 1992. "The Incidence of Criminal Victimisation of Individuals with an Intellectual Disability." *Australian Psychologist* 27:114–17.

Withers, Bethany P. 2015. "Without Consequence: When Professional Athletes Are Violent off the Field." *Journal of Sports and Entertainment Law* 6:373–411.

Wolf, Jonathan, and Avner de-Shalit. 2007. *Disadvantage.* Oxford: Oxford University Press.

Yeatman, Anna. 2000. "What Can Disability Tell Us about Participation?" *Law in Context: A Socio-legal Journal* 17:181–202.

Young, Cathy. 2015. "Consent: It's a Piece of Cake." *Spiked,* November 2. http://www.spiked-online.com/newsite/article/consent-its-a-piece-of-cake/17594#.WYRvP1qGPUr.

Young, Cathy. 2017. "Is 'Weinsteining Getting Out of Hand?" *Los Angeles Times,* November 1. http://www.latimes.com/opinion/op-ed/la-oe-young-weinsteining-goes-too-far-20171101-story.html.

Young, Iris. 2005. *On Female Body Experience: 'Throwing Like a Girl" and Other Essays.* New York: Oxford University Press.

Young Turks. 2014. "This 'Consent Is Sexy' Video Is Anything but Sexy." *YouTube,* November 8. https://www.youtube.com/watch?v=hUwAKhHDXlU.

Younger, Teresa C. 2012. "Official Statement RE: *State v. Richard Fourtin* Conviction." CT General Assembly Permanent Commission on the Status of Women, October 2. https://ctpcsw.files.wordpress.com/2010/07/pcsw-official-statement-on-fourtin-case-10–2-12.pdf.

Yung, Corey R. 2016. "Rape Law Fundamentals." *Yale Journal of Law and Feminism* 27:1–46.

Yuracko, Kimberly A. 2016. *Gender Nonconformity and the Law.* New Haven: Yale University Press.

Zakaria, Fareed. 2012. "Incarceration Nation." *Time Magazine,* April 2. http://content.time.com/time/magazine/article/0,9171,2109777,00.html.

Zavidow, Evan. 2016. "Transgender People at Higher Risk for Justice System Involvement." *Vera Institute of Justice,* May 10. https://www.vera.org/blog/gender-and-justice-in-america/transgender-people-at-higher-risk-for-justice-system-involvement.

Zevgetis, Garrett, dir. 2016. *Best and Most Beautiful Things.* Only Bright Productions.

Zhou, Y. Carson. 2016. "The Incest Horrible: Delimiting the *Lawrence v. Texas* Right to Sexual Autonomy." *Michigan Journal of Gender and Law* 23:187–245.

Index

inequalities: American football as distraction from, 40; child sexual abuse and, 213n13. *See also* sex inequality
insufficiency of consent as to relational status, 23–24. *See also* status sex laws; vertical status relations
insufficiency of consent as to sexual conduct: overview, 22–23; as alibi for violence and inequalities in sex, 35–36, 202–3n2,6; consent defense mobilized via football–kinky sex analogy, 38–40, 45, 47, 204nn11,13; and corporanormativity (privileging the body) of serious injury, 48–54, 205–6nn21,24,27; dignity threshold as inadequate constraint on consent, 23, 54–58, 206nn27–30; "German Cannibal" case and, 23, 32–33, 34, 36, 37, 54–56, 206n28; as not green-lighting all sex, 31, 34–38; physical injury threshold as inadequate constraint on consent, 23, 34, 37–38, 52–53
intellectual disabilities. *See* disabilities, persons with cognitive/intellectual
interests. *See* autonomy
interspecies relations: animal husbandry/ sterilization/veterinary practices, 118, 120, 122, 212n1; capabilities approach and, 212n1; expressions of wants or urges (behavioral analogues), 121, 126, 212n2, 213n8; inappositeness of consent regarding, 118, 121; intelligence and cognitive capacities of nonhuman animals, 121; intimate relationships, 213n17; killing of animals, 122; mass meat consumption/industry, 118, 120, 131, 213n10
interspecies sex: antibestiality laws, 117–18, 122; argument against nature and, 213n9; capabilities approach to, 121, 122, 126, 212n3; consent, inability of animals to proffer, 121, 212n1; consent to sex, erection of horse as, 118; as dehumanizing, 213n9; disgust and, 122, 212n4, 213n9; as exploitation, 212n4; and heterosomething masculinity, 131–34; horse sex death incident (Washington), 117–18, 119–20, 121–22, 132–33; inappositeness of consent regarding, 118, 121, 126, 213n8; love, care, or sympathy approach to, 121; property damage approach to, 213n9; rights-based approach to, 121; as sexual assault, 118, 212n1; sexual autonomy

of animals and, 121; utilitarian emphasis on sentience and nonsuffering approach to, 121, 126; zoophiles and treatment of animals with love and respect, 212n4; zoophilia as sexual orientation, 213n16
Ireland, and sexual education, 170
Israel: *Kashur v. State of Israel*, 95, 211n12; *State of Israel v. Alkobi*, 95

Japan, and sexual education, 170
Jenner, Caitlyn, 97
Johnston, Elizabeth ("Activist Mommy"), 1
Joseph, State v., 219n25

Kant, Immanuel: and the "against nature" argument, 213n9; and autonomy, 141, 142, 143, 144, 148, 216n8; and human dignity, 55, 57
Kaplan, Margo, 50–51
Kashur v. State of Israel, 95, 211n12
Kennedy, Anthony, 81, 82, 88
Kim, Suki, 179
kink, as term, 202n1. *See also* BDSM
Kipnis, Laura, 7–8, 209n28
Kulick, Don, 150, 161–64, 220–21nn37,38,43

Lawrence v. Texas: assault consent defense not upheld by, 20n19, 50–51, 205n22; horizontal status relationships given wide berth in, 81; incest law as moralized, 68; morality as unconstitutional basis to criminalize private, adult, consensual sex, 78–80; and people in relationships where consent might not be easily refused, 74, 82, 88; *Powell* as precedent for, 64; and private sexual conduct, right to, 81; specialness of sex and, 34
Levy, Neil, 212n2, 213n9
Lewinsky, Monica, 68, 89, 209n28
Lewis, Ray, 40
LGBTQ rights: bullying, 98; marriage equality movement, 81, 104. *See also* homophobia; same sex couples; sexual minorities; sodomy laws, invalidation of; transgender and gender-nonconforming people
Limbaugh, Rush, 117, 118, 121
"L.K.". *See Fourtin, State v.*
Locke, John, 48
Louis C.K., 177–78, 180
Lowry, Lord, 203n4